Becoming *a* Teacher *in the* New Society

Studies in the
Postmodern Theory of Education

Joe L. Kincheloe and Shirley R. Steinberg
General Editors

Vol. 139

PETER LANG
New York • Washington, D.C./Baltimore • Bern
Frankfurt am Main • Berlin • Brussels • Vienna • Oxford

Elizabeth P. Quintero
and Mary Kay Rummel

Becoming *a* Teacher
in the New Society

Bringing Communities
and Classrooms Together

PETER LANG
New York • Washington, D.C./Baltimore • Bern
Frankfurt am Main • Berlin • Brussels • Vienna • Oxford

Library of Congress Cataloging-in-Publication Data

Quintero, Elizabeth P.
Becoming a teacher in the new society: bringing communities
and classrooms together / Elizabeth P. Quintero and Mary Kay Rummel.
p. cm. — (Counterpoints; vol. 139)
Includes bibliographical references.
1. Critical pedagogy. 2. Postmodernism and education. 3. Education—Philosophy.
4. Education—History. 5. Multicultural education. I. Rummel, Mary Kay.
II. Title. III. Counterpoints (New York, N.Y.); vol. 139.
LC196 .Q85   370'.1—dc21   00-026745
ISBN 0-8204-4920-2
ISSN 1058-1634

Die Deutsche Bibliothek-CIP-Einheitsaufnahme

Quintero, Elizabeth P.:
Becoming a teacher in the new society: bringing communities
and classrooms together / Elizabeth P. Quintero and Mary Kay Rummel.
–New York; Washington, D.C./Baltimore; Bern; Frankfurt am Main; Berlin;
Brussels; Vienna; Oxford: Lang.
(Counterpoints; Vol. 139)
ISBN 0-8204-4920-2

Cover art: Hervé Constant, *Labyrinth,* 1996
Cover design by Dutton & Sherman Design

The paper in this book meets the guidelines for permanence and durability
of the Committee on Production Guidelines for Book Longevity
of the Council of Library Resources.

© 2003 Peter Lang Publishing, Inc., New York
275 Seventh Avenue, 28th Floor, New York, NY 10001
www.peterlangusa.com

Printed in the United States of America

It was the best of times, it was the worst of times, it was the age of wisdom, it was the age of foolishness, it was the epoch of belief, it was the epoch of incredulity, it was the season of Light, it was the season of Darkness, it was the spring of hope, it was the winter of despair, we had everything before us, we had nothing before us . . . in short, the period was so far like the present period that some of its noisiest authorities insisted on its being received, for good or for evil, in the superlative degree of comparison only.

     —*Charles Dickens,* A Tale of Two Cities *(1859)*

Share with them your spirit and you will change the world.

             —*Anaya (1999)*

Contents

CHAPTER ONE

Introduction

We begin this introduction with a poem that reflects the voices of some of the poets and prophets whose wisdom composes this book.

Long Ago These Sounds Took Sides
—*Mary Kay Rummel*

My language is the tongue of the sea
It sounds like a divine voice
I shall never forget it
As I cannot forget my mother
　　　　　　　　—*Renate Blumberger*

In the Roman Baths
I'm thinking of that boat the tongue is
restless in its mooring

The waters of Bath wear the face of the goddess
Latin Minerva, Celtic Sulis, the Gorgon Medusa
　　　　　each alphabetic snake uncurled
yet headphones translate Latin inscriptions
　　　　　and those words are male to me.
language of priests, male choirs, cathedrals.
I was a child among its roots and syllables
repeating what I didn't understand
　　　　　ave
　　　　　magnificat
　　　　　anima mea dominum

I remember the voices as one singing,
left too soon the Irish of my grandmother,

harsh gutturals of West Seventh,
English novels of my mother
to enter the silence of my father
and the Latin conjugations I was taught
                belonged to God.

> *I think language is a basket woven*
> *from palm leaves by a woman*
> *who cements it with sun dried mud*
> *puts her child in it among river reeds.*
> *Who knows where it will end up?*

In the Roman Baths
I'm thinking of that country the tongue is

Francisco tells me of his Spanish/
English/ translated into Irish poems.
His Dublin audience
would not speak English.
He could not speak Irish.
So he read in Spanish
and they all understood.

Jack's mother in Northern Ireland
spoke Irish when she was stopped by patrols,
pretended to not understand English
when she was searched. Outside the stores
she'd drop all her packages, curse in Irish,
confuse the guards.

The Irish mind is Celtic, says Declan
pre-Roman, able to hold two thinks at a time.

> *And history's a mind that's never still*
> *with its black thoughts—ravens*
> *its white thoughts—gulls*
> *not blends, but digraphs*
> *tossing and cawing among great ruins*

By the waters of Sulis-Minerva
I am thinking of my friends
and that freedom the tongue wants
How do we cure ourselves of silence?

For years the only poetry New Zealand children
read detailed the splendors of the land.
No one mentioned colonization.

Australian Sari writes a story
about a place threatened by words destructive
as the venom of serpents, a beauty overlaid
with visions from a distant land, no mother at all.

> *I think my language is made of water*
> *tongues of rain, that demure*
> *leveler, cloud-sent plain maker*
> *of the angled, twisted swollen green*
> *hungry sea tongues*
> *that hiss about then swallow*
> *the apples cut by horse's hooves on the beach*
> *where the past disappears in seconds*

This book uses an approach that is student-centered and based upon a postformal perspective (Kincheloe & Steinberg, 1996), which includes critical theory, feminist theory, and social autobiographical narrative. This perspective demands that the politics of knowledge and the origins of sustained inequities of modern society be examined. The book is written for all educators who are investigating teaching and learning in a world that demands of its teachers new knowledge and understanding. The pedagogical approach upon which it is based has been used extensively by the authors.

We believe that becoming a teacher means growing in the understanding that the philosophies, beliefs, and pedagogies that influence education in other countries and cultures affect education in the United States of America, both indirectly and directly. Tim Wise (1999), an activist on equity issues, says that we (in the United States) "are an a-historical people . . . we hate history," but he goes on at great length to point out that we are all responsible for the inheritance of the impact of what was done to people in the past—to the American Indians, to the Mexicans whose land was taken away to become California, Arizona, New Mexico, and Texas, and to the well-meaning people who left inner cities because of Federal Housing Authority policies that encouraged whites to move to the suburbs. He is quick to acknowledge that "your grandfather did not do these bad things; you didn't do these bad things, but you are responsible for your life now," for trying to make a positive difference. In addition, Americans travel widely to the far reaches of the globe, but often the histories underlying beliefs of the people they meet are unknown. Maxine Greene (1999) reminds us that "We can be fully human only if we can open ourselves to the complexities of outer and inner experience. Our saving comes when we can recognize ourselves in the other" (Greene, 1999). The other may be an African entrepreneur, a Middle Eastern Muslim, or a Maori elder.

We are committed to looking at the ways historical events around the globe, our nation's relationships with other nations, immigration patterns, and global economies influence education. We are also committed to thinking about how those events may affect all our lives—in our families and communities on a local level and beyond.

Practicing What We Teach

We contend that the goal of education is personal and political empowerment of both teachers and their students. As teacher researchers we believe that all of us must consistently reflect on our work and our convictions. This constant clarification of our own values and action in all areas of pluralistic work with students is the ongoing aim of education. We see this clarification as Freire (1985) does when he defines conscientization (based on the Brazilian conscientizaçao), as "the process by which human beings participate critically in a transforming act" (p. 106). We see our classrooms as communities of learners, which reflect characteristics of the larger communities from which the students come and the global community where we all struggle to live together peacefully. We include here a brief history of our own philosophies of teaching and the experiences which led to their development.

Elizabeth Quintero

My issues of conviction and work revolve around paying attention to parents' and children's strengths. By doing this, I believe educators and leaders in all arenas can learn more about how culture, language, and varying concepts of family affect child development, community development, and ultimately our ability to live with each other with respect and peace. By briefly going back in time, I will highlight a few instances relating to why these issues became so important to me.

I grew up in Florida in the 1950s when it was okay to speak Spanish only at dance class (in Tampa) on the weekends. When I was sixteen, I worked for Project Head Start in the summer of 1966 as an assistant teacher. We visited rural black families in central Florida. All these years later, one of my most vivid memories is of the homes where the family members of various ages gathered on their front porches telling stories and "acting them out." I didn't know then that one day I'd learn that that was a classic example of both art and literacy. Later, I decided early childhood education was what I would do. Yet, I had had friends in teacher education programs who told me about classes of boring texts and superficial memorizing of various "methods" of teaching and "recipes" for discipline. I guess as a result of the combination of life experiences and personal philosophy I wanted to study early childhood education from an alternative perspective. I went to visit the British Infant Schools and Summerhill School in England. Fairly soon after arriving in London, I learned about a training program for preschool teachers that involved much practical experience in various inner-city neighborhood preschools. I plunged in and to my delight I was placed in a school in a Middle Eastern immigrant neighborhood.

Later, back in north Florida, I found work in a small preschool for three- and four-year-old children. After I finished my masters in education in early childhood studies, I expanded my work to kindergarten teaching and literacy and science teaching at the elementary level. It was during this chapter of my life that I became very involved in asking the question, "What's left out . . . of my personal experience, my education, and ultimately, my teaching?" This was the beginning of the conviction about which I talk now when I tell students to always ask the questions about whose stories and opinions are left out of every textbook, every research study, and every news report.

I was still learning about culture, language, teaching, and learning during the next decade when I lived in Mexico, where my three sons were born. After a few years, I went to New Mexico to work on a doctorate in early childhood/bilingual education. This was when Yetta Goodman and others—during the beginnings of the whole language movement—spoke of young children's play and communication as exemplifying the "roots of literacy." I realized that I had been studying and observing firsthand these roots of literacy in the children I had been working with for years, wherever they were—monolingual English-speaking children, African-American children both in rural schools and in inner city schools, monolingual Spanish-speaking children in Mexico, Spanish-English bilingual children in Texas and New Mexico, or the Middle Eastern children in London. I had seen the "roots of literacy" as an integral part of what children do as they understand and take part in their world. Ironically, when families don't speak English, this "world" of language and literacy is often considered less than adequate and even deviant, because it is different.

As I worked with children and parents in a variety of programs, I saw that every parent I had met—from a diversity of circumstances, from difficult to comfortable—cared deeply about their child that was being entrusted to my care. I was becoming a critical pedagogist and developing the perspectives and commitments that would lead me in the directions that guide my work today.

Mary Kay Rummel

The story of poetry in my life and work is a way to describe the foundations of my own teaching and learning. For me poetry has always been an action by which I both come to self-knowledge and affirm that discovery through language. Because I came from a background of silence, it has been a way of breaking that silence. Poetry has always been tied to feeling and personal perception for me and has been a saving gift for me in my life. It meant the loosened tongue to me, prophecy, speaking out.

September 23, 1973, was the day that Pablo Neruda died. His death, and the events surrounding it, changed my life, my view of language, and the way I see and feel about my country, the United States. Allende, the democratically elected leader, was assassinated; the military took over, with the assistance of the United States. I found myself at a memorial service for Neruda in Minneapolis, led by Robert Bly and Meridel LeSueur. I began to understand poetry as a revolutionary act and began reading women poets who lived this belief, like Neruda, integrating belief, life, and writing.

Many years ago I wrote a poem about this writing in my life as a way of connecting all my roles of mother, teacher, writer, and agent of change. It is my first poem to be published in a literary journal and is the first poem in my first book of poetry.

Seamstress

—Mary Kay Rummel, 1989

I remember a sewing machine
a black Singer with a pedal
that tapped all afternoon
beneath my grandmother's foot.
Her thick fingers pushed cotton
and silk into its snapping mouth
until her eyes darkened from strain.
Parades of bright dresses,
shirts, shawls tumbled from her machine.
On our thin bodies
we wore her eyes.

In the mirror
I see my mother's face
and my grandmother's face
a long parade of Irish Marys
with tunnels for eyes
holes where children crawl
eyes made blind
from too much looking
at the sea.

Afternoons
I feed my typewriter
raw fear and strange words
the cotton pieces of my life.
They step out whole
and walk away on thin legs
solid like mirrors
with eyes wide open.

I shared my poems and the poetry I loved with my students. I
strongly believed in the connection of poetry with the body and the
rhythms of our lives. I remember the first snowfall during my first
year of teaching. I recited the poem that ends "the trees are dressed
in silver skirts / and want to dance around" and my whole class of
forty-two second graders stood up and danced around the room
holding hands without any kind of signal from me—it was pure response. Encouraging creative response and guiding children in their

writing was what I loved about teaching children. Poetry with its ground in feeling, its basis in sensory imagery, its compression and rhythm which children love provides a way of saying things that cannot otherwise be said. It is a way of doing what Maxine Greene suggests, "helping students find language to bring dreams into being, language that introduces them to the experience of going beyond."

I always read to my students sections of what I was reading myself—Shakespeare and Tolkien, Emily Dickinson, Elizabeth Bishop, Pablo Neruda, and James Wright as well as parts of the work of Adrienne Rich, Lucille Clifton, and Nikki Giovanni in addition to poetry specifically written for children.

In 1987 I began the literacy work that I loved the most as a Writer in the Schools. I especially loved working in the Dialogue Program. It was a four-year project in the St. Paul Public Schools that brought together professional writers who worked for the COMPAS Writers-in-the-Schools Program and teachers from St. Paul Schools. We developed a collaborative long-term relationship designed to teach the writing process both through the teachers writing themselves and through teaching writing to students. I was able to team-teach with teachers for a whole year in a specific city school. I really got to know the children, and I led a group for the teachers that met once a month where they shared their own writing and their teaching writing experiences. It was so satisfying; it brought together everything I love to do and I could really see the results of my work. There was so much excitement in those classrooms around the acts of writing and sharing writing.

Although I have always been struggling to integrate the different parts of my life, my writing feeds my teaching and in some ways teaching feeds my writing. Virginia Woolf's book, *A Room of One's Own*, and Tillie Olsen's writings about women breaking the silence of their lives through writing really affected me. It has always been a struggle to find time to do creative writing. Yet I know that work is organic; everything feeds off everything else.

This struggle and separation was reflected in graduate school. At that time at the University of Minnesota the field of reading was kept separate from language arts and children's literature. I specialized in language arts and children's literature as well as English composition. Naomi Chase, who recruited me to come to the university and asked me to work with her, was a wholistic language teacher at a time in the late seventies when everything was becoming more segmented. It was hard to integrate various disciplines of study and to integrate work in the English Department and the Education Department. I find the same problem teaching on the university level; I feel a separation between creative work and professional writing. One of my goals is to contribute to the blending of the disciplines.

From the beginning I tried to integrate my life as a teacher of young children and my life as a writer. Now I must integrate my life as a teacher educator and as a writer. I learned much about the importance of audience for children's writing through becoming a public writer myself and publishing my first book of poetry. I learned about the importance of building a literacy community in the classroom from my twenty-five years of participation in Onionskin, a group of highly professional, creative, and productive women writers. Actually, my life's work is that of integration. This is true in the methods classes that I teach for preservice teachers also. I have the same expressive goals for them that I have had for the children with whom I have worked. I want them to grow in their love of and ability to use language and then to pass it on to children. I want them to experience the transforming power of both writing and responding to literature.

We know how to empower children through language. We do it with our lives. We swim in a river of language. Reading leads to writing which leads to reading. We need to hear the poems of the children of the world, for without those voices, those poems, something vital and deep and large is missing from our lives. Seamus Heaney (1984), winner of the 1995 Nobel Peace Prize in Literature, tells us of the power of the perceptions of the young:

I had forgotten for years
Words so seismic and plain
That come back like rocked waters,
Possible again.

Rationale for Book

This book is based on the stories and observations of real educators at work. In addition, this book presents both historical and philosophical perspectives that may underlie who these people are as educators. Some of the perspectives included have been left out or purposefully silenced in some education books. We include primary source essays, articles, and works of fiction and poetry to give the student reader some varied background knowledge. We also include interviews with educators. We intentionally present the words of informants in their own voices, with limited commentary on our part. As Lather (1994) again guides us, we aim "to grasp both specificity and discontinuity, deploy the space of dispersion . . . to make use of drama artistry, literary practices" (p. 3). We believe the complexity, contradiction, ambiguity, and tension which the reader will see in each author's contribution and in each educator's story form the vitality of the information which we have presented here. While the information falls into the educational themes we are addressing, the different life experiences don't repeat themselves, but yield information about educators' variations on the themes. As Lather (1994) suggests, we, the researchers, move beyond referential naiveté in a way that doesn't simply collapse the referent, that doesn't dismiss what Cornell West (1990) terms "a reality that one cannot not know" (p. 20). We believe, as Freire (1998) explains, we must consistently try to "diminish the distance between me and the perverse reality of the exploited" (p. 123). He goes on to say we must be passionate about gaining "the knowledge of how to uncover hidden truths and how to demystify farcical ideologies, those seductive traps into which we easily fall" (p. 123).

In addition, we include some of the information we have learned currently in an ongoing international research project which has enormous potential to augment knowledge about sociocultural issues for teacher education. We began this international research with a previous study (Rummel & Quintero, 1997) in which we interviewed teachers who are sensitive to diversity and have a commitment to communication with parents and collaboration in the education community and the broader community. We believe we have found, and are reaffirming currently as the research continues, some of the common dispositions of educators who integrate culture and language effectively in diverse contexts.

In the past when we asked teachers to participate in our research, we used Casey's (1993) concept of teacher as "artisan," implying the possibility of changing the world through work. These exemplary teachers create curricula which weave their knowledge with the needs and interests of their students. Their commitment to students is part of the fabric of their total lives. In most cases they create or participate in organizations which impact larger systems of school or society. Casey defines the activist teachers whom she interviewed as "progressive" because they "advocate social change

which will benefit" the constituencies they work with, they acknowledge conflicts, and they recognize "contradictions and in-
equalities in society" (p. 13). We used the same criteria when we
asked people to contribute to this book. We have included educators
from a wide spectrum of racial, class, and gender backgrounds who
teach in a variety of contexts. We have identified the educators who
exemplify Casey's "artisans" through personal contacts we have
made in the course of our previous research. We have found that the
educators we have met and interviewed, like Casey's (1993) participants, resist labels. They just want to do their work. They want to
preserve and save energy for what they clearly see as the most important issues in the lives of their students.

Teaching, for the informants in Casey's study, and our book, is
much more than being employed in a school. "When they find
themselves unable to construct social meaning within the narrow
confines of parochial schools, they abandon that environment.
Working outside that established system, and, supported directly by
persons of conscience, these women are able to address the particular material and moral needs of those around them" (Casey, p. 66).

We believe that teachers, both in and outside the classroom, have
the power to change their students' lives. Through our research we
have strengthened our belief that teaching practice of effective educators is an interrelationship of life's activities and priorities both
inside and outside the classroom. Apple (1993) reports Casey's reflections about her informants:

> All educators working for social change have a great deal to learn
> from the care these women give to their students; the outrage they
> feel towards injustice, and the way they dare to use the limited pow-
> ers that they have." (Apple, quoted in Casey 1993, p. xv)

Beliefs of Activist Educators

In previous research Rummel and Quintero (1997) found that these
beliefs are often expressed as metaphors for life. Teaching is a part of
this life. It is clear that any kind of clarification and deconstruction
of personal beliefs has to involve the whole of life, not just the classroom, because these beliefs emerge from a total life experience. "It
is difficult for me," Maxine Greene (1995) tells us, "to teach educational history or philosophy to teachers-to-be without engaging

them in the domain of imagination and metaphor. How else are they to make meaning out of the discrepant things they learn?" (p. 99).

More surely than anything else we are defined by our stories—the cultural myths we hear from our earliest days. At the same time we are defined by the way we "rewrite" the myths we hear. Only as old patterns in our consciousness crumble are new patterns possible. The life metaphors of the teachers in our research seem to provide a mechanism for "remything." All around us, we hear the cracking of old certainties. And yet, in the midst of our confusion and grief, a new mythology is being born. Exemplary educators are involved in midwifing emergent mythologies. They are transforming their school classrooms into mythogenetic zones: places where new myths and metaphors are born. They are vessels through which new mythologies are slowly emerging, creating what has not been. As the exemplary teachers in our previous work (Rummel & Quintero, 1997) told us their stories, it became clear that they began to re-create common mythologies at a young age. This "re-creation" happened during a critical reading of what they were learning in and out of school. In their own lives they integrate knowledge from social sciences and the humanities.

Our main goal in an introductory education course is to help our students critically "read" what they are learning in and out of school. We want them to integrate knowledge from social sciences and humanities and to begin to develop their own beliefs about and metaphors for education and social change as well as to analyze those that have been developed by others. We hope the reader will examine all sorts of new and ancient information and use myth and metaphor, as the late Joseph Campbell (1972) encouraged, "as a parable for our world today, as an exhortation to press on with the work, beyond fear."

In communities and schools in the United States and all over the world, issues of education are becoming very complex. Power and access to all types of knowledge, resources, and education are huge issues. By the year 2030 one half of all the people in the workforce will be people of color, and over half the students in United States schools will be students of color. There is an emphasis on preserving unique cultural traditions and at the same time an emphasis on globalization on many levels. Increasing numbers of refugees and immigrants are living in communities which are new to them. There is also renewed emphasis on maintaining cultural identity and native language within a pluralistic society. While there is an increasing global interdependence, there are increasing inequities, socially, economically, and culturally. Across the world, issues which combine history and culture, traditions, and attempts at new understandings of current and future society are complex and difficult. We believe that only by integrating historical knowledge with the humanities, drawing upon wisdom in the fine arts, can we provide information for future teachers and a framework for continual professional learning (Quintero & Rummel, 1998). A responsible study of education must expand beyond history centered in the United States of America. Information and perspectives must reflect boundary-less realities of the turn-of-the-century globe.

Lisa Delpit (1995) maintains, "We all carry worlds in our heads, and those worlds are decidedly different (p. xiv)." We educators set out to teach, but how can we reach the worlds of others when we don't even know they exist? Growing up as members of a family and community, children learn explicitly and implicitly the rules and expectations of their cultures. Individual children may be members of more than one cultural group and may be embedded in their cultures to different degrees. The cultures borrow and share rules and cultures change over time.

As Csikszentmaihalyi (1996) reminds us, "As cultures evolve, it becomes increasingly difficult to master more than one domain of knowledge. . . . Therefore, it follows that as culture evolves, specialized knowledge will be favored over generalized knowledge" (p. 9). So, there is need for students to learn specific knowledge from practicing teachers in a variety of contexts and, as Casey (1993) tells us

> Language is the way which human beings make meaning, as well as the worldviews which have been socially constructed in that process, while politics are understood as relationships between groups with different worldviews, and the processes by which they contest each others' perspectives. And these contestations are not limited to the verbal level; my definitions assume that words and deeds, policy and practice, are also inseparably linked. (p. 3)

Deep understanding of the assumption that words, deeds, policy, practice, and theory application are inseparably linked in our world today underlies this text. We cannot pretend that teaching is neutral, nor can the practice be done in isolation. Thus, a study of history, social science, and the humanities must underlie a study of education. In this perspective community becomes a context for studying education.

Community and Social Imagination

Freire states in his last published work (1998),

> There are times when I fear that someone reading this . . . may think that there is now no place among us for the dreamer and the believer in utopia. Yet, what I have been saying up to now is now the stuff of inconsequential dreamers. It has to do with the very nature of men and women as makers and dreamers of history and not simply as casualties of an a priori vision of the world. (p.55)

We believe that there is a magical power of art and imagination that has a definite role in creating a sense of place, a community. This relates to the rethinking of the narrative of neighborhood and construction of the "poetry of neighborhood" discussed by Crichlow (1995), who describes different maps of a neighborhood drawn by parents and children. Relatedly, Elliott Eisner (1998) reflects over a lifetime of scholarly work which demonstrates that in the arts nothing stands alone. He maintains that in music, theater, pottery, or painting, every aspect of the work affects every other aspect and that attention to relationships is a fundamental mode of thinking that the arts require. He documents in much detail in many venues that students' ability to translate creation into observation requires students to use a language that is not literal, that employs metaphor, illusion, and innuendo, and through the arts students recognize that problems can have multiple solutions, questions can have multiple answers. Imagination and metaphor are essential to investigations in education.

Varied Ways of Knowing

We have been saying that in order to study education, we must look at various fields of study—all the fine arts, art history, psychology, sociology, history, archeology, astronomy, geology, humanities—and various forms of lived experience as recorded through the arts, media, and more recent forms of technology such as the World Wide Web.

One of our informants in our research, Eamon Slatter (1997), is an activist and sociologist in Dublin, Ireland. He spoke to us about the connections between ancient cultural knowledge from ancestral storytellers and what he calls the "visual mind" in the modern, technological "Celtic Tiger" society of Ireland. He explained that in the last five or six years Ireland has undergone a remarkable transformation in the sense that Irish culture has gone on to a global stage. He said this is happening because of global forces. He mentioned several examples. Rock bands, such as U2, tap into traditional culture and move their ideas from an oral culture into a rock medium. In addition, he pointed out that in music production today, it is also important to sell a visual, a video. Dr. Slatter also pointed out that *Riverdance* has put Ireland on the international stage through its production which marries traditional, participatory Irish dancing with American stage dancing. He also pointed out that there has been a new surge of films being made in Ireland and the fact that historical, traditional Irish pubs have been replicated all over the world. It is all those things that suggest that Irish culture is becoming more global and more visual at the same time. Dr. Slatter adds that the visual aspect is in part because culture is easier to explain to the outside world on a visual level rather than a written level or even an oral level. We see an opportunity for all of us to synthesize old and new ways of knowing with content knowledge that is familiar and unfamiliar, in many media and in the illustration of many ways of knowing.

We present three examples of varied ways of knowing. In her work with university students, Diane Brunner (1994) expands the meaning of the world of objects by emphasizing the central role of media, film, and art in construction of the image and the connection between these images and knowledge of the spiritual in our lives. She describes how image-making constructs identity through a narrative mythmaking as

> embodied narrative seems to be much more than the articulation of what is understood, more than the framing and understanding of one's experiences, more than play with words . . . this applies to narratives we read, narratives we write, and narratives we vocalize, and, indeed, even those we think but never vocalize. (pp. 17–18)

Ways of knowing that combine particular histories often misunderstood by outsiders are poignantly described by Robert Coles

(1990) as he discusses how Hopi children's way of knowing directly conflicted with both the knowledge and social context of the children's teachers.

> Here, for example, is what I eventually heard from a ten-year-old Hopi girl I'd known for almost two years: "The sky watches us and listens to us. It talks to us, and it hopes we are ready to talk back. The sky is where the God of the Anglos lives, a teacher told us. She asked where our God lives. I said, I don't know.' I was telling the truth! Our God is the sky, and lives wherever the sky is. Our God is the sun and the moon, too; and our God is our people, if we remember to stay here. This is where we're supposed to be, and if we leave, we lose God."

Coles asked if she explained the above to the teacher.

> "No."
> "Why?"
> "Because—she thinks God is a person. If I'd told her, she'd give us that smile."
> "What smile?"
> "The smile that says to us, 'You kids are cute, but you're dumb; you're different—and you're all wrong!' " (p. 26)

Our final example illustrates a type of lived experience which is often viewed from a perspective of deficit, when in fact, Raúl Quintanilla describes a complex and positive learning environment in his early family life. Now an English as a second language teacher, Mr. Quintanilla grew up in a family of farm workers who migrated yearly from Texas to Minnesota. He explains,

> *My parents lived in Mexico and then they crossed to the United States. I was born right on this side of the border. I have eight brothers and eight sisters. In the summer I would work every day from 5:00 A.M. till sundown. We didn't work during the school year except for weekends.* (quoted in Rummel & Quintero, 1997, p. 211)

He goes on to describe the days in the fields.

> Everything was very positive. Your father is there, your mother is there, and your brothers and sisters are there too. You are all working together and your father is saying good things all day, every day for a long time. I didn't know at that time, but it was a close family unit.

They talk about supporting a family now with two incomes. With the migrant families we were doing that long ago. (quoted in Rummel & Quintero, 1997, p. 212)

Problem-posing Approach:
Beginning with the Student Reader

Maxine Greene (1999) speaks of the characters which Melville portrays in his novels as metaphors for the kindred blindness of self-righteous people who may be well-meaning but in their desire for creating sameness use the view of certain children as scarcely human. She says we need to dig up moments from our personal experience when we have failed to see and ask, "How come I wasn't able to see?" She says, "We need to have the guts to face this in ourselves." She relates that little by little film and literature have helped her to see these domains of difference and experience the revelation, "Oh, my god, I never saw it that way" (address, NCTE, November 1999). Our problem-posing methodology is designed to lead readers on their reflective, active journey described by Greene.

The exemplary educators included in this book have shown us aspects of how they nurture pluralistic teaching and activism. They relate historical issues, philosophical, pedagogical issues, and sociocultural information. Because of our commitment to what these educators represent in terms of activist education and our commitment to involving the student reader in a very realistic, personal way, we are organizing our book in a framework that highlights these aspects in actual contexts around the world.

The book is presented in sections which contain information included in many introduction to education courses. We have added information addressing multicultural and multinational perspectives. The activities and information will be appropriate for use both in the university classroom and in the larger community of in-service education. Additionally, lists of resources from the World Wide Web, teaching professional organizations, and social action groups will be included for the reader.

The problem-posing (Listening, Dialogue, Action) activities lend themselves for inclusion of a variety of content information and a variety of learning processes. For example, the Listening section may include:

- Self-reflection activities which encourage the student reader to focus on the theme and content being addressed AND encourage the student reader to make a personal connection in some way to the information;
- Educational foundational information according to themes in the form of primary source material, thought-provoking essays, and some short literature segments which relate to the theme;

The Dialogue section may include:

- A discussion with a class member, a small group of participants, an acquaintance in the community, or a family member about the educational foundational information;
- A discussion about if and how the items discussed above relate to the readers' personal reflections;

The Action section may include:

- Opportunities for the readers to investigate various primary source material of interest to them from different cultures and countries around the globe;
- Opportunities for the readers to investigate various art forms of interest to them from different cultures and countries around the globe;
- Suggestions for the readers to pursue action-oriented projects related to the themes;
- Resources from libraries and the Internet. We would like to reaffirm our critical, postformal perspective for these endeavors and remind readers that analysis and reflection are important throughout this investigative process.

As previously stated, most foundational investigations into education address American historical events and trace those events' impact on education in the United States from a rather ethnocentric perspective. However, we believe this approach is outdated and unrealistic in our current world. We are committed to looking at historical events around the world and how those events may affect all our lives—in our families and communities and our nation's relationships with other nations, immigration patterns, global economies, global natural resources, natural environments—and education.

This investigation of education presents both historical and philosophical perspectives that may underlie the work of outstanding educators. While the participants who contributed to this book represent a wide range of geographical regions, cultures, and experiences, we purposefully are not categorizing our information into "a United States" chapter, a "European" chapter, a "South American" chapter, an "African" chapter, or a "South Pacific Island" chapter. We don't believe the issues and content should be superficially divided in such a way. The framework provided and the authenticity of the material presents issues in ways that will help student readers to understand the connections between their own lives and learning and that of others around the globe.

Barbara Kingsolver's (1998) character Orleanna in *The Poison-wood Bible* states:

> I was occupied so entirely by each day, I felt detached from anything so large as a month or a year. History didn't cross my mind. Now it does. Now I know, whatever your burdens, to hold yourself apart from the lot of more powerful men is an illusion. (p. 323)

We hope the reader thinks about this attitude during the use of this book.

References

Apple, M. (1993). Series editor's introduction. In K. Casey, *I answer with my life: Life histories of women teachers working for social change* (pp. ii–v). New York: Routledge Press.

Brunner, D. (1994). Inquiry *and reflection: Framing narrative practice in education.* Albany: State University of New York Press.

Campbell, J. (1972). *Myths to live by.* New York: Penguin Books.

Casey, K. (1993). *I answer with my life: Life histories of women teachers working for social change.* New York: Routledge Press.

Clandinin, J. D. & Connelly, F. M. (1994). *Handbook of qualitative research.* London: Sage Publications.

Coles, R. (1990). *The spiritual life of children.* Boston: Houghton Mifflin.

Crichlow, W. (1995). Rethinking the narrative of urban neighborhood: Perspectives on the social context and processes of identity formation among African American youth. Unpublished paper presented at the American Educational Research Association meeting in San Francisco, CA.

Csikszentmaihalyi, M. (1996). *Creativity: Flow and the psychology of discovery and invention.* New York: HarperCollins.

Delpit, L. (1995). *Other peoples' children: Culture and conflict in the classroom.* New York: New Press.

Dewey, J. (1916). *Democracy and education.* New York: Macmillan.

Dewey, J. (1934). *Art as experience.* New York: Capricorn Books.

Dewey, J. (1938). *Experience and education.* New York: Collier Books.

Eisner, E. (1998). *The kind of schools we need: Personal essays.* Portsmouth, NH: Heinemann.

Freire, P. (1985). *The politics of education.* Granby, MA: Bergin & Garvey.

Freire, P. (1998). *Pedagogy of freedom: Ethics, democracy, and civic courage.* New York: Rowman & Littlefield.

Greene, M. (1995). *Releasing the imagination: Essays on education, the arts, and social change.* San Francisco, CA: Jossey-Bass.

Greene, M. (November, 1999). Reimagining difference and diversity. Unpublished paper presented at the annual convention of the National Council of Teachers of English. Denver, CO.

Heaney, S. (1984). *Hailstones.* Dublin, Ireland: Gallery Press.

Kincheloe, J. L., & Steinberg, S. R. (1997). *Changing multiculturalism.* Philadelphia: Open University Press.

Kincheloe, J. L., Steinberg, S. R., & Gresson, A. D. III (Eds.) (1996). *Measured lies: The bell curve examined.* New York: St. Martin's Press.

Kingsolver, B. (1998). *The Poisonwood Bible.* New York: HarperCollins.

Lather, P. (1994). Gender issues in methodology: Data analysis in the crisis of representation. Unpublished paper presented at AERA National Conference, New Orleans, LA.

Quintero, E. P., & Rummel, M. K. (1998). *American voices: Webs of diversity.* Columbus, OH: Merrill/Prentice Hall.

Rummel, M. K. (1989). *This body she's entered.* Minneapolis, MN: New Rivers Press.

Rummel, M. K., & Quintero, E. P. (1997). *Teachers' Reading/ Teachers' Lives.* Albany: State University of New York Press.

Rummel, M. K., & Quintero, E. P. (1998). Global culture and community: Links to classroom practice. [Online] Available: http:// www.d.umn.edu/educ/mkbq/

Slatter, E. (April, 1997). *Interview.* Dublin, Ireland.

Sleeter, C. (1992). *Keepers of the American dream.* London: Falmer Press.

Sleeter, C., & Grant, C. (1994). *Making choices for multicultural education.* New York: Macmillan.

West, C. (1990). The new cultural politics of difference. In R. Ferguson, M. Gever, T. T. Minh-ha, C. West (Eds.), *Out there: Marginalization and contemporary cultures* (pp. 19–38).

Wise, T. (October, 1999). Speak out on equity. Unpublished lecture at University of Minnesota, Duluth. Duluth, MN.

CHAPTER TWO

What Beliefs Shape
Teaching and Learning?

Belief

—Andrew Rummel

The morning does not begin with light.
It begins with a little less darkness.

The morning begins on Emeishan
with the mist clearing mid-day.
The owl that hides beneath the temple
now sits, without fear, on the dead
limb and knows it has outlived even the tree.

The pilgrims, the monks, the tourists, the ones
who make monkeys pose for pictures climb the stairs.

Outside Beibei, the morning begins.
On the hillside, stones not worn by the constant
rub of water, but worn by the flood
of human feet with faith as strong
as the creations of time and water.
At night the moon outlives
the karoake bars.

Reviewing the Format of the Chapter

The problem-posing activities of our methodology provide a nonlin-
ear framework in which complex information can be connected

with readers' lives. The chapters include selections of information which represent perspectives of varied lives in terms of culture, language, and other complexities that make up social and historical context. Freire's (1973) problem-posing format of listening, dialogue, action is then utilized in flexible ways. Students participate in the activities by relating their own experience and/or choose other activities included to further their reading and background knowledge. They pursue their particular field of inquiry in terms of foundational issues and learn from related issues in other participants' fields. This is especially true for issues relating to sociocultural contexts of communities and schools. A dialogic class begins with a problem-posing discussion and sends signals to students that their participation is expected and needed.

Trueba, Spindler, & Spindler (1989) describe Freire's (1973) method:

> His model goes beyond mere description, however. It aims to educate people in the skills necessary so that they can de-enculturate themselves individually and collectively—thereby reasserting greater control over their lives as social and historical beings. (p. 97)

The problem-posing activities are recursive activities, not a lesson plan in a preconceived, rigid sequence. Sometimes action is needed first, for the concrete experience it provides. Then reflection follows, relating the action, the stories, to the student's life and the student's choices for more action.

Personal Experience and Life Philosophies: Reflections on Student Life and Times

Options for Listening

Choose one of the following sets of questions to reflect upon and write a short journal entry about.

- What is the history of a tradition or a celebration in your family? Where did it originate? In your journal write or draw a past/present "snapshot" of a tradition in your family. What questions do you have about your family?
- Write about a story which has been retold in your family or in a group of your friends. How has this story changed during its retelling? What are the underlying meanings or truth in

this story? What have your family members or friends learned from it over the years?

- Who are the storytellers in your family or group of friends? How did they get this role? Describe them in your journal.
- Try to remember an incident in your childhood in which a parent or other significant adult was giving you some sort of moral lesson. Were you told something to the effect that you should always "do what you know is the right thing to do" and "know that you are a good person"? What happened? Please summarize the situation, the understandings you had as a child, and your current understandings about what was really going on. Write a letter (real or imaginary) to this adult with questions you have about the incident, the intentions, and your new (or developing) understandings.

Options for Dialogue

Discuss your family stories in small groups. How are they similar? How are they different? Do the stories give glimpses of the student reader's educational experiences?

Options for Action

Communicate through a letter, a telephone call, an email, or a personal conversation with a family member. Explain your memory that you wrote about and get a response of your accuracy from that family member. Bring your reports to the next class meeting for discussion.

Learning: In School, Out of School

Choose one of the following sets of questions to reflect upon and write a short journal entry about.

- Think back to an important historical event (either tragic or joyous) and describe in your journal where you were when you became aware of the event. Describe other aspects of the context such as the emotional dynamics of the setting, who was with you, and whether those people were moved in the same way you were by the event. What is a critical question you had or still have about some aspect of the event?

- Write a few reflective sentences in your journal about any factual information you know about a Middle Eastern country, an African country, a South American country, or any country you used to know very little about. Write about a relationship (a close friendship or an acquaintance) you may have had with a person from the Middle East or another country. Write a few sentences about what you learned by knowing that person (factual and/or opinion learnings are important).
- Go back to your life when you were 14 years old. Reflect on and write about some things you learned that year. If you could ask family members some questions now about events from that time, what would the questions be?
- Think back to your high school years. Write about an activity outside of school that you really enjoyed. Where did you do this? Which people were involved, if any? Do you now have a sense of why you enjoyed this so much? Can you see now that you were learning something in the process of doing this activity? What questions do you still have?
- Reflect on a place outdoors where you used to spend time as a teenager. Describe the place in your journal. Was it a rooftop? A vacant lot? A wildlife reserve? A river? Try to capture some details about how you felt when you were in this place. What questions do you still have?

Options for Dialogue

Discuss these memories about learning in small groups. How are they similar? How are they different? Do the stories give glimpses of the student reader's educational experiences?

Options for Action

Communicate through a letter, a telephone call, an email, or a personal conversation with a family member. Explain your memory that you wrote about and get a response of your accuracy from that family member. Bring your reports to the next class meeting for discussion.

Review of Personal Experience

Options for Listening

"Listen" to your experiences by reviewing your work and reflections from the previous sections and look for patterns in your own learning. Are there similar lessons you've learned through different contexts and different people over the years? Are there traceable differences in dynamic or subtle changes in your learning over the years? Summarize what you see. (Remember, you are the expert of your own experience; there is no "right" answer to these questions.)

Options for Dialogue

Discuss your personal history or your life. Can you name a philosophical and/or historical influence on your thinking and learning? In the next section, you will be asked to make connections by responding to the experiences of others. Write this question in your journal: *How are philosophies, stories, and ideas of others reflected in the following essays, stories, and poems?*

Options for Action

Choose a textbook from any class you are currently taking and identify the philosophies and histories (personal or professional) of the authors of the book. Report your ideas to your group and then the whole class. Discuss whether or not the philosophies of the authors of the textbook are similar to your own, different from your own, or a mixture of similarities and differences compared to your own.

Anne McCrary Sullivan, Poet and Teacher Educator

Options for Listening

Research the ideas of Progressive Education in the early part of the twentieth century and the work of John Dewey. *Progressivism* was a movement that advocated the application of human and material resources to improve the American's quality of life as an individual. In terms of education, progressive ideals demanded that the needs and interests of students rather than of teachers should be the focus of all learning in schools. Students were responsible for maximizing their potential with the teachers as facilitators. Write about an experience you have had with a "progressive" educational experience.

Read Dr. Anne Sullivan's introduction to her found poems.

These eight found poems, constructed from the text of John Dewey's *School and Society,* bring into focus some of the critical themes of the book by distilling Dewey's prose and shaping it in ways that heighten attention to key concepts. In constructing these poems, the poet maintained these rules for herself: 1) I cannot add words of my own; 2) I cannot change meaning; 3) I may re-order words or sentences if meaning is not altered; 4) I may change verb endings (drop or add an -*ed, -ing, -s*); 5) I may alter and add punctuation. The resulting poems are proposed as strategies for bringing students, and others who may be intimidated by or uncomfortable with Dewey's prose, into relation with his work. They are invitations, doorways, beginnings.

Read the following found poems and write personal insights and inferences you can make about John Dewey as you read.

Eight Found Poems from John Dewey's School and Society
—Anne McCrary Sullivan

Mathematical Problem

There is just so much desirable knowledge.
There are just so many needed accomplishments

in the world. Then comes the mathematical problem
of dividing this by the six, twelve, or sixteen years

of school. Now give the children every year
just the proportionate fraction of the total;

by the time they have finished
they will have mastered the whole,

covering so much ground during this hour
or day or week or year. Everything comes out

perfectly at the end—provided
the children have not forgotten, provided
the children have not forgotten. (p. 33)

Learning Cotton and Wool

The children are given the raw material
flax, the cotton plant, wool as it comes from the sheep.

Children in one group work thirty minutes
freeing cotton fibers from the boll and seeds,
get less than one ounce. They
easily believe that one person could gin
one pound a day by hand, understand why
their ancestors wore wool (pp. 20–21)

Learning

Here is a certain disorder
and chairs—artistic, hygienic,

There is not silence.
Persons are not engaged

in maintaining fixed
physical postures.

Their arms are not folded.
They are not holding
their books
thus and so.

There is confusion, the bustle
of doing things to produce results

and there is born a discipline
of its own kind and type.

The only training
that becomes intuition

is that got through life itself. (p. 17)

In the School Supply Stores

I was looking, trying to find desks
in any busy workshop.
and educational. Finally, one dealer
more intelligent than the rest,
remarked: "I am afraid we have not
what you want. You want something
these are all for listening."

Just as the biologist can take a bone
or two, reconstruct the whole animal,
so, if we put before the mind's eye
the ordinary schoolroom with its rows
of ugly desks in geometrical order,
crowded together, as little moving room
the same size,
with just space enough to hold books,
pencils, paper, and add a table,
some chairs, the bare walls, possible
a few pictures; we can reconstruct
the only activity that can go on
in such a place: listening.
Studying lessons out of a book
is only another listening,
dependency of one mind
upon another: passivity.
Plato somewhere speaks
of the slave as one who in his actions does not
express his own ideas
but those of some other. (pp. 23, 31–32)

On School

To
    School

rigidly set

give
a shock. (p. 15)

Criminal

For one child
to help another;
school crime (p. 16)

Revolution

There has been a revolution,
the face of the earth making over,
political boundaries wiped out and moved.

Population from the ends of the earth
gathers into cities.
Habits of living alter.

Go back one, two, three generations,
find a time when clothing was made in the house,
members of the household were shearing the sheep,
carding and spinning, plying the loom.

Instead of pressing a button
and flooding the house with light,
illumination followed its toilsome length:
the killing of the animal,
the trying of fat,
the making of wicks
and dipping of candles.
Flour, lumber, foods, building materials,
household furniture, hammers, hinges, nails,
produced in open shops, centers
of neighborhood congregation.
The industrial process stood revealed,
and children initiated into the mysteries. (pp. 9–10)

Reference

Dewey, J. (1920/1990). *The school and society.* Chicago: University of
    Chicago Press.

Options for Dialogue

- Please discuss with a partner what you see of Dewey's ideas of schooling coming through in these found poems.
- Discuss with a partner which issues raised in the poems reflect your own thinking about teaching and learning.

Options for Action

- Visit your library and choose a philosophy or a school of thought. Read about a proponent of that philosophy and write a few Found Poems using Dr. Anne Sullivan's guidelines, 1–5 (In the Listening activity above).

References

Allen, P. G. (1991). *Grandmothers of the light.* Boston: Beacon Press.

Freire, P. (1973). *Education for critical consciousness.* New York: Seabury Press.

Freire, P. (1985). *The politics of education.* Granby, MA: Bergin & Garvey.

Rogers, Annie G. (1993). Voice, play, and the practice of ordinary courage in girls' and women's lives. *Harvard Educational Review, 63* (3), 265–295.

Shannon, P. (1993). *Becoming political.* Portsmouth, NH: Heinemann.

Sleeter, C., & Grant, C. (1994). *Making choices for multicultural education.* New York: Macmillan.

Trueba, H., Spindler, G., & Spindler, L. (Eds.). (1989). *What do anthropologists say about dropouts?* New York: Falmer Press.

CHAPTER THREE

. . . Creating Dialogue about Culture and Beliefs

We are living in a time of a consciousness of paradox. Many of the values of childrearing, education, and living are being called into question. The events of the autumn of 2001 have forced many people to reinterpret the world as we know it.

In Faith Ringold's *Tar Beach* and *Aunt Harriet's Railroad*, the character, Cassie, uses her imagination and her stories which nourish her to overcome oppression and limitations. In a *New York Times Book Review* (9/30/01) Margo Jefferson wrote,

> . . . Real art matters now—the lyric, the epic, the satire, the memoir and the essay. In the *Nation*, Edward Said had written that intellectuals should work like artists, accepting "overlapping yet irreconcilable" realities. What is more difficult than to "truly grasp the difficulty of what cannot be grasped, and then go forth to try anyway"?

Richard Rothstein (9/19/01) wrote in the *New York Times* shortly after the attack on the World Trade Center that while school reformers promote critical thinking, there is a question about what that means on a practical level. He believes that teachers need to answer questions from students about personal safety, about what motivates others to attack us, about how we should relate to fellow citizens who are Muslim or Arab, and about whether civil liberties should be curtailed in a time of crisis. He says that if unasked, these questions should be provoked. This is true of the important questions that arise at any time in history or in any particular place.

We believe that by using a problem-posing, critical approach, even the complex issues of a world in conflict and confusion, issues of culture and belief can be addressed in an on-going dialogue. One of the purposes of this text is to guide those readers who are or will be teachers as they discuss critical issues with their students. In the same way we want the readers to engage with the issues raised by the authors who appear in the book. In the following four selections authors share insights in very different voices about the interactions of culture and belief. The questions listed above are central to writing from many different perspectives.

Cynthia Shearer writes about storytelling in many forms, especially music and its grounding in culture and belief. In a poem written in two languages Francisco Alarcón explores the connections among nature, language, and beliefs. Following that, Carlos Aceves describes the struggle of an indigenous people to reclaim identity and at the same time proclaims that identity. Jeffrey Thomas Leong recreates through complex images the interactions among the conflicting cultures that have influenced his life. Finally, activist artist Faye Kahn documents her personal responses through her diary entries on an extended stay in Israel. She questions much about culture and belief.

References

Anzaldúa, G. (1995). *Prietita and the ghost woman*. San Francisco: Children's Book Press.
Jefferson, M. (September, 2001). *The New York Times*. New York.
Rothstein, R. (September, 2001). *The New York Times*. New York.

Cynthia Shearer, Author and Museum Curator

Options for Listening

- Write about your earliest memories of lessons about how to be a good human being. Did your family members or significant elders tell you stories? Did you get the "lessons" through songs? Through organized "classes" at a church or synagogue or your school?
- Write about your thoughts about popular music and film currently in terms of "messages" or attitudes and opinions portrayed by lyrics, dialogue, and stories.
- Read the essay by Cynthia Shearer. Write any personal connections you have to her thoughts on parenting, gender, respect, and music.

Planet Absurdo

—Cynthia Shearer

There is a particular bend in the road to our home outside Oxford, Mississippi, that seems to deepen my daughter's thoughts and cause her to inquire about weighty matters. Once, when she was about eight, we were passing through the woods there, and she turned her white face to my white face and asked, "Are you some kind of racist?"

"How can you ask me that?" I stammered.

"Because you only listen to black people's music," she said. I had a blues tape on in the car. I laughed, but the question rankled a bit.

Not long after, she discovered the music of James Brown and could be spotted dancing like a dervish in her pink room, big poufy bunny slippers and all. Her question became moot. She owns more black people's music than white people's, too.

But ever since, I've wondered, should I tell her the truth? I have spent a good part of my life as a Southern white female trying to get inside the skin of blacks. Music, literature, painting, even cooking—I've tried all these venues as a way to shuck my white skin even momentarily.

My earliest memories of black skin: Rosalie Smith, the woman who took care of me when my mother had to start teaching school, after my father skipped out. I must have been about three. In the chaos of our home life, the race thing went like this for me:

The black woman is the one who takes time to hold you on her lap and sing to you.

The white woman is the one who ignores you and smokes cigarettes and reads Faulkner.

The black woman is the one who will come calmly with the hoe to kill the copperhead that is coiled between your feet under the flowering peach tree.

The white woman is the one who wrings her hands and does not know how to cook, iron, or pay the bills, but she can order from a menu in French.

The black woman is the one who knows how to feed you and your siblings like field hands, even when there is no money. She is the one who holds you in her arms on the afternoon your sister has shot you with your brother's BB gun, and you are not quite sure that belonging to the human race is a viable option.

It never occurred to me as a child that blackness and whiteness constituted a problem until I saw some news reports of riots in Johannesburg, South Africa. I asked my mother what was going on. She said, "That is what happens when human beings are not treated as human beings." She divided people into two categories: Human beings, and those who refused to be human beings. The human being moniker she attached only to the worthy.

I have another memory of those years. Some men in white robes and pointed hats set up a kind of road block near our house and were handing out pamphlets. I was too young to comprehend my mother's words, or what was in the pamphlets, but I can still remember the tone of her voice, a kind of vitriol she spoke to them to make them go away. Not long after one of the stock characters in my nightmares became a white man in a white robe and a white pointy hat. He had a Snidely Whiplash moustache, and he was always coming after me, meaning harm.

Black skin signified safety and decency to me. Human beings.

By 1968, the year the public schools integrated, the whites in our town had stopped speaking to us, mostly because of my mother's outspokenness in support of integration. She was educated, divorced, liberal, not religious, a pariah many times over. Our family could go into a store or a public gathering in the town, and everything would fall silent. We were the only white faces south of Macon, it seemed, who believed black faces and white faces should go to school under one roof. I can describe to you the day the word detrimental became a part of my vocabulary. I was thirteen. About two minutes after school started one winter morning, I was summoned to the principal's office. It would be detrimental to me, he tried to explain, if I continued to be friends with black students.

Before that year was out, I'd seen my mother level another barrage of vitriol at some redneck farmers standing in the schoolyard with loaded shotguns. She seemed not to know much profanity, but that didn't cramp her style. She knew there was a vein of decency in those men, somewhere, and she was going to find it. I understood then that a woman can use the power of her words to shame a man who happens to be holding a loaded gun. He can be tranced forward, if you choose your words carefully, back into the fold of human beings. Nobody got shot at that day, or ever, in my hometown. No crosses were burned. But I remember a lot of silence toward us from white people.

When I became a mother, it was my black mother's patois of baby talk and dialect I spoke to my own baby at first. My husband, who was born white in Manhattan, was concerned about it at first, but I explained. Where I come from, that's the tongue used to speak love to babies: you say "chile," instead of "child" when you mean love. White women of my generation didn't hand over their babies to hired black women. (If anything, we stayed home and watched black women with fancy degrees rise up the ladders of academia and commerce.) But all of us raised on those loving sounds carry them as a deep memory. This legacy of nurturing is what I have to pass on.

I was a latecomer to black blues music. I got my first real taste of the blues at age thirty-seven in a black juke joint in Marshall County, Mississippi, half an hour down the highway from my home. You have to cross the Tallahatchie Bridge to get there. I was finishing my first novel and had it in mind that I needed to understand how it was that my father's fifteen-year-old brother, Weyman Shearer, could have been gunned down by MPs in Montgomery, Alabama, in 1947 for being AWOL and refusing to leave a black juke joint.

A couple of hours in the juke joint near my home and it almost made sense. Listening to R. L. Burnside, a sharecropper known to his familiars as "Rule," I wanted to go AWOL, too, from my lily-white faculty wife life back in Oxford. I wanted to stay all night in that tiny shack in the middle of somebody's pasture. Burnside wore a buffalo-plaid flannel shirt and a hat that said something like "Caterpillar" on it, and the music was all the sweeter for being practically free. There were few white faces in sight.

Burnside, now seventy-two, once exiled himself to Chicago, then exiled himself back home to hill country. When you see him in the hardware store, he looks like any other Mississippi farmer. I've heard that when he plays in Amsterdam, it's standing room only. When he plays in Mississippi, he is perfectly capable of looking into a white woman's eyes without begrudging her whiteness or her femaleness. When he does that, it is like a long drink from a deep, dark well. It's great to meet up with someone so at peace with his black skin, and at peace with your white skin.

All other blues music I hear, I tend to measure against the night I first heard him. I found myself listening to a CD of his over and over, teaching myself something without a name to it, something about disorder and exuberance. The late Robert Palmer once wrote that Burnside's guitar was as good a way as any to illustrate chaos theory. I have learned to apprentice my white mind to certain black musicians, no questions asked.

A few months after my daughter's racism question, we were again in the car together, this time on the way to the mall to get ready for summer vacation at the beach. When we were stopped at a traffic light, there was a young black man in a pickup truck in the next lane, his rap music booming so loud that my sternum was vibrating in perfect

The general argument of the song had something to do with how women are not to be trusted because they are of only two kinds: the kind that rhymes with witch and kind that rhymes with woe.

It all registered crazily in my mind like a syllogism from Planet Absurdo:

1. People of any skin color have the right to express themselves, to live.

2. To insure this, white women like my mother stood and fought.

3. Therefore, the young black man is now free to signify the death of all women.

I looked over at him, blew my horn. He looked back, dissing and dismissing my white face all in one glance. I wanted to get out of the car and invoke my mother's sharp tongue, ask him, "Did you buy that music with your mother's money or your own?"

Instead I laid the palm of my hand down on the horn, and I kept it there. I decided that if he was free to play his music, I was free to fill the air with my car horn, to drown out what he was forcing my daughter to hear. Other drivers stared at me as if I'd lost my mind. I drove alongside him, slowly, sending a silent prayer to the local constabulary: Chief, if you get reports of some white woman harassing young black guys who play their music loud, it's me. Me and my car horn.

I know allegedly educated men who will suggest to me that there is something a tad bourgeois about me that prevents me from appreciating the absurdist conventions of rap. It resembles farce, they tell me. Perhaps I am not qualified to critique it, they'd say. Better to leave interpretation up to women who are qualified to talk about it because they are against it, like Susan Sontag.

In the meantime, I understand clearly that my daughter will have something to contend with that I did not, once she begins to fall in love with men. I went through my adolescence listening to music that made me feel good about being a woman. My daughter is headed into hers exposed to massive doses of music that wants to assign her a place at the back of the cosmic bus.

The music is successful in part; not only because it fills the corporate white man's coffers, but also because it fulfills some white men's wet dreams somewhere about the ultimate taboo. Thousands of years human beings have lived with the gift of imagination, and some seem able only to use it to get off in a dark corner with the guys and say the nasty about women.

Later in the summer I picked up the local newspaper and read that a young black woman I once taught at Ole Miss had been found strangled in a field here. Her name was Charlotte Simpson. I remembered that her mother had moved back down South to get her out of Milwaukee, so she could grow up safe. I drove around alone in the country and had myself a good cry. A closed car, a country road—it's a good place to scream whatever bitterness you wish, without hurting anyone. I couldn't stop thinking of that rap music from weeks before. I kept mulishly dragging those words of contempt towards woman forward, like admissible evidence.

On the one hand, Charlotte's dead body in the grass.

On the other, the memory of that hate music released like a virus into my town. No, pumped into my town by corporate profiteers.

It was like holding live jumper cables. When I brought those two facts too close together, the rage would arc. A dead woman's body in the grass is not farce.

Even now, it all makes me want to go do some crazy thing, like call up Ice-T on the telephone at an odd hour, wake him up out of a dead sleep.

Hey, come visit Mississippi. I'll take you to a juke joint out in a pasture.

We'll go hear Burnside rule. He plays real good for free, as Joni Mitchell says. And when the music raises the hair on the back of your necks, Africa lives in all our veins, along with Israel, Italy, Russia, and France. We'll step outside and search the night sky for the sight of Tupac's sharecropper soul. And we will ask him if it was worth it, bootlegging all that hate for the white man's corporation to sell to the masses.

As for me, I will dwell in the house of worthier musicians than Ice-T. There is simply too much good music out there for me to subsidize the hate profiteers.

Finishing up my second novel, I am as apprenticed as ever to Mississippi's black hill country blues men. I'm particularly drawn to the music of Joe Callicott, who died penniless up in Nesbit. Near the end of his life, he opened his door to the folklorists and played, and the little white boy who was his student that day grew up to be Burnside's side man.

Callicott could sustain two kinds of music on one cheap guitar. One line is heavy and dark, the other is light. After years of solitude and silence, he answered the dark undertow of history with songs about love and magic.

So many years after I used to find shelter and safety in Rosalie's lap, I still feel like the white child with her nose pressed to the glass door that always seems to bar whites from entering culture. Some black musicians hang a "Blacks Only" sign on their music, to bar whites from taking a drink from the dark well.

More and more, I ignore the sign that excludes me. There is probably only one door worth pressing one's nose to, the door that opens to the place where we learn to become human beings. I like to imagine that if I push hard enough on that door, the spirits of Rosalie Smith, Rule Burnside, and Joe Callicott could enter me, like Africa, and abide under my white skin.

Options for Dialogue

- Please discuss in small groups: What are Shearer's "issues?" Why?
- As a group, list the multiple ways the issues relate to each other.
- Are her issues specific to her gender, community, generation?
- Discuss any parallel issues that relate to your life.
- As a group, brainstorm about any of the ISMs mentioned previously that relate to Shearer's ideas.

Options for Action

- Listen to a blues singer that you are familiar with. Choose a particular song or series of songs and prepare a short oral presentation about the music, the message, and why you like the artist.

- Read in the Annals of Pop section of the *New Yorker* magazine (October 11, 1999) "Bold Mary's Word: A former Public Enemy follows the career of the Queen of Hip-Hop Soul" by Sister Souljah. Relate this article to Shearer's essay and report to your class.
- Interview an elder about a favorite vocal or musical artist. What do you learn about the artist? What do you learn about the person you interviewed? Search out the artist and bring a sample of the music to play when you report on your interview.
- Poet Laureate Rita Dove talks about her belief that there are good rap and hip hop creations. Research Ms. Dove's writings and interviews and document some of her comments about rap artists she respects. Look into some of the music and poetry by these artists. Report to the class.
- Listen to the interview of Bill Moyers with playwright August Wilson in The Moyers Collection: A World of Ideas, Films for the Humanities, 1994. In the interview Moyers and Wilson discuss the artist's use of music to create and participate in culture. They discuss the blues, rap, and hip hop. Report what you learn to the class.
- Choose a writer, musician, or visual artist of the Harlem Renaissance era and create an oral, visual, or written presentation about what you learn about this person. Share with your class.
- Read one of the following books and create an oral, visual, or written presentation about what you learn. Share with your class.

George, N. (1998). *Hip hop America.* New York: Viking.

Hughes, L. (1997). *The first book of jazz.* Hopewell, NJ: Ecco Press.

Jones, K. M. (1994). *Say it loud! The story of rap music.* Brookfield, CT: Millbrook Press.

Watson, S. (1995). *The Harlem renaissance.* New York: Pantheon.

Francisco Alarcón, Poet and Teacher

Options for Listening

- Think about the language you use in the company of very close friends or family. How is this different from the language you use at work? At school? Do the words you use define anything about your identity? Do the words reflect your beliefs about things? Does the language include any "secret" codes or meanings? Write about this in your journal.
- Make a list of words that you use every day, in your native language, that are derived from a different language. For example, if English is your native language, did you know that Milwaukee and Minnesota are words which originated in American Indian languages? Did you know that Colorado and Los Angeles are Spanish?
- Write about an experience in which you felt close to nature. Did you have a sense of the human connection with nature? Write briefly about your experience or represent it in a drawing.
- Read the following poem by Francisco Alarcón. Think about the connection between nature and spirit.

In Xochitl In Cuicatl
—Francisco Alarcón

cada árbol	every tree
un hermano	a brother
cada monte	every hill
Una pirámide	a pyramid
un oratorio	a holy spot
cada valle	every valley
un poema	a poem
in xochitl	in xochitl
in cuicatl	in cuicatl
flor y canto	flower and song
cada nube	every cloud
una plegaria	a prayer
cada gota	every rain
de lluvia	drop
un milagro	a miracle

cada cuerpo	every body
una orilla	a seashore
al mar	a memory
unolvido	at once lost
encontrado	and found
todos juntos:	we all together:
luciérnagas	fireflies
de la noche	in the night
soñando	dreaming up
el cosmos	the cosmos

Options for Dialogue

- Discuss with a partner what you believe are some of the poet's beliefs. What's your evidence?
- Discuss a situation in which you have seen language forms which are closely connected to belief. Was the situation connected to a religious ceremony? Was it at a political meeting? Was the situation in a family or community story? Why were the language choices made?

Options for Action

- Research information about one of the few existing treatises on the culture of Nahuatl—the Indian language primarily spoken by the Aztec. This treatise was written one hundred years after Hernan Cortez's conquest of Mexico by Hernando Ruiz de Alarcón, a Mexican Catholic priest (1587–1646). He had been commissioned by the Spanish Inquisition to compile, translate, and interpret the spells, chants, and invocations of the Indians. Spaniards were afraid that the Indians were still practicing their traditional beliefs and had not truly accepted Catholicism, so the Inquisition intended to educate other priests about Native customs with this treatise so that the offenders would be punished, usually by death.
- Find some retellings of traditional stories about Coyote or other magical or "trickster" characters in cultural folklore. For example, the African trickster is Anansi, the Spider; the Norse trickster is Loki; the African American trickster is

Br'er Rabbit. (Language note: "trickster" is often defined as "one who deceives." Yet, in some folktales the trickster uses cunning and magic for positive purposes. Notice this as you read.)

- Individually or in a small group create a trickster figure of your choosing. Relate an episode showing how she or he outwits others by means of magic, cunning, or trickery. You may choose to illustrate your story using some visual or electronic representation.
- Look up the definition of "manifesto" and then read the following manifesto written by Carlos Aceves, kindergarten teacher and Chicano community spiritual leader.

Carlos Aceves, Activist, Bilingual Kindergarten Teacher

A Mesoamerican Manifesto:
An Indigenous Struggle to Reclaim Our Human Identity
—*Carlos Aceves*

We the Mesoamerican People, having found a voice in the civilization left to us by the original inhabitants of this continent, proclaim our self-determination to nurture and express our humanity as citizens of the Family of Creation.

A litany of labels has been created for us over the centuries through which to proclaim a cultural identity: Mexican, Chicano, Hispanic, Mexican American, Latino, Spanish, Mestizo, Indio. None of these can completely express who we are.

We are human beings, the two-legged nation placed on this Earth by our Universal Creator to care for the land as our Mother and respect all our relatives of Creation. The cradle of our civilization is Mesoamerica, called Anahuac in one of our traditional languages. But as citizens of Creation we are not bound by geography or political borders but by the universal truths each human being carries in their heart-truths that when spoken through the language dictated by five centuries of pain become twisted and misunderstood words.

The late mesoamerican scholar Octavio Paz wrote that culture is the ability to name things. For five hundred years we have continually lost our ability to name. Human became Indio. Anahuac became America. Meshica became Mexicano. A thousand years of history was erased and replaced with 1492. But as we stand on the bones of our ancestors already reintegrated into the dust of our path, we reclaim the original meaning of our terms without denying their new place in contemporary existence.

MEXICO is a country forged in 500 years of anticolonial struggle. Meshico is also the place where the Moon's navel touches the Earth and life is created. We are Meshicameh, children of Earth and Sky. Mexico is the island-state in middle of Lake Texcoco, capital of the Confederacy of Anahuac, cultural center of Mesoamerica.

NAHUATL is the language of the Aztecs. We also remember that when our ancestors were asked what language they spoke they answered—the truth. Nahuatl is that which has harmony, and that which is in harmony is truth. The Nahuatlaca family of languages is called Uto-Aztecan and includes the Shoshone of Wyoming and the Nahua speakers of El Salvador in Central America. We are Nahuatlaca. Tlaca is person. We are persons seeking harmony and we choose to speak our language, the truth.

TONANTZIN is la Virgen de Guadalupe, our Sacred Mother. She is also Tlecuauhtlacupe, the Morning Star riding on the Moon's crescent symbolizing the spark in the womb, the moment that is the miracle of Life. That is how we were conceived and how we came to be who we are, Anahuatlaca. She is Coatlaxompe, Mayahuel, Coatlicue, Chachihuiltlicue, Tlazolteotl, and Coyolxauhqui. She is our mother, our wife, our sister, our daughter, and ourselves.

QUETZALCOATL is a god, according to western thought. We also know this title to embody a concept, an understanding that the Earthbound (coatl) also has the ability of transcendence (quetzal) to the sky. To be aware of the unity of body and spirit is Quetzalcoatl. Knowing that, we can see the coatl (serpent) in the natural curving motion of the universe, the patterns of Venus, and in the flow of the wind and water. This motion is the beauty (quetzal feathers) of Creation. As a human incarnation Quetzalcoatl was born in Amatlan, Mexico, 1500 years ago, founded the Toltec Civilization, and traveled throughout Mesoamerica until his death at age 114. Toltec means one who uses instruments to create beauty. Quetzalcoatl is part of what we carry and whom we can choose to be.

We are not a single name, nation, or language. Like Creation, one reflects the many and all the one. We are a civilization, way of life whose seeds were planted millennia ago and whose trees, though plundered of their fruit, give us today the faith that is their roots. Those roots also have names. They are living entities, spiritual bonds with our communities of origin and tribal nations from whom we were severed through disease, war, poverty, and forced relocation. When we name these ties to history, culture, and civilization we do not seek power or glory but the fellowship of all who see Mesoamerica, Anahuac, the Great Turtle Island as their home and not their property.

MAIZ: Among certain native people of New England corn has retained its Mexican name—maiz. Originating in Mexican territory and now a staple of diets all over the world, corn is truly one of our gifts to humankind. It came to us as a gift also from an ant who told Quetzalcoatl where it was hidden. Transforming himself into this tiny creature, he took seven grains, each tinted with a color of the rainbow, and gave them to the People. From the ants he learned and taught us the tekiotl, laboring with instruments to harvest this essential part of our sustenance. Our Creation myths tells us we are made of maiz. That is what we are and continue to be.

COYOTE: One of our Creation stories tells us that Huehuecoyotl, Old Coyote was asked by the Creator to blow the conch shell and break the silence to initiate Creation. Then the Creator gave him a gourd rattle to guide Creation into a dance across space. As a grand protagonist of the Beginning, Coyote often has trouble being in awe of such a role but cannot escape the humility of his task. So he is a trickster who teaches by being a victim of his own tricks. We call people who cheat but never profit by their cheating coyotes. Those who smuggle people across the U.S. border for money are coyotes. Coyotes in our corridos (ballads) are people who fall because they are not able to transcend their character despite opportunity or insight. Originally a word of Meshica origin, coyotl, coyote is now even an official term of the French language. Coyote is part of what we recognize as an aspect of our human nature, part of what we are and can become.

CURANDERO: Despite the development of western medicine we still have our curandero (folk healing) tradition, our faith in herbs and ritual to restore harmony to an ill body, community, or soul. Although we use doctors and hospitals, in our communities we still use this way of healing. We have seen in contemporary times that the use of natural medicine and herbs has been a multibillion dollar industry. In this way, western civilization has attempted to catch up to ours. But no healing approach is complete without its spiritual aspects, without its peyotl, the center of the heart, the residence of the spark of life, the act of faith which is the essence of our spiritual traditions.

PIRAMIDE: Pyramids are the temples of Mesoamerica. These temples dot the landscape from Central America through regions along the Mississippi up into the Great Lakes. Temple mound cultures abound in Arizona and Colorado. There are pyramids from Casas Grandes in Chihuahua to Chichen Itza in Yucatan. They are not tipped like the Egyptian, but truncated into levels decreasing in size towards the sky. The missing endpoint is a unity with Creation, a becoming one with our Creator. Given our physical limitation, our truncated nature, we can strive for this but always are aware we will never achieve it. For only when we are capable of creating everything are we capable of thinking will we have perfection. But then we would be gods and not creatures who are capable of grand technological feats but completely ignorant of our place in Creation. Our teokalli or tekpan remind us of the struggle in our human nature between the ego, which tells us divinity is attainable, and spirit, which accepts the struggle towards the unachievable, towards the realm of the Great Mystery, of which only the Creator is Master.

CALENDARIO: In public buildings and private businesses south and north of the Mexican border we find the Sun Stone or Aztec Calendar displayed. Many of us may be illiterate in the language that governs its symbols but in our minds and hearts we know it is part of what we are. Its center is a mirror holding our human face telling with tekpatl tongue the vision of truth as we see ourselves in the Universe. Astronomers even today recognize it as one of the most accurate in the world. Accurate but not complicated, for it was formed with the simplicity of standing daily in one place year after year and taking the time to observe the movement of heavenly bodies across the sky day and night. The record of generations, needing no power source or moving parts, is freely given to those who seek a place of purpose and not of power in the Cosmos.

NAHUATL: If we choose to speak the language of truth, it does not matter which sounds we use. When we are identified with the Spanish language we do not automatically lose our identification with this continent. Linguists have identified hundreds of words of common use in Spanish of Nahuatl origin. The language of truth had a profound impact on the evolution of the Spanish language. Spanish is our common language in a civilization that has many traditional languages. It is a vehicle by which to talk with those who still live in their communities of origin and are citizens of their traditional nations. Mesoamerica is a civilization of linguistic diversity. We are not ashamed of that. It is part of what and who we are.

DANZA: We still take our children to see the matachines, concheros, danzantes Aztecas, and voladores de Papantla. Our traditional dances are repetitions of the natural movements of Creation, especially Nature. Motion is Her language. That is the way she teaches us. When we stand at a plaza or church steps watching these warriors honor Creation our heart strives to beat to the rhythm of the drum, the noise of our minds is eased by the shaking of the gourd rattles. Amidst the sounds of the carrizos and ayoyotes suddenly there is no question who we are.

DIA DE LOS MUERTOS: Death as a celebration and renewal is a concept indigenous to Anahuac, to this Great Turtle Island. It is one of the 20 day glyphs in the Aztec Calendar, the symbol mikiztli. Every November first and second we remember those who were here before us. It is a thousand-year-old covenant with our Way of Life. From the Spirit World, Mictlan, they return and we, their reflections, their seed, their inheritors are still here.

These are by no means our only bonds to a Tradition that began long before 1492. Their immediacy is part of the urgency we feel to break the silence of a civilization that has had to go underground since then. Our voice can be heard through those symbols and practices, which still shape our lives and conscience.

There are laws and treaties that promise the free exercise and expression of our ceremonies where we can voice our symbols through prayer, meditation, and ritual. There are also great obstacles that make those laws and treaties seem nonexistent. How do we overcome them and water those roots still nestled deep in Mother Earth?

LA LLORONA: Years before the arrival of the Europeans in Mexico-Tenochtitlan a woman was heard wailing in the night along the edge of Lake Texcoco. No one could see her, but everyone could hear her agony. The medicine people at the time told Moctezuma that it was the Spirit of Mother Earth, Coatlicue, crying for her children. "Men who are half beast will come," they said, "and turn the waters of the lake red with our blood. She cries for us. But she will be with us until we can again be her children." After the Spaniards mounted on horses arrived and completed the prophecy, this history was transformed into the story of La Llorona. In this way Coatlicue is with us until we can return to her as her children.

KALPULLI, THE LONGHOUSE: Our traditional form of organization is the kalpulli. Kal means house, pul means extended, thus kalpulli means "extended house." This social unit was developed by our civilization as a means of creating community, self-government, and economic development. It is similar to the longhouse concept of the Iroquois and the kibbutzim of Israel. China's Chairman Mao used it to improve his country's agricultural communes after reading *Organizacion Poltica de los Pueblos de Anahuac* by Agustin Vargas de Iturbide. It is a simple concept though not easy given the influence of western styles of organizing. Whether it can prove effective for the challenges of today remains to be seen. We will not know without an act of faith in one of many things left to us by those that came before us.

If we need to struggle to be who we are, if we need to remove the barriers that have kept our civilization underground, we choose to do it through a process that is itself part of who we are. How else can we test our faith and know that what we fight for is truly valuable?

Human beings can choose to see ourselves as part of Nature or separate from Her. Exercise of either choice brings consequences. Mesoamerica is a civilization founded on the principle that we are part of Nature. Our symbols, our ceremonies, our covenants, our temples instruct us how to act on this choice. No matter what the circumstances of the world, we choose to continue learning.

Five centuries ago began the sunset of our civilization. Its light gave way to darkness. We accepted the departure of our Sun as a time to gather and hide in the center of our hearts our most precious treasure. Our way of life continued in secret, fearful of persecution. In the home, fathers taught sons, mothers instructed daughters. So it was for centuries, from one generation to another.

Our civilization never died, only remained hidden. Its sunrise has begun, first in our hearts filling our conscience, urging us to come together and place before the world without fear or shame that which we are. With our hearts in our hands and our hands in the soil we declare that the call to act with love and create beauty is our destiny. Earth is not property but Mother. Creation is our family and our home. We are human beings, the two-legged nation, relatives to the families of the waters, the land, and the air. Ixachilan, Mesoamerica, Zem-Anahuac, the World is our womb.

Today we are born to be who we are.

Investigate the Web site from the film, *La Otra Conquista (The Other Conquest)* at *http://www.theotherconquest.com/.* Compare ideas, philosophies, histories of the filmmaker to those of Alarcón and Aceves. Report to your class.

Jeffrey Thomas Leong, Poet and Health Professional

Options for Listening

Please reflect and write some personal thoughts about the following questions:

- How would you describe your racial background if you could use twenty-five words? When you hear the words, "American citizen," whom do you visualize? How would you define "American culture"? In what ways have you used the color of your skin to advantage? In what ways has the color of your skin been a burden to you?
- As a small group, read aloud the poem "Myths of Whiteness" by Jeffrey Leong. Have different readers dramatize different parts or voices in the poem.
- Write questions you have about this poem, questions about both content and about opinions.

The Myth of Whiteness
—*Jeffrey Thomas Leong*

In the beginning there was myth . . .
Sitting around the Formica kitchen table before bowls of steaming rice,
quivering egg custard, and stinky tofu baby bok choy,
the near gods told us of Fan Gwei Loh, the ghost

of whiteness, a pale pretender, and Haahk Gwei Loh, black
devil, who I was told to keep an eye on in canned goods,
Yahp Bun Jai, the Japanese, to whom we lost the family home
in Kwangtung, our anger and shame, Fee Loh Bun Jai, and Leih Soong.
These eight immortals we feared or guffawed or praised
seeming so much like us.
Gods reduced to "ghosts," devils," and "boys,"
are one dimensional, a cartoon enemy,
for a rough-cut, three-dimensional world.

. . .

Somewhere in A hall, Michael Viebrock created the concept of B Hall.
Pale cool, surfer 60's, his tight-ass white Levi's and multi-hued
madras cotton short sleeves, declared
Ben Davis black chinos "out", we were in.
We, mixed-up children of the tired, poor and unwanted, once- removed.
the Italian, Irish, poor white and Jew,
and we, blanco de blanco Asians,
gathered around the concept of "Secretary of General Activities",
wore wool high letters on varsity belles
while the chinos and chulas cruised down their own streets,
snickered at painted-on jeans where the most important cahuengas
had no room to breathe.

. . .

White is the absence of color, black is the presence of all colors.

This is not chromatically true.
Except in Blackhawk, where it doesn't matter,
what counts is how you feel.

. . .

Every rainbow has its natural order, colors coordinated in distinct bands.
The marriage arc was no different.
Closest to center, the golden glow of sweet Chung Shan village,
next, J-town's deferential beauty,
then, the white mysteries, the blonde ephemeral uncertainty.
Last, a degradation into brown and black: Filipino, Mexican, and African-
    American.
those links fade into a dark rejection,
a lifetime of pariah messiah-dom.

. . .

White is "mo' bettah", I was told
reinforced by my 16-year-old summer school classmate's
poetry-hating, hip-boot-wearing, Highway Patrolman father,
who said, "You better (mo' bettah) leave my daughter alone!"
But my cousins from Hong Kong said more better too,
their pure translucence shown under skin,
a diet of non-dairy, non-animal fat foods,
while my opaque Asian-American brownness
belied many Happy Meals from smiling cows and delirious potatoes.
When I was in Taiwan, the women whipped out
umbrellas against the strong tropical afternoon sun,
so that their skin stayed clear and light.

. . .

The village peasant picks the beans, plants fists
of rice in muddy fields, pushes his melanin to the max,
while the landowner picks his teeth, plants sons
in faraway California, impales himself into prosperity.
According to the Cantonese, this is good,
if you are Wah Kue, overseas Chinese, with relatives in Golden Mountain.

. . .

The dinner table myths continued . . .
    One cold Shanghai winter, paternal grandfather's science experiment,
jamming a pail upside down on a seaman's head who just poured
dishwater on a boat family selling jook from their sampan. This ancestral
god hid in the Chinese woman's hold (at ship's bottom) for the rest of his
journey home.
    In '43, my mother fired from a cotton mill in Greensboro, South
Carolina because Chinese were neither white nor black, and the company
was busting African-American union organizing. As she walked slowly
through city streets, the church bells tolled for Roosevelt's empty body as
it passed on a train north for Washington.
    The Twitchells, white rancher neighbors, who during the scratched out
days of the Great Depression, supplied endless milk and eggs from plucky
chickens to one poor Chinese share-cropping brood.

. . .

Lying beside Lauren, her Jewish-Arab Pasadena history,
similarities of olive and gold-toned skin on chest and abdomen,
but too, her pink fuzzy cheeks, my sun-browned hands,
and the penultimate pale wrinkling into of her breasts,
her disappearing nipples.

In the 70's, Lauren's blonde surfer locks passed for,
while her sister's frizzy and dark Arab hair,
became a rainbow of sisterhood, night and day of culture.
What surfaces from the gene pool is random.
Lauren's nephew, Miles, runs a radiance never seen before,
a mix of mysterious elements, a complex stew of trace and base,
which steams through the living room.

. . .

At Berkeley in '69, we in the Movement tore down walls
of political economy in favor of true ethnic history,
against the lies of African-American slavery,
reviving Lakota warrior legends, remembering Wounded Knee,
exorcising dust-blown ghosts, the shame of
WW II Japanese-American concentration camps.
And yesterday, a Chicano farm-worker averts his eyes from mine
at the Cal Mart in downtown Calistoga.
His, the hands of the great Napa Valley,
its vines and wrinkles now owned by a corporate body.
What was once affirmative action, slips slowly back
into the myth of whiteness.

. . .

Ultimately, I believe myth is made
in the words passed after love-making,
when the story of Uncle Ameen, godlike maker of poetry in the schools,
is shared, his lyre or aboud at his side
while he creates the ghazals of post-modem immigration.
I believe Coyote is a woman, and Coyote is a man.
Coyote is the two halves of the same being
necessarily talking to itself,
reinventing story,
again and again.

Options for Dialogue

- With a dialogue partner, please discuss: What is the author telling us about his experiences? What kinds of learning does the author describe? What does the concept of "whiteness" have to do with education and its foundations?
- How can a poem such as this one challenge or change a society? Please discuss.

Options for Action

- Attend a play, opera, art film, or some artistic presentation in which you are immersed in the visual. Try to pick out a concept that is hard to explain in words but that is shown visually as Jeffrey Leong does with the complexities involved with the concept of "whiteness" in the poem.
- Choose a term or concept regarding a historical reference in the poem; find some research or other reading about this concept, and write a critical review about it.
- Go to the research around the definitions of "race." Why do people in different fields such as sociology, anthropology, and history disagree?
- Share one of the coyote or folk stories you found in the previous assignment.

Faye Kahn, Playwright and Actress

According to the Bible, Abraham had two sons, each of whom received a promise from God to beget a great nation. For Isaac it was the Jewish people, for Ishmael, the Arab. Together these sons, Isaac and Ishmael, buried their father in the cave of Machpelah. Yet Ishmael had been exiled so many years before, I wonder if they felt like brothers.

Options for Listening

- Think of an event in history (history from long ago or the recent history of your own family) and write about a disagreement between men and women. Now write about a disagreement of people with different belief systems. Now write about an example of "hope"—however small—that differences can be respected and peace restored.
- The author of the next selection introduces her work:

Recently I spent almost a year in Israel as a theatre artist-in-residence. I had the opportunity to perform my work, teach school children theatre improvisation, network, and begin research for a new theatre piece based on how Israelis view themselves and the issues facing their country. While trying to lead a normal life in Jerusalem, I began a journal of essays, my observations and experiences as I tried to negotiate this different culture in a foreign language. The following pieces are the end result of this record. I believe they capture many of the contrasts and paradoxes that are Israel.

- If you had the opportunity to visit Israel, Palestine, Jordan, other Middle Eastern countries, what would be some personal questions you would like to answer? Write a few of these. Listen to some of Faye Kahn's questions about her learning experience in Israel:

Why should I, a left-wing Reconstructionist Jew from Philadelphia, want to visit the Jewish settlement within Hevron, or want to visit the holy sites of the matriarchs and patriarchs? I want to see if there is meaning for me. I want the chance to experience what it is that Jews and Moslems die for. I don't know what I will experience. I am prepared for a lot of right-wing rhetoric and public relations.

- Read the selection from Faye Kahn's diary. Write questions you have as you read—questions about facts, questions about feelings.

Diary Entries
—Faye Kahn

Glossary

kipah/kipot (pl)—same as yarmulke, the skullcap worn by Jewish men

haredi—ultra-orthodox

shiur—lesson, study session

rosh chodesh—new moon, in the Jewish lunar calendar; also beginning of new month, traditionally celebrated by women, while the men celebrate together at the full moon

davven—pray

tzit tzit—fringes worn as undergarment or on the prayer shawl, to remind one of God's commandments

Purim—celebration from the Book of Esther, where the entire book (the whole megillah) is read, while participants dress up in costume and get rowdy and drunk

Tisha B'Av—literally means the 9th day of the month of Av; is a day

of mourning and fasting for the Jewish people, being the day of
commemorating the fall of both the first and second temples in Jerusalem as well as some other national tragedies

Baruch Hashem—blessed is The Name; more loosely, thank God, or
God willing

hailliam—soldiers

heblish—combination of Hebrew and English

erev shabbat—Friday night, the beginning of shabbat, the day of rest,
as all days in the Jewish calendar begin the evening before

shul—synagogue

davvening Shlomo Carlebach style—Shlomo Carlebach, who died
about 7 years ago, was an Orthodox rabbi but also a musician; he
taught passion in prayer through the new music he wrote for traditional liturgy; there are some synagogues who base their service
on his music and physical way of praying

minyan—in Orthodoxy, a minimum of 10 men to make a group for
prayer; more loosely, a congregation

kavannah—intention

Yom reshon (The First Day)

It's raining in Jerusalem. It's also *motza'ei shabbat*. After waiting
patiently for the restaurant to open and prepare our food, we now have to
rush to Yakar where we are going to hear Archbishop Desmond Tutu
speak on the truth and reconciliation process in South Africa. We hail a
taxi, jump in, and bark our directions in anxious Hebrew. The taxi
doesn't move. The driver says calmly, "*Shavua tov.*" Ahhh. To a good,
new week.

Yom reshon, Sunday, the first day. Already I have a tradition in
Jerusalem of celebrating the new week by taking an early morning class,
Torah and Yoga. I hop the number 18 bus, which takes me to the yuppie
neighborhood of Baka. I won't apologize for how at home I feel here. The
yoga class is held in the Reform synagogue. The class is filled with cool
women, some Israeli, some English-speaking, and one or two men
wearing *kipot*. I smile and say *boker tov* to a few participants I actually
know.

This week's *parasha* is, for the fifth consecutive week, on the building
of the *mishkan*, the sanctuary. Our teacher reads in Hebrew the text that
says, build it that I may dwell among them. She explains how the
sanctuary had to be built in order to contain God's essence. Through yoga
we build and strengthen the temple that is our body, in order to create a
holy space for the presence of God within ourselves. I do forget my own
essential divinity.

In the afternoon I have my weekly doctor's appointment in Bayit Vegan. I worry about the public transportation today because there is to be a huge *haredi* demonstration at 3:00 with an anticipated crowd of 300,000. Plus, there is to be a counterdemonstration by non-*haredi* groups. It's all about a complaint by the *haredi* against the High Court. The Court voted unanimously that the draft exemption for yeshiva students is illegal. They voted that Reform and Conservative representatives will sit on the Jerusalem religious council alongside their Orthodox counterparts. These decisions oppose the desires and customs of the *haredi*. Like Torah this is but one layer of meaning. Dig a little deeper, you find the very soul of Israel being pulled in two directions, bound and gagged by its very definition as a Jewish and a democratic state. How can these two concepts fit together? Will decisions regarding religious freedom be made by a body that is, ideally, divorced from politics, and thus from the direct influence of *haredi* constituents? Or will religious freedom be defined by the body which represents "the people" politically, where the *haredi* stand a better chance of wielding influence?

I decide the demonstration will be a good photo opportunity. It is still early, so I don't expect to see much action. As I walk toward the site of the rally, I see some buses parked at the central bus station with logos of out-of-town yeshivas. I see a lot of men and women in blue, extra police brought in. I see a few groups of young girls in tight pants carrying posters. Mostly I see a steady stream of religious school children. I wonder, are they part of that large count?

I ask my doctor about it, as I suspect he is *haredi*. He in turn asks his daughter, who tells him there is to be a special children's area, sort of babysitting, while the adults have their prayers. I nod approvingly but I'm not convinced.

Hours later, as I wait for the bus, group upon group of young men in black suits and hats are walking home. I notice a few families, too. On the bus, I pass by the site again. There are no people. The streets are covered in white leaflets, like a fresh, still snowfall. For a party that lasted less than two hours, I learn later that the cost to the city for cleaning up the trash was 15,800 shekels, $4,000.

I am in need of self-nurturing, so I stay on the bus all the way back to Baka, where I began the day so many hours ago. At my favorite restaurant I order Mexican chili. I walk to Yakar for an evening *shiur*. The rabbi has selected a text to relate to today's event, from Exodus 15:22–26. The people have come to water, but the water is bitter. They complain to Moses and ask, "What shall we drink?" Moses cries out and God instructs him about a tree. Moses casts the tree into the water and the water becomes sweet. And there, God gives him a statute and an ordinance.

I think about the connection between bitterness, sweetness, and rules. Does it all boil down to civility? Does it all hinge on faith? Will sweetness come from all this bitterness, too?

Yom Sheni (The Second Day)

The number 38 bus is smaller than a full-size bus. It makes a continuous loop around the center of Jerusalem, beginning and ending in the Jewish quarter of the Old City. At 7:15 in the morning, it acts almost as a school bus. Instead of lurching off and practically spilling passengers in the usual race for what, it waits a few moments as young yeshiva boys with sleep on their faces appear from different directions on the Jaffa Road. They board the bus on the way to their schools in the Old City, where authentic Judaism is taught.

While we idle in city traffic, I think about the young Arab woman who was stabbed to death on a Jerusalem street by a young Arab man, because he thought she was Jewish.

I get off at the last stop and head for the *kotel*, the wailing wall. It is *rosh chodesh*, or so I think, and from above as I pass through security, I scan for Women at the Wall. This is a group of women who, once a month, pray and sing out loud at the *kotel*, where such behavior is banned by law. No one is there. I guess *rosh chodesh* was yesterday. No matter. Now that I am here, it is a glorious morning and there is no crowd in the women's section. I walk right up to the ancient stone, lay my forehead against its cool soothing hands, pray. I pour out my heart. My tears require no explanation.

According to the Bible, Abraham had two sons, each of whom received a promise from God to beget a great nation. For Isaac it was the Jewish people, for Ishmael, the Arab. Together these sons, Isaac and Ishmael, buried their father in the cave of Machpelah. Yet Ishmael had been exiled so many years before, I wonder if they felt like brothers.

Back on the bus, the woman in front of me, hair modestly covered by an attractive scarf, looks down her nose at the man in ultra-orthodox black hat merrily gabbing on his *pellaphone* as the woman next to her, in red wig, *davvens* from a worn prayer book. On this bus, every woman is wearing a skirt; every man and boy has his head covered. Even the bus driver wears a kipah, a sign that he, too, is religiously observant. I am wearing a long skirt. Underneath are my long pants. My head is covered, as well. It's cold outside.

As we circle the downtown, a few more young boys board the bus. With their velour *kipot*, their *tzit tzit*, and Snoopy book bags, they look so cute. Not one of them has a Jewish nose.

The bus pulls up to a red light. Next to us two soldiers are having trouble with their van. Our driver gets out of his seat and stands at the door, advising them and laughing. As the light changes he turns directly to us, his audience, and with Shakespearean seriousness, delivers his aside. Spoken all in Hebrew, I don't understand a word.

Yom Hameshi (The Fifth Day)

One day after Purim I calculate to be a safe day to visit Hevron and the Cave of Machpelah, the Cave of the Patriarchs and Matriarchs. More than a thousand years ago, when the Sanhedrin was deciding which texts would be included in the *Tanakh,* the Bible, Queen Esther wrote to them, requesting her story be included. Make for me a book, and a festival. At first the wise men refused on the grounds that we Jews shouldn't brag too much about our victories over the gentile nations, *Amalek.* Just so, the Arabs like to humble us on Purim. It's a mitzvah for them to do some violence to Jews in Israel on Purim. Last year and this year, nothing happened, *baruch Hashem*. But I also remember Baruch Goldstein murdering the 30 Moslem worshipers in the Cave on Purim. Were the Arabs planning a pogrom against the Jews? They had knives aplenty for cutting him to bits. Whether he was villain or hero, better to go after Purim, when bad memories are already waning.

Why should I, a left-wing Reconstructionist Jew from Philadelphia, want to visit the Jewish settlement within Hevron, or want to visit the holy sites of the matriarchs and patriarchs? I want to see if there is meaning for me. I want the chance to experience what it is that Jews and Moslems die for. I don't know what I will experience. I am prepared for a lot of right-wing rhetoric and public relations.

We begin at the Tomb of Rachel, the only matriarch who is not buried in the Cave at Hevron. The Kever of Rachel, a small cave, is actually covered by a new building. Six women seated in plastic patio chairs are already lined up against the tomb itself, so the rest of us stand around the room, praying in our own ways, and surreptitiously taking photographs of each other standing close to the tomb. I think about Omar, the Palestinian I interviewed who lives practically around the corner from this place, in Bethlehem. He declared Rahel an important matriarch for the Moslem Arabs, a symbol of mercy, until the Israelis took land to build what they called an Institute to house the kever, and installed Israeli soldiers outside, here in Bethlehem which is already under the Palestinian Authority. For Omar the thought of Rahel now brings up only bad feelings.

The Biblical city of Hevron was founded some 4 millennia ago. When Joshua was preparing to enter the land, he sent scouts to see who was in the land. Reports came back that giants dwelled in Hevron. Three thousand years ago, King David ruled from Hevron for seven years before ascending to Jerusalem. During the second temple period, King Herod constructed a huge building over the cave, in order to make it a more impressive holy shrine. In 1267, the Mamluks conquered the whole area. For 700 years, until the 6 day war in 1967, the cave was closed to Jews and Christians, as the Moslems converted Herod's building into a mosque and only Moslems can pray in a mosque. For 700 years Jews prayed at the cave by standing on the seventh step, outside the entrance, where the wall is now blackened from their candle smoke. After the expulsion from Spain, Sephardi Jews came to Hevron in the 16th century and built the walled Jewish ghetto. From that time until 1929, there was continuous Jewish presence in Hevron.

I so believe that peace will never come so long as we, both Arabs and Jews, dwell on the past, on who is more entitled, on who lived where from how long ago, on who has suffered more, on who started it and who is seeking revenge. As in South Africa, there must be acknowledgment of cruelties and injustices through a truth and reconciliation process that will enable both peoples to move into the future as peaceful neighbors.

Sitting in the playground surrounded by the 7 caravans housing 7 families that were permitted by Begin to move here in 1984, creating a tiny neighborhood outside of the Jewish quarter, our guide tells us about the 1929 Arab massacre of Jews in Hevron. On shabbat, in 10 short hours, while the British stood by and did nothing, the community was decimated, until the British themselves felt threatened and fired a gun into the air. At the sound of gunfire, the Arabs fled. The surviving Jews were bused to Jerusalem that evening. After centuries of continuous Jewish presence, there were no Jews in Hevron.

I want to feel entitled as a Jew. I want to see the Jewish people in strength and glory. I must also feel compassion for the Palestinians. Our guide's telling seems to me to fan the flames of Arab stereotyping. I ask her what caused the riot, what provoked it. Caught off guard, she promises to explain, later.

We are given a tour of the small Jewish quarter and hear the story of the Levenger family and others who, bravely or selfishly or arrogantly or stupidly, put themselves on the line to make a Jewish presence again in Hevron, in 1979, 50 years after the massacre. We are taken to a small darkened stone room. The room is an altar to the victims. The photos are in the dark while our guide tells us more details of the massacre.

She does explain that two things occurred, one on the Jewish side, one on the Moslem. Only one day a year were Jews permitted to pray at the Western Wall, under the British mandate. That day was Tisha B'Av. For some reason, in 1929 the British forbade the Jews from coming. There was such an outcry that the British said okay, come one week after Tisha B'Av. Many, many more Jews than usual came to the Wall to pray. Apparently this made the Arabs nervous. On the Moslem side, the British-appointed Mufti of Jerusalem hated the Jews. Inflammatory sermons were preached at the local mosques. Cars from Jerusalem and elsewhere began to stream into Hevron.

Our guide then switches on lights which illuminate the photographs, showing Jews with fingers cut off, hands, arms, a neck slashed, blood dripping down the steps of the Bet Cholim, where the massacre began. The hospital, a free hospital built by Jews which served both Arab and Jew. I am sick at heart, sick to my stomach.

I know all of this is carefully choreographed to provoke exactly this reaction, a revulsion and total hatred of Arabs. And what of the British? I want to scream all the way to England, what are you Jews doing there, giving your contributions to that society? Get out of there! A year after the massacre, the British issued a White Paper which put all the blame for the massacre on the Jews.

Like all good Reconstructionist Jews, I can't get celebratory over the 75,000 killed by the Jews on Purim. Just for today, however, I say Long live Queen Esther.

Our tour ends as close to the Cave as anyone can get, in rooms dedicated to Abraham and Sarah, Isaac and Rebeka, Jacob and Leah. I lean my head on the iron grillwork and cry noiselessly.

Yom Shishi (The Sixth Day)

So much of Judaism is about making distinctions. In this way our consciousness is raised to appreciate each little thing. Above all, shabbat is about making distinctions. We make a distinction between the work week and the day on which we take in that it is good.

In Jerusalem, Friday is the hardest day of the week. Everything must be done, all errands, all shopping, all banking, all cleaning, and all cooking. Everywhere is jammed with people. My neighborhood is by the Mahane Yehuda, the big open-air market where people from all parts of the city do their shopping. One of my important pre-*shabbat* errands is to swim at the YMCA. The bus stop by the market will be overflowing with fragile old people and their bursting bags of produce and cheap housewares. The stop by the central bus station will be packed with sturdy young soldiers on their way home for shabbat, plus their duffels and their rifles. I choose to cast my fate with the haillim and set off upstream for the bus station. I can pick up a schedule for my trip to Haifa as I pass through.

When I get to the information counter, I am informed by the young man, in unbroken American, that we are out of Haifa. Out of Haifa. What does that mean? There are a lot of Palestinians still carrying keys to their homes that would like us out of Haifa.

I arrive at the Y in time for the women's swim. I am becoming more Israeli by the day. I actually let loose on a bunch of women standing in the middle of the pool just talking while I am trying to swim laps. *Eze kef*: this is fun. As we yell at each other in heblish, I am saying "you see that I am swimming here. Why do you stand here? He (the lifeguard who is busy talking to his friend) told me to swim on this side. You stand over there." The spokeswoman says, "Ah. He told you that? We know better than he. You swim over there."

It has started to rain. Waiting for the bus, I begin to fantasize that a taxi pulls up, already with some passengers, and offers me a free ride. I decline, at first thinking I misunderstand. He urges me, I decline again, this time with an uneasy feeling. Later I hear that a taxi driver made a suicide bombing in his own taxi. I snap out of my fantasy when the bus comes and I must board along with 18 tourists from Baltimore. In the back of the bus I hear them discussing when on *motza'ei shabbat* they will be able to return to Ben Yehuda Street to pick up their purchases of silver jewelry. How quickly the shadow of detonated bodies is disappeared by the light of new eyes seeing Jerusalem for the first time. Eighteen: double chai, double life.

Distinctions. God made the sixth day the hardest in order that we appreciate the seventh day, the day of rest. I look forward to its sweetness.

Yom HaShabbat (The Seventh Day)

On *erev shabbat* it pours rain. All day I have cleaned and cooked in preparation for Friday night guests. When the horn sounds to announce shabbat, it is time to light the candles and say the blessing. Because of that horn, even though I am alone, I don't feel alone when I light. I know that many people are doing just what I am doing at approximately the same moment. I wear my genuine Israeli dress, teal velour down to the floor. At 6 o'clock my friends arrive with their contributions to the meal. For the first time, I am using my plata, the electric hot plate that keeps food warm for the entire shabbat, so there's no turning on the electricity once shabbat is in. I have turned everything on, the two heaters and all the lights, because I believe it is important to them. And why not? I never do such things when I am alone, but tonight I enjoy this ritual of making shabbat, making distinctions.

We dance through the raindrops to Beit Simcha, a small shul with davvening Shlomo Carlebach style. Melissa and I try to stand behind the *mechitza,* a sheer white curtain. The women's section is so crowded, we're half in and half out. It doesn't seem to matter. David stands on the other side of the curtain but near to us. The singing has already reached a frenzy, with young men jumping up and down and shrieking. Children crash into my ankles. There is a little girl alone in the women's section. I have noticed her before. She has pigtails and glasses. Her normally pale face is flushed with color. I watch her pray, the book pressed to her heart as she rolls her eyes towards heaven. I wonder how she landed here.

During the silent standing prayer, after my own personal prayers, I take time to notice the men who are standing in front of me. Several are dressed in work shirts or sweaters, with knitted *kipot*. Others are in white shirts and black hats. A few are old, most are very young. Some, looking more like babysitters, carry small sons on their shoulders. One has a full bushy head of curly hair. Another sports a long ponytail, *tzit tzit*, and a leather jacket. Two wear gigantic fur hats.

In the women's section Melissa and I receive stares. Melissa whispers that it's because she's blond. She must be a wasp shiksa. I'm sure they're staring at me. My Reconstructionism must be showing somewhere. Most of the women also are very young. Two or three women are nursing babies. The women are lined up in neat rows of plastic chairs. Melissa and I stand, as do most of the men. Better to receive our extra soul.

Yom HaShabbat (The Seventh Day)

Shabbat morning is an entirely different thing. The air is crisp, the sun shines on this day that for the first time in Israel I will read from the Torah. At the Reconstructionist minyan there is no *mechitza.* No one stares. The room is warm and friendly. A group of Reconstructionist, Renewal, and Reform rabbinic students have divided the leadership of the service, both men and women. They warmly congratulate me after the service. The energy of this service is staid in comparison to the energy of last night, which was more like Evangelism. But here I feel a palpable bond, of a minority, a minority that believes in egalitarianism, that honors the voices of women. Back in the Diaspora, we are becoming the majority within a minority. Here in Israel, I don't know what we are. We are a minority voice in relationship to the religious establishment, but is that establishment a majority? I think not. Yet the nonobservant majority are not ready for this evolution in Judaism. We stand alone.

Last week I interviewed a settler in Gaza, a religious Zionist. He said he appreciates what the Reform movement has been in the Diaspora, a means of maintaining Jewish identity in the face of the pull of assimilation. But here in Israel we cannot live under one roof. He prefers the secular Israelis to the Reform, because when they don't want to keep *halacha,* the religious laws, at least they agree on what is the *halacha.* With Reform, he claims they bring a different Torah. They are changing *halacha* and telling him he is wrong. Israel is not ready for these kinds of changes to Judaism. The rabbinate feels threatened. The Reform movement is destroying spirituality in Israel.

His last statement jolts me, reminds me of that form without content that Judaism can appear to be. Reminds me of how, at age fourteen, I cast aside all religion as a too tight skin. I have come to Israel to try to understand these conflicts within Judaism firsthand. A thousand years ago we were cast out of the land while having these same debates. Now that we have returned the beat goes on. Sometimes I think the fourteen-year-old was right.

After services we have a potluck meal. I sit next to my friend N, who is preparing to become a Jewish Renewal rabbi. She tells us how she explained to some Orthodox women why she wears a *kipah* but not the hair covering that married women wear. She says men wear a head covering in deference to God. Married women cover their hair in deference to men. Her kipah is worn in deference to God and that's enough. Just as she thought about her head covering and came to her own decision, in Jerusalem I am trying on Jewish practices in a way I never do at home. All week long I am conscious of how I dress, where I sit on the bus, which dishes I use, what errands I must do before shabbat. I swing between a love and hate of the structure, a love of the kavannah, a hate of the arbitrariness.

All form and formality aside, what I love about shabbat in Israel is how many people actually observe it by attending shul. I am inspired to pray hard. Sometimes I pray for peace with justice and an end to oppression. Sometimes I pray for healing for others. Other times I pray for myself. Lately I have been focusing my prayers on my children. When I see the changes in my children, I know that prayer works. Especially prayers Made in Israel.

Options for Dialogue

- Dialogue with a partner about events and feelings of each day's diary entries. Discuss what stands out most for you and why.
- What are some of the things the author is learning in Israel?

Options for Action

- Research information about a government (your choice of which) policy on the issue of separating church and state. Describe the process and how this differs from or is similar to what the author describes regarding modern Israel. How does this policy affect education?

- Go to the following Websites and read at least two essays by Edward Said, noted Palestinian author, intellectual, and activist.
  http://www.iap.org/politics/esaid-pl.html
  http://www.leb.net/tesa/
  http://www.palestine.html

CHAPTER FOUR

... Creating Dialogue about Histories and Beliefs

What does history mean when studying education? From our post-formal (Kincheloe & Steinberg, 1997) perspective, education is a process of both reading history (the world) and creating history (what do you believe is important?). No one develops knowledge out of the context of family, community, country, world at the present time or without a connection to the past—the stories of those who have gone before. Education develops among particularities, among persons and objects in families and communities.

The history of the Armenian peoples provides an example of this. Their survival owes much to their attachment to their native language with its distinct alphabet, although the largest Armenian community in the world today is in the United States. For 1700 unbroken years they have expressed the beliefs at the heart of their identity through text illuminated with art. For hundreds of years manuscripts were illuminated, embellished with luminous color with either literal or symbolic decoration to help with the layout or reading. In modern times this oneness of the written with the visual was lost except in books for children or more recently in conceptual art. The written and visual are moving together again this new graphic age and so literacy has to be intertextual. A literate person must be able to read between and within these different texts. In order to help students develop these multiliteracies, the curriculum must consider and include their individual communities and personal histories.

Cannella (1997), among others, believes that the construction of knowledge is rooted in power relations (Cannella, 1997). She traces the genealogy of childhood education and reminds us that childhood did not exist during the medieval period. She goes on to show the dramatic connection between historical and social context, including the power brokers of a given society at a given time, and the accepted notions about childhood. Cannella's (1997) work raises questions in terms of social justice and early education.

- How do we eliminate the two-tiered system? Does the curriculum respect the multiple knowledge and life experiences of younger human beings from diverse backgrounds?
- How does our current practice perpetuate a classed structure in the society?
- Is the message provided by education to each human being equitable regarding his or her background, beliefs, and life experiences? Does the educational/care system treat everyone fairly with respect?
- Are there those whose life experiences create privilege for them within the school contexts that we have created? Is this socially just? (p. 164)

These questions are central to learning to teach. They are also central to the following selections in which the authors confront and interrogate historical lives and beliefs in the light of culture. It is the hope of the authors that the reader will connect these works in various genre to their own lives and work. Syl Jones discusses the meaning of whiteness in American culture from a historical and contemporary perspective. Mary Gallant used primary source documents in the form of personal diaries, newspapers, and archival data to write the biographical essay which tells the story of a woman who was a pioneer in the education of females in Victorian England. Ann Green gives an example of a classroom teacher using traditional folk literature to help students make connections among cultures and with their own lives. Fairy tales are one of many ways traditions are passed along. Fairy tales are constantly being rewritten in the context of culture. An example is *Ash Girl* rewritten by Sarah, Ms. Green's student, to express her beliefs.

References

Cannella, G. S. (1997). *Deconstructing early childhood education: Social justice and revolution*. New York: Peter Lang.

Kincheloe, J. L., & Steinberg, S. R. (1997). *Changing multiculturalism*. Philadelphia: Open University Press.

Richardson, L. (1994). Writing, a method of inquiry. In N. Denzin and Y. Lincoln (Eds.) *Handbook of qualitative research* (pp. 516–529). Thousand Oaks, CA: Sage.

Syl Jones, Playwright, Essayist, and Columnist

Options for Listening

- Reflect and write about how you describe or define your racial or ethnic identity. What is important and not important to you about this aspect of yourself? If it is important, why? If unimportant, why? Is your ethnic identity tied to a particular place? In what ways? What are some of the details of that place that are a part of your life now or of a memory you hold dear?
- How did you learn about your racial or ethnic identity? What are your earliest memories of it? What was enjoyable or painful as you learned about these aspects of your identity? Write about this.
- In your notes, create an idea web around the words in your home language that reveal some of your people's histories.
- Read the essay and write any questions that come to mind as you read.

Bound by the Chains of Whiteness

—*Syl Jones*

> *White people have not always been 'white' nor will they always be 'white.' It is a political alliance. Things will change.*
> —*Amoja Three Rivers*

What if you, an innocent, intelligent Caucasian, learned that you had been born into a system, an ideology, that stripped you of your true identity and imposed upon you a cradle-to-grave facade? What if you discovered that this same tautology had been responsible for the oppression of others? That your elected officials, corporate leaders, and major institutions—some unwittingly—had used this belief system to keep us from embracing our humanity and thereby demanding an end to economic exploitation?

Would you have the courage to pull back the layers of supposition, tradition, and deceit? And, once you came face-to-face with the truth, would you be willing to change? With indisputable evidence of its destructiveness, would you be willing to participate in the abolition of that way of life and the creation of something new, unifying, and positive?

These are among the most interesting questions to emerge from a rather beleaguered field known generally as Whiteness Studies. For years, African-American writers have mused on the question of what it means to be white but have seldom been taken seriously. That may be about to change as, ironically, white scholars from nearly every discipline—many of whom have puzzled for years over the intractable nature of racial prejudice in the United States—are beginning to ask similar questions. These questions aim at nothing fewer ambitions than the unmasking of whiteness as an invisible system of oppression.

Here I offer a caveat: The study of whiteness isn't simply or primarily about skin color. First and foremost, it postulates that the very concept of race is an artifice and that the true differences between us are minimal at the biological level. In other words, race has been constructed as both an explanation for cultural differences and, second, as a barrier to true unity between and among cross-cultural classes. Although it would seem ridiculous to say that race itself was created in America, there can be little denial that racial oppression—on the basis of skin color—was refined in this country as a strategy for ensuring white supremacy.

For example, laws passed in Virginia in the seventeenth century forbidding nonwhites—whether slave or free, black, mulatto, or native—from testifying in court against Englishmen, from "raising a hand against" the English, and exempting slave owners from prosecution on the charge of rape were the first of their kind to be based solely on skin complexion. These laws were unique because they allowed all Englishmen, regardless of class, to benefit from a kind of carte blanche protection because of their whiteness.

This strategy was not imported from Europe, as some have mistakenly assumed. It was instead an American invention that was given widespread acceptance through the simple legal requirement that these laws be read aloud at church services and public gatherings on a quarterly basis in Virginia and, later, in other colonies. In this way, white supremacy was inculcated into the hearts of all Americans at the same services where the laws of God and the love of Christ were taught.

The reasons for such laws transcended pure cultural chauvinism or hatred. They were prompted by very practical concerns like the alarming specter of bloody rebellion by united blacks and whites and the potential loss of a growing slave and/or low-cost labor force. White landowners—fearing actions such as Bacon's Rebellion, where working-class men of all races united in an unsuccessful attempt to overthrow a growing aristocracy—worried that they might lose their livelihood and perhaps even their lives unless a powerful wedge could be driven between blacks and whites.

They were so successful that more than 300 years later, in this year of a presumed "national conversation about race," not a single leader has raised the question of the origins of whiteness, why the concept appeared when it did, and what purpose it has served. In fact, many people, when confronted with the invention of whiteness, respond that they've never thought about the issue before and find it hard to do so now. That's because the most dominant aspect of whiteness is its invisibility caused, paradoxically, by its ubiquity.

Whither Whiteness?

There was, in fact, a time in American history when whiteness as a presumed biological fact did not exist, when citizens were known by their ethnic traditions and language distinctions, not their skin color. Theodore Allen, author of *The Invention of the White Race*, points out that "In colonial Hispanic America, it was possible for a person, regardless of [physical appearance], to become 'white' by purchasing a royal certificate of whiteness." If whiteness can be located in history as a commodity that could be bought and sold, what does that say about its authenticity as a personal descriptor?

This question has been explored for decades by African-Americans and some whites on the fringes of American history. What has changed recently is that the debate has lately turned toward the controversial idea of "abolishing" the concept of whiteness and is being advanced by many Caucasian scholars. Their thesis, as expressed in dozens of books, is that studies of whiteness will help us understand white privilege and its destructive aspects. And that once understood, even those who consider themselves white will want to abolish the label in order to end the ordeal of racial separatism and oppression.

The New Abolitionists

One of the most important modern critiques against whiteness has been raised by David Roediger, professor and chair of American studies in the history department at the University of Minnesota. Roediger's book, *The Wages of Whiteness*, brilliantly illuminated the historical forces that have conspired to make whiteness the most dominant invisible political force in American history.

Roediger's work emphasizes that the central implication arising from the insight that race is artificial "is the specific need to attack whiteness as a destructive ideology." His aggressiveness in pursuit of a new racial landscape in the United States marks him as one of a coterie of historians I like to call the New Abolitionists. Like the abolitionists of old, they are passionate to the point of alienating many, if not most, Americans. But their astute reading of history—including analysis of the English oppression of the Irish—and their dedication to unifying working-class people of all ethnicities—separate them from the old abolitionists.

Taking his cue from W. E. B. DuBois's towering work, *Black Reconstruction*, Roediger asserts in one of his essays, "It is not merely that whiteness is oppressive and false; it is that whiteness is nothing but oppressive and false." Lest you take that personally, his point is that whiteness as a racial construct was designed by the rich in order to ensure that working-class people remain in constant competition with each other. Roediger is not the first to make this observation, but his writing hammers home the point with more conviction than others have managed to muster.

Radicalized by Experience

How did a Caucasian American like Roediger manage to shift his personal paradigm so that he could see the invisible chains of whiteness binding him? Perhaps growing up in a small, all-white town near East St. Louis, Illinois helped. Roediger spent summers in nearby Cairo as well, where a particularly explosive mix of populism, racism, and antiracist activism has existed since before the Civil War.

Through the influence of a local priest, Roediger realized early on that the interests of working-class whites overlapped those of African-Americans. As student body president of his high school, Roediger spearheaded efforts to fund the United Black Front, an antiracist organization then despised by local whites. The resulting "pitched battle" with his school board helped radicalize Roediger and prompted a lifelong inquiry into U.S. labor history, racism, and class struggle.

What Roediger wants to know—what all of us should demand an answer to—can best be summed up in the question, "When people say they're 'white workers,' why is the emphasis always on the word 'white'?" That question is perhaps the most important race-related inquiry we can make at this moment. It heralds answers that may awaken those who've been sleepwalking through generations of racial conflict.

The Race/Class Axis

Over the years, the national debate on race has focused almost entirely on people of color. We have been examined and labeled in such minute detail that popular culture is filled to overflowing with descriptions of our music, food, political inclinations, social mores, habits, faults, and so on. This has conveniently allowed commentators to avoid all but humorous examinations of whiteness (see Martin Mull's all-too-true analysis, *The History of White People in America*).

In fact, some readers of this article are currently engaged in the same tired "quid pro quo" debate that always emerges whenever the spotlight is turned on white history. They're asking themselves smugly, "If whiteness is abolished, does that mean blackness should be abolished, too?" The answer is twofold: First, blackness came about in reaction to whiteness. It will not need to exist as an artificial racial category if the glorious day ever comes when whiteness does not exist. Secondly, blackness has begun a healthy evolution into "African-Americanness," emphasizing cultural affinities rather than skin color. When Caucasians re-create themselves and their histories to the same extent, the possibility will emerge for a new Americanness based on shared values. Scrutiny of whiteness and its invisibility is highly useful to all. It invariably leads many to ask what social purpose is served by whiteness. The startling answer—in part, that whiteness is a kind of false merit badge awarded to working-class whites so that they remain open to exploitation by the upper classes—ought to shock many into consciousness. Once the shock wears off, it is possible that working people will unite regardless of color and that the great middle class will reach down to give its support to those who make our high standard of living possible. As racial awareness gives way to class awareness, will Americans fail to see the opportunities for uniting?

Who of us, regardless of race, can deny that companies like General Motors and Northwest Airlines are economically exploiting their workers by not sharing the profits the company has gained over the past five years? Those profits are a direct result of concessions made by working people who delayed their financial reward so that their companies could run more efficiently. In the case of GM, those efficiencies have failed because of management errors, and management should be penalized for such failures—not those on the bottom of the pile, who have little or no decision-making powers.

A number of books, papers, and conferences have been produced on the subject of whiteness. But as Roediger remarks, the popular media have often ignored the subject, preferring instead to focus on more sensational issues.

"At a conference on whiteness held at Berkeley a few years ago," says Roediger, "we received quite a number of calls from the media. But once they found out we were not advocating white supremacy, they lost interest."

What Roediger and his fellow scholars are advocating turns out to be a careful examination of how our institutions blindly support whiteness as somehow natural and DNA-induced instead of socially constructed. And, how the continuation of the lie of whiteness robs Euro-Americans of their true identity and of the natural affinity with Americans of color, both of whom are struggling in comparison to the top one percent of Americans.

Roediger is of special interest to Minnesotans because he lives and works here and is blazing a trail that many would do well to follow. His newest book, *Black on White,* contains a series of pieces by African-Americans on the subject of whiteness, some dating back 150 years. Roediger's own intellectual debts are acknowledged in this book, which gathers together essays, tales, cartoons, poems, and short stories by African-American thinkers analyzing whites. Ranging from slave autobiographies to works by such contemporary writers as Alice Walker and Greg Tate, the collection samples a rich tradition of black studies of whiteness.

For a more in-depth treatment of this complex subject, readers should also consult Theodore Allen's *The Invention of the White Race, Parts 1 & 2,* Alexander Saxton's *The Rise and Fall of the White Republic,* Toni Morrison's *Playing in the Dark: Whiteness and the Literary Imagination,* and "The White Issue" of the *Minnesota Review,* published in 1996.

Once the subject is exposed, additional questions will be asked, and whiteness will become more visible and, perhaps, less powerful as a social construct.

Options for Dialogue

- Please discuss whether anyone in your small group has read about or heard about "whiteness studies" in the media or in any classes. What do you know about the topic?
- What was new information for you in this essay? What information was something you already knew?
- Mr. Jones brings up historical information which may or may not have been included in history books or history classes that you've been exposed to in your education. Please discuss your groups' thoughts about what is often included and what is often left out of text books and course content.

Options for Action

- Read Alexander Saxton's *The Rise and Fall of the White Republic,* Toni Morrison's *Playing in the Dark: Whiteness and the Literary Imagination*, Theodore Allen's *The Invention of the White Race, Parts 1 & 2*, and "The White Issue" of the *Minnesota Review*, published in 1996. Relate anything you find interesting in what you read to Mr. Jones's essay and report your findings to your class.

- Read *The Bluest Eye* by Toni Morrison. Discuss how Shirley Temple in the story is a metaphor for the forced acceptance of a certain kind of identity forced on children who cannot imagine an alternative.
- Design 7 to 10 interview questions, based on the information in the essay and/or the above reading suggestions, and interview a history teacher. Does this educator include in classes any of the information discussed? In what ways? Report to your class.
- Ask your parents, grandparents, or other members of your family to read this essay and discuss their reactions.

Mary Gallant, Librarian and Historical Researcher

In his poem in the preceding chapter, Jeffrey Leong describes the present that carries the past in many obvious and subtle ways. The following historical essay describes past events that are related to philosophy and education from the perspective of a pioneering female educator. We will ask you to look for bridges between her story and the present issues in education.

Options for Listening

- Think about your family or close friends. Try to remember and write about the schooling history of the eldest woman you know. Where did she live and what were the conditions surrounding her schooling? What was her age when she had to or wanted to stop attending school? How has she talked about it or did she talk about these experiences during her life? Write about this woman.
- Briefly describe what you know about the educational system in England, Ireland, Scotland, and Wales.
- Think back to your own schooling and remember when you had the opportunity to learn from a "primary source" document, or set of materials (original letters, a treaty displayed

in a museum, an archaeological artifact). What was the situation and what were the materials?

- Read the following historical essay about the life and work of a nineteenth-century British educator. Pay attention to the philosophies of education that prevailed at that time. This essay was, in part, composed as a result of the author's reading original diaries of Anne Jemima Clough.

Charleston to Liverpool: Shaped by Two Cultures

—*Mary P. Gallant*

Anne Jemima Clough was many things. She was the only daughter of James Clough, a cotton factor who left his home in Liverpool to seek his fortune in the American South. She was the beloved sister of Victorian poet Arthur Hugh Clough, who reaps posthumous fame as a resident of the second tier of nineteenth-century Victorian poets. And as the first principal of Newnham College, University of Cambridge, she was acknowledged and venerated among educators as a luminary in the field of nineteenth-century women's education in Britain.

Much has been written, particularly in Britain, about the nineteenth-century movement for women's education. Anne Clough's role as the first principal of Newnham College in England has thrust her onto the stage of history. But in accounts of her life and intellectual development, most attention is paid to her years as a teacher among the poor of Liverpool and the crofter families of the English Lake District. Conspicuously absent from these works is a discussion of the period of her life which Clough herself considered "American South." Through her recollections of this formative time in her life, including her rather novel view of Charleston and Charleston society in the early 1800s, we see the antebellum South through the eyes of a young, foreign, female observer. Indeed, her views about race, class, and women's roles in society were markedly influenced by her Charleston experience.

Born in Liverpool in 1820 and reared in Charleston, South Carolina, Anne Clough's exposure to two different cultures before she was sixteen years old caused her to see things differently all her life from most others of her class. Understandably, she was never comfortable with her own identity; always lurking in the back of her mind was the conviction that she was indeed "different," although she never truly assimilated the main reason for her "differentness."

Anne Jemima Clough was the only daughter of the four children of James and Ann Perfect Clough. In 1822, shortly after her second birthday, she and her family moved to Charleston, where James hoped to find the prosperity he found so elusive in Liverpool. When his business in Liverpool began to flag, James looked to America to rejuvenate it. The family settled in "a large, ugly, red brick house on the East Bay . . . [The children's] father's office was on a lower storey, and there they played among the heaps of cotton, and saw the captains of the merchant vessels who came in about their business" (Clough, 1897, p. 2). A solitary and quiet child, Anne was an astute observer of what went on around her. As she laments in her recollections, "[Our] Father & Mother were too English to let us go to school which was perhaps a pity" (Clough, 1897, p. 6). Nevertheless, although she was not permitted by her parents to attend school or to participate in many of the activities of her peers, Anne made up for the lack by peopling a vivid imaginary world with people she observed. Although the Clough children were insulated from that potential threat to a proper English upbringing, personal contact with the natives, they treasured their few contacts with others. Indeed, Anne Clough's views about race, class, and women's roles in society were markedly influenced by her Charleston experience. The idea of female self-sufficiency was ingrained in her consciousness early. In a society often only one or two generations removed from a frontier culture, women tended to be less fettered by tradition than they were in the circle of British society in which the Clough family was rooted. Filtering through Anne's later diaries and writings is the idea, formed from close observation as well as from her somewhat limited contacts in Charleston, that women should have opportunities equal to those of men. For instance, many women in Charleston kept dame schools in their homes; not only were they paid for their services, they were admired for their independence and their industriousness.

Another of the imported ideas that remained with her during her career in Britain, and one that she frequently tried to implement in later life, was the concept of the lending library. It was often only among the pages of books from the lending library in Charleston that the lonely child met lifelong friends and visited other lands and cultures. During her life Clough remembered and commented frequently upon the lending libraries of Charleston.

Probably related to these early memories was her lifelong promotion of the establishment of school lending libraries. "One point which she frequently urged upon the mistresses was the desirability of establishing school lending libraries, from which the girls could obtain general literature and acquire a taste for it. She not infrequently presented some small sum with which to start such libraries" (Clough, 1897, p. 266).

Unfortunately, James's hoped-for success as a cotton broker in Charleston did not materialize. But in spite of the instability of his financial situation, he managed to send his boys to school abroad for an English gentleman's education. Anne's three brothers, Charles, Arthur, and George, were taken to school in England as soon as each reached what was considered a suitable age. But convention dictated that the education of a girl was secondary to that of a boy, and Anne's attendance at school in the South was not a viable option, either financially or socially. Even in America "[a]n English-style education [for a girl] . . . cost approximately $150 a year although this amount varied from institution to institution and region to region, with costs steadily increasing during the antebellum era" (Clinton, 1982, 135). In fact, much female education, in America as well as in Britain, was sorely lacking in any but the most rudimentary intellectual substance.

For the first fifty years of the nineteenth century all the daughters of the upper and middle classes, except for a few in exceptional nonconformist and intellectual families, received an education which was specifically designed to be useless. They were carefully brought up to be ornamental and not to have any vocation. . . . This useless education concentrated on accomplishments: smatterings of foreign languages, playing instruments and singing, decorative sewing (Delamont, 1978, p. 135). And although the schools for girls in and around Charleston, like many others in the South, "offered an array of academic subjects including literature, science, languages, and the social sciences, . . . [the main thrust of women's] education was to enhance . . . women's chances in the marriage market" (Friedman, 1985, p. 100).

So Anne was taught at home by her mother, a stern woman with a decided religious bent. She pursued a course of study, chosen and overseen by Mrs. Clough, consisting mainly of history and religious works. She recollects that "[o]ur Mother taught [me] about great men & their noble deeds & with her [I] read the Bible & learnt to look up to our Heavenly Father" (Clough, 1897, Newnham Archives). Thus, aside from this early, intellectually constricted course of study, Anne was virtually self-tutored.

The Cloughs returned to England in the summer of 1836. Anne was sixteen years old. Her childhood and much of her adolescence had been spent in Charleston, and as much as Ann Perfect Clough had attempted to shield her children from "American" influences in order to preserve their "Englishness," her daughter would never forget her childhood home and her acquaintances there. And despite her social isolation she now had ties with Charleston and her life there that it was hard to sever. Although she was never again to visit America, she always remembered her life there with fondness.

Although the Cloughs were middle-class socially, their economic situation was far from well defined. Anne was reared in an atmosphere of Victorian middle-class values that were often at odds with the family's precarious financial situation. From adolescence she was torn by the conflict between her desire to conform to the expectations of her social-class-marriage, child-rearing, household management, and perhaps her performance of charitable social work outside the home. An examination of her social and intellectual development from childhood through adulthood may help us better understand the paradox of Anne Jemima Clough and her quiet decision to work for change within the system, rather than outside it.

When the Cloughs returned to Liverpool, James Clough's financial affairs were more unstable than ever; his hoped-for business success in America had not been realized. In fact the period of the late 1830s and 1840s continued to be one of uncertainty and financial insecurity for the family, precluding yet again Anne's desire for more structured education. In an attempt to give some organization and purpose to her life, she proceeded to do charity work in Liverpool. She began assisting and then teaching in the Welsh National School, which James Clough had been instrumental in founding. Although she performed her duties with a dogged determination admirable in one so young, she found visiting the families of the poor grueling and emotionally trying. Arthur accompanied her on occasion during his periodic visits from Oxford, to distribute "the only supplies—coal, potatoes, and flour—that stood between them and starvation" (Greenberger, 1970, p. 58). But in spite of her revulsion for the filth and poverty of Liverpool's slums, Anne showed great compassion for her pupils, children from the city's back alleys and courts. There are passages in her first diary in which she recounts instances of "sweet" appreciation from one child or another, which must have counterbalanced, at least somewhat, her loathing for the conditions she encountered and her dread of visiting the homes of her students.

Although he did assist her on occasion, her brother Arthur's letters between 1838 and 1852 indicate that he did not support her venture. He remained ambivalent toward her work with the poor; "Annie's dirty little children" (Clough, 1957, p. 283) and their constant claims on her time continued to confound him. "[Although] Arthur encouraged [Anne] intellectually, . . . he did not encourage her to break away [from the characteristic Victorian dependency of a daughter and sister] in practice" (Chorley, 1962, p. 64). On the one hand was his aversion to the squalid conditions that confronted his sister in her frequent visits to the poor families of her pupils. "[T]o work for her livelihood was considered a 'misfortune' and 'ungenteel,' indeed, by such action she became a 'tradeswoman,' looked down upon by friends and relatives as the 'poor relation' who had to provide for herself" (Horn, 1989, 217). On the other was his reluctant pride in her and a sense of relief that she had found a way to occupy herself.

In a display of self-awareness uncommon in one so young, Anne appreciated that her milieu was not to be the drawing room or the dinner party. She saw herself as clumsy, without personal style, and she was never able to learn the "flirting slang" required for successful social performance among her peers. As she more than once confided to her diary, she "could not talk to gentlemen." Just how earnestly and diligently she did try, and fail, in her interaction with the opposite sex is evident from many diary entries; for example: "I don't much fancy men often understand women; they don't know how restless and weary they get" (Clough, 1841–1849, Diary 3, Newnham Archives).

Not only did the goal of matrimony seem out of reach, it was beginning to seem less and less desirable. In another diary entry she voiced her opinion of that blissful state: "Far would I be from desiring to upset the ways of the world, but . . . [s]urely married life too often becomes dull and hard" (Clough, 1841–1849, Diary 1, Newnham Archives). Furthermore, the Clough family's worsening financial situation made recompense for her labors increasingly necessary.

The increasingly precarious state of her father's finances led Anne to consider seriously the future necessity of earning money. She introduced to her family the idea of going out 'day governessing,' for she saw that "[i]f a [proper middle-class] girl remained single and could not live in semi-idleness at home the only occupations open to her were those of paid companion or governess" (Kamm, 1971, p. 24). At first Anne's proposal was met with strong disapproval from her family; convention asserted that "[t]he governess was a lady fallen on hard times, and as such had no education except in the useless accomplishments herself. She was rarely a teacher by choice, had no training for the work, and her unmarried state was a living testimony to her failure in the only contest open to the lady, husband-hunting. She was, therefore, unlikely to be regarded as skilful at man-trapping, and had little else to impart" (Delamont, 1978, p. 134).

But as the years passed and financial stability seemed no closer, Anne's idea became more attractive. James Clough continued to flounder financially; his prospects receded as each year passed. Charles was continually trying out new occupations and succeeding at none. Also, evidence was accumulating that Arthur was not realizing his own intellectual potential.

Because of this series of misfortunes which had beset the Cloughs, "the family were in great difficulties, and had to apply to their relations for help . . . Anne also set her mind on earning money to pay off what had been lent by their friends, and pressed for leave to keep a small school . . . she got her way in the end, and in time found three or four pupils, and with them started a small class, which she kept on for about four years" (Clough, 1897, pp. 20–21). In January of 1842 she confided to her diary that she had begun the school; she kept it, at least sporadically, until 1846 when she finally gave it up for good.

In 1844 James Clough died of a recurrence of the fever which he had first contracted many years previously in Charleston; his death was yet another blow to the family's unstable economic situation. More worried than ever about finances, Anne became gloomy and despondent. She wrote in her diary in September[?] 1845 that "I often feel very much out of sorts, and half wish we were out of Liverpool. We lead such a very solitary life, and I am beginning to fear I shall not see much fruit of my labours" (Clough, 1841–1849, Diary 3, Newnham Archives).

Since she no longer had her school, Anne found herself without occupation or pursuit. She again broached to her family the possibility of governessing, that and teaching being virtually the only two occupations open to girls of her class. Although both Arthur and Ann Clough reacted negatively to that scheme, Anne never completely relinquished the idea of work outside the home. In a diary entry dated March 1847 she wrote ". . . Told her [Anne's friend Jane Claude] some of my notions about its being right in certain cases to quit even one's Father and Mother and family for work as well as for a husband" (Clough, Diary 3, entry for March 1847, NA).

As the months progressed ennui and enforced idleness were her constant companions. She retreated more and more into a dream of living with Arthur, probably in London. For a time it appeared that her dream would be realized. But early in 1849 Arthur was offered the principalship of University Hall, London, and he withdrew his offer. He took up his duties at University Hall at the end of the summer of 1849; the responsibilities and demands of the position led him finally to reject the possibility of his mother and sister living with him.

Again Anne was left without options. She wrote in her diary in March [?] 1849: "I . . . wish very much we could have come up to live [with Arthur], supposing I could have got a school, for I would not have liked to be idle; but that plan seems impracticable" (Clough, Diary 3, entry undated but presumed March, 1849, Newnham Archives). And in a letter to his mother dated April 2, 1850, Clough finally put to rest the feasibility of the move to London: "On the whole I incline to think that the question of your coming to London had best be reconsidered. [Although] it would be a change for Annie, no doubt, and might do her good . . ." (Clough, 1957, p. 1, 283).

He did return for a time during the winter of 1849 to visit his mother in Liverpool, thereby enabling Anne to attend teacher training in London. His career had stalled and his finances were depleted. Thus his temporary residence in Liverpool would both free his sister from family responsibilities to pursue her own interests and, he hoped, allow him to regain control of his own life.

When her dream of living in London evaporated, Anne devised another plan. Her niece recounts that "Miss Clough had often considered the desirability of leaving Liverpool, where they [sic] had not now many friends, and lately she had begun to be anxious about her mother's health, for she had had a slight paralysis stroke, and her daughter thought a quiet country place would suit her better" (Clough, 1897, p. 78). After consultation with her mother and brother, Anne settled on Ambleside, in England's Lake District. She was acquainted with the area through numerous holidays spent there; as well, she perceived that the village of Ambleside would give her the opportunity to work, because "as she said, she could not live without teaching" (Clough, 1897, p. 78).

So in 1852 she and her mother moved to Ambleside and with, a loan from Harriet Martineau's building fund (Martineau, 1983, p. 308), purchased a newly built house outside of town up a steep hill called Eller Rigg. There Anne "decided to establish a regular school for the children of the tradespeople and farmers, and went round . . . to all the tradespeople who had children, and asked them to send [their children] to her to be taught" (Clough, 1897, p. 87). The house, Eller How, was to be her school as well as her home for the ten years she lived in Ambleside.

Anne Clough and her school at Eller How evidently fulfilled a need among the villagers of Ambleside. A testimonial was presented her by the parents of her students upon her departure from the village; in addition, there exist descriptions such as the following: "She brought her own cultured mind to bear upon [her students], and won their love and respect . . . and her gracious, gentle dignity was itself an education" (Clough, 1897, p. 91).

Mrs. Clough died in Ambleside in the summer of 1860; Arthur passed away the following year. The deaths of these two close family members in such quick succession, following immediately upon years of administering a school and nursing an invalid, took their toll on Anne's health. And so, urged by her doctor and her friends to give up her school, she reluctantly agreed to do so. The money troubles were finally a thing of the past. A modest inheritance from Ann Clough had now left her daughter financially independent for the first time in her life.

Before she left the village, however, Clough worked to assure that the educational work she had begun would not be abandoned. She arranged with one of her teachers to continue the administration of her school; she also made a considerable donation to repair the boys' grammar school in Ambleside and to build a library there (Clough, 1897, pp. 97–98).

Upon reentering the field of women's education, Anne Clough was somewhat dismayed to find that as the headmistress of her Ambleside school she had garnered a modest reputation within the field. Her reputation sprung not from any new and innovative ideas in the discipline, nor was it grounded in organizational skills; in fact, from childhood she had struggled constantly to impose some sort of organizational discipline upon herself and her work (Clough, 1841–1849, Diary 2, Newnham Archives). It grew instead from her very persona, her kindness and tact, as well as the interpersonal skills honed by her early years of teaching in the Welsh Charity Schools and later in the village of

Ambleside. She never forgot the great gaps in her own education, nor did she waver in her determination that other girls would find no such hardships.

In 1866 Anne moved back to Liverpool, where, among her other accomplishments, she was instrumental in founding the Liverpool Schoolmistresses' Association. And as secretary of the Ladies' Educational Society of Liverpool she, with the support of Josephine Butler and her husband, the Reverend George Butler of the Liverpool College, and others, assisted in formulating a plan of lectures in that city for women (Stubbs, 1982). "[Clough's] . . . chief concern was for the plight of schoolmistresses, their isolation and lack of training in mental discipline" (McWilliams-Tullberg, 1977, p. 127), a lack she had always felt sorely in her own life. A common theme in her diaries written throughout her teens and twenties is her constant search for an intellectual regimen of her own. For example, as early as 1838 she noted, "Have wasted time by not being careful of small bits" (Clough, 1844I–1849, Diary 3, Newnham Archives).

Henry Sidgwick, a professor and former don at Cambridge had been involved in the women's education movement since its inception. He was instrumental in convincing the University Syndicate to grant women permission to take the Cambridge Higher Local examinations. During the autumn of 1869 Sidgwick brought forward the idea of an informal series of lectures for women to be offered in Cambridge; a plan of lectures was then drafted and printed in readiness for the Lent term of 1870 (Clough, 1897).

By the end of 1870 it was becoming increasingly clear that permanent provisions must be made for lodging students who came from a distance to attend the lectures. So Sidgwick took it upon himself to let a house with his own capital, and early in 1871 began to look for a lady to take charge of the house and the visiting students. "He determined to ask Miss Anne Clough, with whom he was personally acquainted through her sister-in-law, Mrs. Arthur Hugh Clough" (Clough, 1897, p. 96). He saw Clough as the perfect choice; progressive enough to lend support to his scheme without being radical in thought or action. He was well aware that for his plan to meet with success he had to project a cloistered, homelike atmosphere at Cambridge. "In the early days few parents were eager to send their daughters away to college. It was expensive and seemed superfluous except for those intending to teach. . . . The chief difficulty was the widespread belief that young women should not leave their homes except under dire economic necessity" (Clough, 1897, pp. 97–98).

The first house of residence was at 74 Regent Street, let and furnished privately by Henry Sidgwick. When term began, there were five students; by the Long Vacation the number had risen to eight. But as Sidgwick's plan caught on and more women came to attend the lectures, living space became increasingly cramped. By 1872 it was necessary for Miss Clough and her charges to remove to Merton Hall. In 1873 so many more students applied to be taken in that a supplementary house was taken in Trumpington Street. When in 1874 the landlord found that he needed Merton Hall for his own use, Clough and her little band removed to two adjacent houses in Bateman Street (Clough, 1892, 101).

Ultimately, it being evident that the women were there to stay, Newnham Hall was built in 1875 at Newnham, a village on the outskirts of Cambridge. Anne Clough was active in raising funds for the construction of the hall of residence. Indeed, no task or duty was ever too menial or beneath her dignity to perform.

In 1880 Newnham College was formally acknowledged by the University of Cambridge, and Anne Clough was duly appointed as its first principal. "She looked upon [her work] as the fulfillment of her desires, and once said to a friend, who was impatient for happiness, "I had to wait for mine till I was fifty" (Clough, 1841–1849, Diary 1, Newnham Archives). Anne Clough's main function at Newnham was to manage the hall of residence, a task that she carried out in a quixotic, although ultimately effective fashion. She insisted on the strictest propriety among the women students, for "the . . . superintendents of the 1880's and 1890's were much occupied with social propriety and the whole business of defining relationships between the sexes in the co-educational environment of the new universities. There is plenty of evidence of what Sara Delamont has termed 'double conformity,' that is the need to reassure authorities and parents that women students could be ladies as well as scholars" (Stubbs, 1982). Indeed, in spite of the support of many in the academic community, many more disapproved of the presence of women in the university. In addition, most of Clough's charges were unknown to her at first, and all were older than the school children she had dealt with previously. And, most uncomfortably, her authority was not yet defined by tradition or rules. Looked at from such an angle, one realizes that the undertaking must have appeared daunting, to say the least.

Clough was unwavering in her belief that the utmost circumspection in dress and demeanor was necessary. She maintained a strict regard for the appearance of propriety both on the part of herself and her students. Stories of Miss Clough and Newnham abound. Most are affectionate and most, knowingly or unknowingly, illuminate the cultural quagmires through which she maneuvered on an almost daily basis.

> Many Victorians believed that scholarship and ladylike behaviour were incompatible, so the schools and colleges set out to prove them wrong. They demonstrated that their students were perfect . . . ladies, pure in thought, word and deed, suitably dressed and ruled by etiquette. This insistence on the students—and of course the staff—being ladylike was confining because the standards of ladylike behaviour were so rigid, and there were so many rules and conventions to be adhered to. (McWilliams-Tullberg, 1977, p. 127)

From a Newnham student comes the following:

> I remember someone had been complaining that Newnham students went along the streets buttoning their gloves. The Principal gave us a sympathetic address on the subject. "I know, my dears, that you have a great deal to do, and have not much time; but I don't like people to say such things about you, and so, my dears, I hope you'll get some gloves that don't want buttoning." (Clough, 1841–1849, Diary 3, Newnham Archives)

Clough always projected the image Henry Sidgwick had sought: ladylike, proper, and above reproach. "[I]t never occurred to her to talk of 'rights,' and the abstract ideas involved in the expression did not appeal to her; she hoped that it would in time be seen that the women students were worthy of further privileges, and that they would then be granted to them" (Clough, 1897, p. 108).

Clough had long been a champion of teacher development, even to structuring a plan which provided for supervisory teachers. From 1871 women teachers had been attending Newnham, but generally for only one or two terms. In 1878 Cambridge University appointed a Teachers' Training Syndicate, which became the starting point for the Cambridge Training College for Women established eight years later due in large measure to the enthusiastic support of Clough and educator Frances Mary Buss.

In the milieu of late-nineteenth-century feminism, Anne Clough was a study in contradictions. She spent her life struggling to improve women's education, but always in ways that were nonthreatening to the acknowledged patriarchal power structure. And not only did she have no desire to challenge that power structure, she actively worked within it to achieve her ends. In fact, she appears to have been unable to commit herself wholeheartedly to the feminist cause. Until the end of her life she was torn between idolization of women of previous generations and sympathy and admiration for her contemporaries who needed and demanded more from their society.

> I recalled chiefly the Grandmothers of my own generation. . . . They had a vocation in their surroundings, in their pursuits, & were satisfied. They did not ask for careers.
>
> But it is true, only too true, that there is another side to the question. That among the women of the generation of Grand Mothers a very great many were very unhappy & found it very difficult to make interests & occupations for themselves. Their minds had been awakened by the changes that were going on around them, they could no longer be satisfied with the small family occupations & pursuits that had served their Mothers . . . They were quite aware that Women had many more difficulties & fewer resources. (Clough, 1866, Newnham Archives)

Anne Jemima Clough died in late February, 1892, in her suite in Clough Hall, in the college to which she had dedicated the last 20 years of her life. The winter had been cold and damp; she had been ill but seemed to rally somewhat. Suddenly her health took a severe turn for the worse and within 48 hours she was dead. "She had expressed a wish that her remains should rest in a churchyard rather than a cemetery, and as she possessed a little property in the parish of Grantchester, the burial was in the pleasant ground attached to the church there" (Eichens, 1859, no page numbers available). In accordance with that wish, she was buried there, less than two miles from Cambridge. She had built two cottages in the village, and as a property owner she was entitled to burial within the town limits. Her remains lie in the Grantchester churchyard in companionable proximity to the English countryside she loved.

Anne Clough influenced the lives of countless women, not only her own students but also those fortunate enough to have come under her influence at Cambridge. Quietly, with remarkably little encouragement or guidance, and within the boundaries of convention, she pursued her dream of making education accessible to all women. She merits her own recognition, not just as a sister or a committee member or a footnote, but as herself, a personage in the broad historical sweep of nineteenth-century education. She deserves a place of her own in the annals of the Victorian past. The history of women's education in Britain will not be complete until the contributions of women such as Anne Clough are recognized.

References

Chorley, K. (1962). *Arthur Hugh Clough, the uncommitted mind: A study of his life and poetry.* Oxford: Clarendon Press.

Clinton, C. (1982). *The plantation mistress: Woman's world in the Old South.* New York: Pantheon Books.

Clough, A. H. (1957). The *correspondence of Arthur Hugh Clough.* (2 Vols). Mulhauser, F. L. (Ed.) Oxford: Clarendon Press.

Clough, A. J. (1841–1845). *First recollections.* Cambridge: Newnham Archives, University of Cambridge. Cambridge, England: 1865.

Clough, A. J. (1866). Hints on the organization of girls' schools, *Macmillan's Magazine,* David Masson (Ed.) London: Macmillan.

Clough, B. A. (1897). *A memoir of Anne Jemima Clough.* London: Edward Arnold.

Delamont, S. (1978). The contradiction in ladies' education. In Delamont, S. and Duffin, L. (Ed.) *The nineteenth-century woman: Her cultural and physical world* (pp. 134–163). New York: Barnes & Noble Books.

Duffin, L. (Ed.) (1978). *The nineteenth-century woman: Her cultural and physical world,* New York: Barnes & Noble Books.

Dyhouse, C. (1995). *No distinction of sex? Women in British universities, 1870–1939.* London: UCL Press.

Eichens, M. (1859). *A first reading book.* Oxford: Clarendon Press.

Friedman, J. E. (1985). *The enclosed garden: Women and community in the evangelical South, 1830–1900.* Chapel Hill: University of North Carolina Press.

Greenberger, E. B. (1970). *Arthur Hugh Clough; The growth of a poet's mind.* Cambridge, MA: Harvard University Press.

Horn, G. (1989). Education in rural England. In Purvis, J. (Ed.). *Hard lessons: The lives and education of working-class women in nineteenth-century England* (pp. 131–143). Cambridge, England: Polity.

Kamm, J. (1971). *Indicative past: A hundred years of the girls' public day school trust.* London: George Allen & Unwin.

Martineau, Harriet. (1983) *Harriet Martineau's Autobiography.* Vol. 2. London: Virago Press Limited.

McWilliams-Tullberg, R. (1977). Women and degrees at Cambridge University, 1862–1897. In Vicinus, M. A *Widening sphere: Changing roles of Victorian women* (pp. 125–140). Bloomington, IN: Indiana University Press.

Stubbs, J. (1982). Miss Anne Jemima Clough (1820–1892): A reconsideration of her work in the field of women's education. M.Ed. (Hons.) Thesis. Cambridge: Newnham College.

Vicinus, M. (1985). Women's colleges: An independent intellectual life. In Vicinus, M. *Independent women: Work and community for single women 1850–1920* (pp. 121–162). Chicago: University of Chicago Press.

Options for Dialogue

- What did you learn by reading the essay that was new information? Please discuss this in small groups. How would you describe the governing educational philosophies in Britain at the time?
- Please discuss any contradictions you noticed as you read about Ms. Clough's life and work.
- Have you read of or heard about any "pioneering" women who had some of the same responses as Ms. Clough to social "expectations" of her time? Discuss this.

- Relate anything you can from the essay to your reflections about the woman in your family that you wrote about in the listening section.
- Identify anything you can from the essay that may have been a foreshadowing of the educational systems in the United Kingdom or the United States.

Options for Action

- Research the history of women's education in the United States, one of the sovereign American Indian nations, an African country, a European country, an Asian country, or a South American country. Report to your class and include a comparison between the situations of the women of your research and the situation of Ms. Clough in the essay.
- Investigate the Website for the National Women's History Project at http://www.nwhp.org/index.html. Relate your findings to any work done so far in this section.
- Investigate this Website: http://www.womenwholead.org. It is described: "Women Who Lead is a project of the Sophia Foundation that focuses on women leaders in world history. England's Queen Mary Tudor, Hatshepsut of Egypt, and the Rani of Jhansi, India will be subjects of our first three young-adult biographies." To quote from their mission statement, "Women Who Lead seeks to encourage young women and men to expand their view of leadership to include women, and to use this knowledge to develop strong enlightened future adults." Find a person whom you would like to introduce to your classmates and plan a creative presentation.
- Investigate the history of another woman educator, from any country, who "merits her own recognition, not just as a sister or a committee member or a footnote." Give a report.

When asked about current historians he admires, Howard Zinn says:

E. P. Thompson, I think, is one of the most extraordinary of contemporary historians . . . he wrote the classic work, *The Making of the English Working Class*. To me he was exemplary not just because he was a historian who unearthed the history of class struggle and class conflict and the awakening of working class consciousness in England, but because he acted out his beliefs in his personal life. (Zinn, p. 142)

- Research the work of E. P. Thompson and report to your class (1999, Monroe, ME: Common Courage Press).

Ann Green, Elementary Teacher

Options for Listening

- When you were a young child, what was your favorite fairy tale or folktale? Do you have any idea why you especially liked the story? What did the story teach? What beliefs were represented by the story?
- Listen to Ann Green explain some teaching activities using fairy tales:

I started my fourth grade reading program by teaching through genre. After I introduced a genre to my class, the students would read and respond to literature that fit into that genre. I would meet with them in small groups two to three times a week to ensure comprehension and to discuss what they were reading. I would culminate each unit with a project that would allow the students to demonstrate what they had learned about the genre. My students wrote fiction, poetry, and fairy tale books. They wrote biography reports and created puppets of their characters; they made historical fiction mobiles, and performed mystery skits.

Our fairy tale unit was a class favorite. To prepare for the unit I gathered as many different versions of the Cinderella story possible. These stories came from a variety of different countries and cultures. I introduced the unit by asking the students what they already knew about fairy tales. We made a list on the board. Their ideas were very limited to what they'd seen in Disney movies and books. I then gave the students a compare and contrast chart. For the next several days the students read the Cinderella stories in pairs. After each book they had to fill in the following categories on their chart: title, country/culture, main character, evil characters, magic person or objects, and the reward. When the charts were complete, we made a class list of the elements found in all of the fairy tales the students read.

The students then wrote their own Cinderella tales based on the list of elements.

- Read the following tale written by Sarah Fretschel, one of Ms. Green's fourth grade students.

Ash Girl
—Sarah Fretschel

A long time ago, in a far away place, a widower and his wife had a baby. Her name was Matilda. She was very pretty, probably the prettiest baby in all the land. That very same day Aurora was born. She was the queen's daughter. Matilda lived happy until one day, when her mother was away and Matilda was at school, her father died. Matilda was very sad. That same day, if not at the same time, Aurora's father the king died. It was a great tragedy for the whole Kingdom.

As if that wasn't enough, Matilda's mother became mean. She made Matilda clean the house and do the dishes. So Matilda grew up in a world full of cruelty. No one liked her. Aurora grew up in a place of rich people and great love. One day when Matilda was doing her chores, by getting an egg at the market, on the town bulletin board it said the sorcerer would be giving her powers away pretty soon. Matilda wanted so much to get the powers but she thought that probably Aurora would be getting the powers because she was the princess. But Matilda never lost hope, even when her mother was mean.

About a week before the judgment time, Matilda grew restless. She wanted to be the first girl there so she decided to run away from home to get there first. Matilda packed all her things, which was not hard because she did not have many things. She planned to leave when her mother was out. Matilda's chance came when her mother went to her neighbor's house for tea. She grabbed her things and started running. When she got to the forest she saw an old man. She asked him, "Can you tell me the way to the castle?" The old man spoke quietly and slowly. "Go over the magic stream, over the great rock, through the forest, and then you will come to a very tall tree. If you climb the tree, you will see the castle. Follow that path." Matilda said, "Thank you" and started walking.

Pretty soon she came to the magic stream. She was surprised to see that it was purple! It was also bubbling. She crossed over the stream and came to the great rock. She stopped but only for a second to catch her breath. Then she climbed up and over the great rock. She went through the forest and came to the tall tree. She just stood there awhile and looked at how tall the tree was. Then she finally started to climb the tree. The climb took her one whole day. But when she got to the top, what she saw was worth the climb. She saw the tops of trees, clouds like she could touch them, and far off in the distance she saw the castle.

She quickly climbed down and started toward the castle. She walked for about three miles until she finally came to the castle. The doors were three times the size of her. She knocked on the door and a little man came to answer it. This is what he said; "This is the palace and the sorcerer is busy. How can I help you?" Matilda answered, "I would like to see the sorcerer about the powers." He answered, "You, you . . . NO WAY. You are an Ashgirl and will never get picked." Matilda sputtered, "But . . . bu . . ." but before she could finish the door slammed in her face.

Just then a little wizard appeared. He was wearing a little hat with stars on it, and a blue cloak, and he was holding a wand that glowed. He asked, "Can I help you in any way, Matilda?" Matilda said, "Yes, could you get me out of these rags, which I have traveled so very far in, and give me elegant clothes so they won't call me Ashgirl." In a flash of light her rags were gone and she wore a beautiful dress as bright and as yellow as the sun.

Then she went up to the castle door again and rang the bell. Again the little man answered the door. This time he said, "What do you wa . . ." but couldn't finish when he looked at Matilda. Then he stared again, "My how lovely you look. You must be here for the giving of the powers. Come right this way, the sorcerer is waiting." He led Matilda down a long hallway. Then they entered a room full of young girls waiting to get picked. Matilda joined the crowd.

In a few minutes the sorcerer came in the room and went up on the stage. Every person was silent. Not a single voice could be heard. Then the sorcerer spoke up, "I know that you all have come a long way. I will try to be as fair as possible when it comes to picking someone." Just then some loud music could be heard and in walked Aurora, the princess. She walked up to the crowd and made her way up to the front where a chair was waiting for her. Then the sorcerer began to talk again. She said, "I have a list of names of all the girls in the kingdom. What I will do is close my eyes and run my finger up and down the list. When I open my eyes, I will stop moving my finger and whomever my finger stops on will get the powers." She closed her eyes and ran her finger up and down the paper. Then she stopped, opened her eyes and said, "The lucky girl is . . . is . . . is Matilda."

Matilda ran to the front where the powers transferring machine was waiting. She and the sorcerer climbed inside and started it. The machine rattled and shook and finally it stopped. Out stepped Matilda and the sorcerer. Just to see if the machine had really worked, Matilda gave a little zap. It did work! From that day forward Matilda lived happily ever after. But what happened to her mother you ask? Some say that Matilda turned her into a frog and she lives down in the old pond! And some are just not sure. What do you think really happened to her?

Options for Dialogue

Please discuss in small groups:

- How did Sarah Fretschel rewrite the Cinderella tale in her story of Ashgirl?
- What beliefs of her own came through in Sarah's retelling?
- What is the difference between Ashgirl and the Disney version of Cinderella? How does she see the female character?
- What recent films present the Disneyized version of the Cinderella story? (e.g. Pretty Woman)
- In what ways are the women characters portrayed?
- What is the "truth" underlying Sarah's story?
- If you were rewriting this tale, how would you change it?

Options for Action

- In small groups follow Ms. Green's class Elements of Fairy Tales list and discuss and create a group tale:
  1. The story starts with, "Once upon a time" or a similar phrase.
  2. Magic events, characters, and objects are part of the story.
  3. At least one character is wicked or evil.
  4. At least one character is good.
  5. There is usually someone of royalty involved.
  6. The main character always gets a reward in the end (goodness is rewarded).
  7. The story ends with, "They lived happily ever after."
- Share your group's tale with the whole class.
- Find versions of the Cinderella story from at least five different cultures. What are the underlying teachings about women in these stories? Compare traditional Cinderella stories with stories in contemporary media with a Cinderella theme such as the films *An Officer and a Gentleman* or *Pretty Woman*. How is the underlying message of Cinderella stories presented to girls in the media? Present your findings to the class.
- Read copies of *New Moon* (Duluth, MN) and other "zines" written by and for preadolescent girls. Compare these to popular magazines which are designed for the same market. What differences do you see? Write a report about places in which young girls can find "voice."

CHAPTER FIVE

How Do Families Guide Our Work as Educators Within a Community?

Bus Duty

—*Norita Dittberner-Jax*

The school buses lumber toward the curb
discharging dead-eyed students in the dark,

white, black, and Asian, hundreds of them;
two teachers and I, plus my student teacher

stand by discussing nothing new, the sorry
state of students, a complaint as old as Socrates,

knowing that if the students could talk this early,
they would be discussing the sorry state of teachers,

a complaint as old as Socrates' students;
the baby bus rolls up and the mothers get out,

heading for daycare, their babies snug
in their cradled plastic; and Tom, the Liberian captain

of the football team, limps toward the door, injured
in last night's game; we are all at our posts,

the daily grind, but over in the baseball field,
a new sight, seagulls white in October darkness,

dozens of them nattering about the diamond,
pecking at the gravel and bumping into each other,

a few lift their long wings and fly to second base;
they were heading south from Duluth, when they saw

a field of green and alighted. Seagulls stopping
at Johnson High School augurs well for all of us.

Wider possibilities, friends. Migration.
I, for one, have been to Brazil and I grew up in Frogtown.[1]

Wider possibilities. Remember the seagulls.

Personal and Family Strengths in Communities

All societies, as reflected in their schools, are a collage of strengths
and barriers, voices seldom heard and voices more often heard. Research shows that when schools bring in the strengths of the families and their communities, in all their pluralistic complexities, the
educational experiences are more effective (O'Brien, 1997; Rummel
& Quintero, 1997; Weinstein-Shr, 1992). The strengths of the families and students may be valued and used by the schools or they can
be ignored and wasted.

Relatedly, Rummel & Quintero, 1997 have found that teachers
bring their past experiences and present values and priorities into
the schools. Teachers' beliefs and their life experiences cannot be
separated from what they do in the classroom. Outstanding educators show an interest in and acceptance of many students' families,
cultures, and differences.

Schools can reflect the strengths of families. Unfortunately, Polakow (1993) vividly points out how public schools in the United
States are "a mirror reflection of public perceptions of the poor"
(p. 107), thus perpetuating the tragic misconception of minority and
poor children. Yet, schools

> . . . Can also be a place for change. As teachers learn to read children's
> texts more critically they will help children learn to be resisting
> readers and writers of their own and other texts and explore through
> language new metaphors and structures that challenge. (Kamler,
> 1992, p. 32)

1. Frogtown is a low income neighborhood in St. Paul, Minnesota.

Greene (1986) notes, sadly, "I think of how little many teachers know about their students' diverse lives and thinking processes, how little they can know because of the paucity of dialogue in the classroom space" (p. 80).

However, teachers can promote dialogue in classrooms and listen to the students as they tell us about their families. This brings families' strengths, in often interesting detail, into the classroom whether or not the parents are physically able to be present. Children in schools are often vocal about their connection to their families. One child expresses it in a poem describing "the day I was born." This child's fantasy about her birth uses the power of metaphor to connect herself, her family, and her world (Quintero & Rummel, 1996).

On the day I was born
The sun shown
Bright n' high.
The birds started singing.
My mom and dad
Started to cry
'Cause they were so happy
I came.
On the day I was born
All the land animals
Started to gather
All around my room
To see me.
The rivers flowed
More than ever.
It rained
But after that
A beautiful rainbow appeared.
And my mom and dad
Said the rainbow was perfect
And so am I.
They said I made their lives happy.
On the day I was born
I made the sun show bright.
And made my mom and dad cry.
On the day I was born
Everyone was on my side.

In learning activities teachers can encourage students to use language that gives importance to their personal experiences. They can also orchestrate situations in which students are able to create new images of themselves in different cultural contexts. Teachers can guide children's voices through use of expressive writing, including poetry and fiction, and through drama, music, and art, whatever the age of the students.

In order to be effective in this promotion of students' voice in authentic ways, teachers must be aware that linguistic choices are socially constructed. By listening sensitively to children's messages, teachers can pick up clues about their students' lives. Lisa Delpit (1996) says that

> I believe that teaching the skills and perspectives needed for real participation in a democratic society is one of the most revolutionary tasks that an educator committed to social justice can undertake. It is only through such education that we can hope to create a truly just society where the most disenfranchised of our citizens can gain access to the political power needed to change the world. (p. 41)

Rummel & Quintero (1997) found that teachers who support children and their cultural, linguistic context in school have some common approaches to pedagogy. They all exhibit a belief that it is their responsibility to find ways of engaging all their students in learning activity. They accept responsibility for making the classroom an interesting, engaging place. They persist in trying to meet the individual needs of the children in their classes, searching for what works best for each student. Their basic stance is a continual search for better ways of doing things.

Trueba, Jacobs, and Kirton (1990) say :

> Educators, especially teachers, need to become aware of the contributions of immigrants and refugees to America in order to inculcate in all students genuine appreciation for the richness of American culture and of immigrants' commitment to the continued existence of democratic institutions. (p. 1)

We would like to introduce you to excerpts from a teacher's story about his childhood as an immigrant and his work now with immigrant students. It is an example of how, by learning from our own experiences, we can be more sensitive to others.

One Teacher's History

The resilience of children and families from immigrant and minority communities is dramatic. All his life, with a passionate loyalty to and love for his Mexican roots, Raúl Quintanilla has worked for change in communities and in schools. He was born the son of migrant farm workers in Minnesota who had immigrated from Mexico. He has lived and worked in various contexts with people who represent many diverse groups. Now he is an English as a second language teacher for the St. Paul Public Schools in Minnesota. His activism demands that his convictions about people, learning, democracy, discrimination reach far beyond the classroom walls. His background, his reading, and his current work take him throughout the state and region as an advocate for various Latino groups, their potential, their differences and similarities.

Quintanilla's personal story illustrates how his family's strengths supported him as a student reader and resisting reader and teacher. Quintanilla noted that by third grade, he was blatantly aware that

> *Dick, Tom, Jane, Paul, Tim and Sally, the old reading books in school. . . . I couldn't understand the one where mommy dropped daddy off at the airport, with a suitcase. And daddy always had a tie. We would go home and say, "My father never wears a tie," and we didn't know anything about airports. But that is what the book was teaching us. The food, too. You know, if there was a breakfast, it was eggs, milk, and toast and orange juice. But with our breakfast it was cup of coffee and a piece of Mexican sweet bread. We could make no relation between the school and the home setting.* (quoted in Rummel and Quintero, p. 165)

However, the home setting for him and his brothers and sisters was condusive to learning.

> *My parents never read to us, but I saw them reading. They read novels and magazines. They read magazines like* Superman, *these were Spanish, the comic type. Very simple. That is how I learned to read. Nobody taught me to read.* (p. 166)

Issues regarding bilingualism and biliteracy are always, and were for this teacher, complex.

I was curious because I went across the border. My cousins in Mexico, across the border, were learning to read in Spanish. They had all these magazines laying around. I can still remember reading, La Bruja, *and many others. Spanish seemed really easy to me. I learned to read and not to write. There is a difference because we were right on the border. We were sometimes criticized because they would say you can't speak English correctly and you can't speak Spanish correctly. . . . Like still in the 8th grade, I'd turn the radio on and I'd be listening to a song and I still couldn't understand what they were saying; it was too fast. Because when we went home from school you know, we didn't speak English at home. Because the parents didn't speak any English and it would be disrespectful. The other thing was that we were all Mexican American and you spoke English and your brothers would say, "Hey, he thinks he is a big shot, because he knows English." It was kind of a shame thing to do. That doesn't help you when you are learning the language. I didn't have trouble with reading and comprehension because I had very good teachers. I think. I learned the library quickly. . . . A lot of teachers need training on this.* (pp. 165–166)

As a child in school Quintanilla realized:

We didn't have any heroes to identify with. We didn't have General MacArthur, we didn't have Roosevelt. We couldn't identify with them because we were Mexican Americans. People that they would consider heroes like [James Bowie] and [Davy Crocket] were white people. To Texas history or American history they are heroes. But if you look at Northern Mexican history they are not heroes. They are the crooks who kicked people out of areas. In fact the school I went to was Sam Houston Elementary, and they would praise him. We didn't know him so we tried to learn. We didn't really have anything or anyone to identify with, except for the "Cinco de Mayo." We had one person. General Zaragoza. The reason that we identified with him is because he was born in an area of South Texas, which is now Goldeanne, and he was the one that won the final battle. (p. 163)

Relatedly, Quintanilla went on to explain a common problem for young Mexican Americans in terms of identity:

The Mexicans didn't want us because we were Chicanos, and Americans didn't want us because they think we're Mexican. So we made this guy our hero. Then John F. Kennedy. He was a hero.
When I got into high school there was a Chicano movement so I got

into that. I got into migrant Mexican American Chicano literature.
I did a lot of that type of literature reading . . . All of my favorite au-
thors were from Southern California: Valdez, Sipuedes, Guerra,
más y más. I got very involved. When teachers asked us to write a
report I would use one type of literature. I would say, "Why can't I
use Mexican American books?" Everybody else did the opposite.
But it was good because the teachers started to learn or understand
about diversity. (p. 163)

Not only was this teacher, Quintanilla, influenced by his life experiences, but also by his reading choices. When asked about a book
that influenced his life, he answered:

Teaching as a Subversive Activity. *It opened my eyes to the messages*
and methods of teaching. It was a strong book. I don't remember the
author [Neil Postman]. We felt that they were only teaching us one
side of the story. So, the book said, when the professor talks about
his side, question. Question the book that you are reading. Again
this is more factual . . . I was going to major in Texas History, but I
got in an argument with a professor because he had a Texas history
book according to "Texas" history. There was nothing else included.
So I dropped that class and didn't major in Texas History. At that
point I wanted to change things. But you need more than one person
to change a book. That professor said this is the book and this is it,
and I said this is not it. I will bring you a book from across the border
and it will be the opposite of what this book says. So, I think they are
better now. It was the 60's and 70's. (p. 166)

Not surprisingly, Quintanilla is an activist in the classroom:

I work with Kindergarten through sixth graders. We have our own lit-
erature books from Addison Wesley, ESL books. What I do is a lot of
oral language. We feel that the books are not adequate. We have to
jump around and figure out what to do for different levels of stu-
dents. Many many different levels. They have stories in there like the
"Little Red Hen," "The Three Little Pigs," so we have the stories that
everybody else has, only they are at an appropriate level. I also read
to them a lot. Books like Rosie's Walk. *ESL students need a lot of vis-*
uals, especially in the first grade. A lot of poems, writing. We read a
lot to them. We do a lot to get them interested in us. Because if they
are not interested in you they will not be interested in what you have
to say or do. So you have to show interest. (p. 167)

Regarding satisfying the interests of the students, he says:

> It's not easy. In the summer I had a class of two Africans, four His-
> panics, seven Hmong, and about seven Vietnamese. I had never had
> that type of class. I had to go home and think a lot. And they were all
> at different levels. You have to do a lot of individualized instruction.
> You have to do a lot of walking around and you better have some-
> thing for them. You have to be aware of their level. If you lose them,
> they get a negative thing about ESL. When you have a group like that
> you do a lot of individual work, it is a lot of work. A lot of teachers
> don't do that. (p. 167)

Regarding teaching Hmong and Latino students, Quintanilla ad-
vises:

> Number one when working with the students: use a lot of positive re-
> inforcement. Instead of using negative statements, turn them into pos-
> itive statements. That is one of the things that we went through that
> the Hmong also went through. You have to respect their language. You
> have to learn about them. I didn't know anything about the Hmong
> students. But I have read about them and their culture. I learned
> about the style that they use for teaching. In my country too, they had
> to recite everything from memory. They still have corporal punish-
> ment. It is way different here. Not because they are right or know a
> word. Just because they are sitting; just because they came. About
> speaking their language (the positive aspects of that). Some teachers
> say no, no don't speak in your language; practice your English. I have
> learned a lot. (Rummel & Quintero, 1997, p. 167)

The following selection describes the work of three educators in
southern Africa. It is an example of listening to student lives and
utilizing that knowledge in school contexts. We believe that the
strengths of the individuals, their families, and their communities
come through in the poetry and the questions raised.

References

Ada, A. F. (1988). The Pajaro Valley experience: Working with
   Spanish-speaking parents to develop children's reading and writ-
   ing skills in the home through the use of children's literature. In
   T. Skutnabb-Kangas & J. Cummins (Eds.), *Minority education:*

From shame to struggle (pp. 46–60). Philadelphia, PA: Multilingual Matters.

Delpit, L. (1996). *Other people's children: Cultural conflict in the classroom.* New York: New Press.

Greene, M. (1986). Reflections and passion in teaching. *Journal of Curriculum and Supervision, 2* (1), 68–81.

Greene, M. (November, 1999). Reimagining difference and diversity. Unpublished paper presented at the Annual convention of the National Council of Teachers of English. Denver, CO.

Kamler, B. (1992). The social construction of gender in early writing. Paper presented to the American Educational Research Association, San Francisco.

O'Brien, R. (1997). Migration patterns and teachers readiness to respond: The New Zealand experience 1840–1996. Paper presented at the International Seminar for Teacher Education. Brock University, Ontario, Canada.

Polakow, V. (1993). *Lives on the edge.* Chicago, IL: University of Chicago Press.

Quintero, E., & Rummel, M. K. (1996). Something to say: Voice in the classroom. *Childhood Education, 72*(3), 146–151.

Rummel, M. K., & Quintero, E. P. (1997). *Teachers' Reading/ Teachers' Lives.* New York: State University of New York Press.

Sleeter, C., & Grant, C. (1994). *Making choices for multicultural education: Five approaches to race, class, and gender.* Upper Saddle River, NJ: Merrill/Prentice Hall.

Trueba, H. T., Jacobs, L., & Kirton, E. (1990) *Cultural conflict and adaptation: The case of Hmong children in American society.* New York: Falmer Press.

Weinstein-Shr, G. (1992). Learning lives in the post-island world. *Anthropology and Education Quarterly 23* (2), 160–165.

Ann McCrary Sullivan, Michelle Commeyras, Mercy Montsi: Teacher Educators and Poets

Options for Listening

- When you were a child did you ever wonder what it would be like to be the other gender? What did you think about? Write about this experience.

- Some creative teachers have brought the reimaging of African students into the classroom dialogue. The strengths and meaning of their expression makes the content of school study much more meaningful. As you read this section think about the beliefs the teachers must have about students in order to work with them the way that they do in the following article.

- The following article is a collaborative work by three women educators. Anne Sullivan is a published poet and teacher educator. In the dialogues after each of the poems, you see her asking Michelle Commeyras, a teacher educator and researcher, guiding questions so that Michelle can develop a poetic way to describe her research information. Mercy Montsi is a Botswana educator who will later describe how she used these poems in her university class. "Data poem" is Anne Sullivan and Michelle Commeyras's term to describe poetry from qualitative information gained in research in the field—in this case, Botswana.

- The following article contains several poems written by women of Botswana about gender issues. Before you read the article, prepare one of the poems to read with a partner(s) to the class. What is the perspective of the author of the poem you read? What are some of your strongest impressions of the students' lives? After answering these questions, go back and read all the poems and the dialogues that follow them, to give you some more information about the situation.

Nothing Else But to Be a Woman:
The Poetics of Gender in Southern Africa
—Michelle Commeyras, Anne McCrary Sullivan, and
Mercy Montsi with Bontshetse Mazile, Ilke Dunne,
Bontle Menyatso, Thala Montsi, Doreen Yorke

Batswana[3] Boys Imagine Life as a Girl

—(a data poem) by Michelle Commeyras

People would laugh at me.
If I woke up tomorrow as a girl . . .

Everyone would scream.
Everyone would hate me.

If I woke up tomorrow as a girl . . .
I would feel disturbed, frightened, shocked and worried.
I would feel embarrassed, humiliated and disappointed.
I would feel lonely, depressed and mentally disturbed.
"I might as well commit suicide."

If I woke up tomorrow as a girl . . .
I'd have to cook and clean.
I'd have to do my hair and nails.

If I woke up tomorrow as a girl . . .
I might get pregnant and drop out of school.
I might get beaten up.

If I woke up tomorrow as a girl . . .
I'd have to stop burping
and swearing
and grooving
and pissing around the corner.

If I woke up tomorrow as a girl . . .
My studies would be affected.
My life will be complicated.
My plans and dreams and future would change.

If I wake up tomorrow as a girl . . .
I will blame God.
And get drugs to change me back.

3. The term "Batswana" refers to the people who live in the country of Botswana.

Batswana Girls Imagine Life as a Boy

—(a data poem) by Michelle Commeyras

If I woke up tomorrow as a boy
Shocked, surprised and puzzled
It would be difficult
but interesting.
I'd adjust
    I FEEL VERY PROUD
    AS A GIRL.

If I woke up tomorrow as a boy
I'd feel great, excited, happy and honoured.
Always wanted to be a boy.
Always imagined myself a boy.
    I WOULDN'T LIKE ANYTHING
    ABOUT BEING A BOY.

If I woke up tomorrow as a boy
I'd . . .
go wherever I want.
have a wonderful career.
marry a wonderful woman.
feel free.
be respected and
very successful.
    I'M A BLESSING FROM GOD
    AS A FEMALE.

If I woke up tomorrow as a boy
I would not worry about . . .
clothes, lipstick, eye shadow, and hairstyle.
falling pregnant.
labour pains.
being beaten
and raped.
    I LIKE MYSELF
    AS A GIRL.

If I woke up tomorrow as a boy
I would not . . .
bully others.
impregnate a girl and run away.

I WOULD LIKE TO BE THE NEXT
MOTHER TERESA
AND PROMOTE GIRL POWER.

If I woke up tomorrow as a boy . . .
I'd show my wife I loved her.
I'd be a wonderful father.

ANNE: How would you explain the existence of these poems to
someone with no prior knowledge of them?

MICHELLE: I wrote these poems from essays written by youth
between the ages of fourteen and twenty in Botswana. I lived and
worked there for one academic year (1997/98). Mercy Montsi, a
friend and colleague at the University of Botswana, was running
a workshop for youth in the YWCA's Peer Approach to
Counseling by Teens (PACT) program. She decided to use an
activity that I had used with a smaller group of PACT students.
The peer counselors had written one-page essays in which they
imagined waking up the following day and finding they were a
member of the other sex. They were asked to write about how
their lives would be different. I had found this activity in a book
by Myra and David Sadker (1994), who used the activity with
hundreds of students in the United States as part of their
investigation of sexism in schooling and society.

ANNE: What does Mercy value in this kind of activity?

MICHELLE: She thought the exercise would sensitize the peer
counselors to ways in which gender socialization influences and
contributes to problems experienced by their male and female
age-mates. Self-knowledge, self-awareness, awareness of one's
sexual environment, social skills, self-concepts, self-esteem, and
responsible boy-girl dating behaviors are among the many topics
covered in the PACT education program.

ANNE: What do you think is the value of the activity?

MICHELLE: I think that some issues viewed as personal youth
problems might be viewed differently if you look at them within
the larger framework of gender and society. This activity helps
you do that. For example, if I were counseling a girl in U.S.A.
who is bulimic, I would encourage her to consider her situation
from the viewpoint of living in a society that defines beauty as
being thin, a society that places a great deal of emphasis on body

image. Thinking about gender expectations and stereotypes that emanate from socialization allows a counselor to see an individual problem as a societal issue.

ANNE: What can you tell us about the "larger framework of gender and society" in Botswana?

MICHELLE: According to the customary laws and customs of Botswana, a woman is a child for life. First she is her parents' child. Then she is her husband's child. Should she not be married, she is her brother and uncle's child. Should she have children, they are her husband's children; they bear his name and follow his culture. Should a woman have children out of wedlock, they are brothers and sisters to her—not her children. In family life and in public spheres preference is given to males. A woman who only bears daughters has failed in her most important duty. I think Mercy would agree with me that personal problems need to be considered within the larger social context that supports these kinds of gender differences.

ANNE: What led you to make poems from the essays written at the PACT workshop?

MICHELLE: The two poems represent one outcome of Mercy's and my analysis (Commeyras and Montsi, 1999) of fifty essays (half written by females and half by males). I was interested in the language and modes of expression the Batswana youth were using. I didn't want to lose that. I got the idea of composing data poems because I wanted to retain their voices while showing what we were learning from the content.

ANNE: What were you learning?

MICHELLE: I was learning that boys basically don't think that they would like life as a girl. Whereas generally girls could see a greater advantage to being a boy, but they didn't necessarily want to stop being girls; they just wanted to have all the opportunities that boys have. Also girls seem rather disappointed in what they were seeing in the way boys live their lives. When girls do imagine life as a male, they imagine themselves being a better boy or man. For example, a father who pays attention to his home life and is loving to his wife and children.

ANNE: So you feel that these poems highlight significant themes and retain human voices. Is there anything you think they fail to reveal?

MICHELLE: I'm concerned that readers will read the poems and think African men and boys are unlikable—terrible. While the poems accurately portray the gender issues and concerns found in the essay data, they do little to communicate that the women and girls have lots of loving feelings for the men and boys in their lives. I'm afraid that what gets lost here is what is endearing about African males. I have found them to be wonderfully sociable, smart, and concerned about issues of fairness and justice.

ANNE: This positive generalization about men seems almost as dangerous to me as the negative one. Where's the complexity in this?

MICHELLE: Yes, there is complexity. There is paradox. Take for example our friend Fidelis in Zimbabwe. We both know how charming and smart he is. But when Zodwa [his girlfriend] became pregnant, he still presumed, as was customary, that she would come and live in his parents' household where she works like a second wife helping his mother do all the cooking and housework while most of the time he is out of town pursuing his career as an engineer. This is the paradox. This is not communicated in the poems because it was not written about in the essays. It's been my observation that even though men and women love each other, that doesn't mean that there isn't a form of patriarchy at work.

Exciting Batswana Women
—(a data poem) by Michelle Commeyras

Mmapheto says	Most men don't value women's voices.
	But I know
	where there is progress
	there is always woman.

| Nolly says | Men do not want women who are educated. |
| | But I love school. |

Dintle says	My father would be happy if I were a boy.
	But I am a person
	of miracles.

Tedro says	My husband was focusing on his self-development.
	But on my family side
	they are giving me support.

Keletso says   My father always wanted me to go to school.
                      But, my boyfriend said,
                      Do not go beyond your B.A.

Sesame says   Males are more supported.
                      But my husband
                      who supports me
                      is the mother now.

Lorato says   A man's voice has to be heard all the time.
                      But, women in the university
                      are not women of the past.

Phatsimo says   Men think intelligent women will dominate them.
                      But, I really loved
                      being in engineering.

Chibuya says   On rare occasions men value women's voices.
                      It is exciting to be a woman
                      Now that things are changing.

MICHELLE: I wrote this poem in response to interview data that my
    friends Bontshetse Mazile and Nancy Austin had collected. They
    wanted me to read their data and meet with them to talk about it.
    They had interviewed nine women students at the University of
    Botswana who ranged in age from 20s to 40s. The research focused
    on finding out how these women ended up in higher education
    and what they thought of being a woman student at the university.
    While I was reading the interviews and making notes on key
    phrases and themes, I had the impulse to write a data poem.
        In the poem, I tried to capture some of what I found interesting
    and significant. I knew that Nancy and Bontshetse were going to
    be meeting with the nine women again for a focus group
    interview. I hoped they would share the poem with the women. I
    had never had the opportunity to take a poem back to research
    participants to see how they would respond to it. Nancy and
    Bontshetse decided to use the poem to launch the focus group
    interview.
ANNE: Do you know what happened in that focus group?
MICHELLE: Yes, I was there. The women were very interested. They
    had not read or seen each other's interviews, so the poem brought
    them very quickly in relation to the data. In a brief format, they

got a sense of how their responses to the interview questions were comparable. They talked about congruences among their views of gender. The poem launched a far-ranging discussion of gender issues.

ANNE: How would you name the key issues that this poem brings into focus?

MICHELLE: On the one hand, as a woman, there are difficulties and challenges in going on for a university education. But, on the other hand, it is an exciting time to be a woman because things are changing for the better. Several women used the word exciting in their interviews to explain how they feel about being a woman. And my take on the focus and individual interviews is that these women are excited and exciting so I titled the poem "Exciting Batswana Women."

ANNE: Is there anything else you'd like to say about this poem or its issues?

MICHELLE: I think it is important that the poem conveys that some women are feeling supported by men in their lives as they pursue a university education.

Unfound Freedom — Untold Wealth
—*Thaala J. B. Montsi (Gaborone, Botswana)*

Drink, smoke, beat,
Betray, lie, steal!
It's okay,
I'm only a boy

Commit every crime,
Live to minimum expectations:
It's all right—I'm simply a boy.

Love is a cliche
Love is a tool,
Fool them, use them; They like it.
It's my duty . . .
After all, I'm only a boy.
The world is mine
I'll rule it;
I'll run their race,
Feed my pride,

Kill my heart,
I'll live,
I'll grow,
I'm a man.

MICHELLE: Thaala wrote this poem when her mother (Mercy) showed her the two poems composed from what Batswana youth wrote about waking up as the other sex. When her mother showed me Thaala's poem I thought it was wonderful with music and message. I assume that Thaala is speaking about what she perceives as women's difficulties with men's behavior.

ANNE: Did you talk to Thaala?

MICHELLE: I didn't even meet her then. Most of the time she is away at boarding school in South Africa. I met her a year later when I returned to Botswana. I asked her to reread her poem because I had added some punctuation and broken some lines, so I needed to see how she felt about that. She found those changes acceptable. And I found out that she likes to write poetry.

ANNE: If Thaala were here right now, what would you ask her about this poem?

MICHELLE: I would be interested in how she interprets her poem now. Does it still represent her thinking? And, of course, now that I have met her boyfriend and seen how nice he is, I would ask her how she thinks about him in relation to what she wrote in that poem.

THAALA: In a twisted, cynical way, I still feel that my words hold true; although they may not apply to all men. I would say that my words encompass society's norm; what our world has raised to be "a man." I, however, am lucky enough to have a boyfriend who is his own man. His values and principles don't belong to this world but are a result of the positive side of our social conditioning. It would take a cataclysmic change to alter the perceptions manifested in my poem, which to me is sad because there is so little good in it. But such is life.

A Sense of Freedom
—*Ilke Dunne (Melville, South Africa)*

If I woke up as a boy . . .

A sense of freedom . . .
no more juggling work and home

no more broken time
no more interrupted thoughts

A sense of responsibility . . .
To remain sensitive to self and others
to remain self aware
keep listening

A sense of power . . .
Earned respect is mine
to retain it is no struggle

I'll spend a whole day watching cricket
and not feel as if I've wasted the day.

I Wanna Be a Momma

—Doreen Yorke (Melville, South Africa)

I wanna be a momma, I wanna be a momma
But if I had to be a daddy or a husband instead . . .
I'd sure be one like me right now!

You know, it could be kinda good to drop
all the baggage and just be a
MAN!!!

A man who goes right for the career-path.
Never mind the supper or the laundry or
music lessons or the car pool or, or, or, or . . .

ANNE: What do you remember about how these poems came to be?
MICHELLE: These two poems were written during the workshop you
    and I presented at a conference on qualitative research in
    education at Rand Afrikaans University in South Africa. It was the
    final day of the conference and our workshop began at 8:30 in the
    morning. I was surprised that so many people came to it
    (approximately eighty people). We began the workshop by asking
    everyone to write the "suppose you woke up tomorrow and
    discovered you were a member of the other sex" essay. Then I told
    them about analyzing the essays collected from fifty youth in the
    neighboring country of Botswana. I read them the Batswana boy
    and girl poems I had written from that data. Then you took over.

You gave them some ideas about how they could transform their essays into experience poems. You told them to break their essays into lines, take out extraneous words and try to put the most significant ideas at the ends of lines. You talked about the importance of concreteness and specificity. Then everyone worked on that. After that they shared their poems in small groups. Finally people volunteered to read the poems they had written to the entire workshop group. The poems we have included here are just two of those shared that day.

ANNE: What observations would you make about Ilke's poem?

MICHELLE: I often get this sense of learning a lot about the person from reading the poem. When Ilke includes "no more juggling work and home" I know that she is telling me what her life is like. When I read "remain sensitive to self and others" I think that this must be what she values in herself and desires to see in others—like men. I learn something of importance about Ilke when I read her poem and about Ilke's views of gender issues and about her gendered self. These poems are personal.

ANNE: How is that potentially useful?

MICHELLE: I think it's useful because education is far more effective when relationships are developed and working well. Sharing poems is a way for people to know each other. It is different from the invitation to tell something about yourself or the practice of discussing our views and opinions of common readings. I think we need lots of strategies for developing good relationships in communities of learners. This is one good way.

ANNE: What observations would you make about Doreen's poem?

MICHELLE: She's repeating a theme from the Batswana girls-imagining-life-as-a-boy poem. She starts out "I wanna be a momma, I wanna be a momma . . . . . But. . . ." Like the Batswana girls, she acknowledges advantages men enjoy but she doesn't want to be a man. I heard many thematic similarities between the experience poems read aloud that day and the two Batswana data poems. People weren't mimicking the Batswana poems. They generated the material for their own poems before they saw the data poems. I view these similarities as confirmation that there are certain themes in people's lives that seem significant in relation to gender.

In Doreen's poem, I get the sense she loves being a mother. She envies men for being able to concentrate on career. I suspect that career is important to her because she was at this conference. But she is thinking about all her other responsibilities—ones she thinks men generally don't assume. Like Ilke's poem, it tells you something about what her life is probably like.

If Tomorrow I Woke Up and Found I Was a Man

—*Bontle Menyatso (Gaborone, Botswana)*

Oh my god!
what about my compassion?
have i lost that, too?
will i now forget to feed the old woman next door
who is living by herself and is so sickly?

Oh my god!
what about my responsibilities?
have i lost that, too?
would i forget about taking and fetching the kids to and from school
as well as asking about their day?

Oh my god!
what about my sincerity?
have i lost that, too?
will i tell lies, say i missed dinner
because i was in an important meeting
when i have actually been playing snooker at the bar?

Oh my god!
what about my caring spirit?
have i lost that, too?
would i demand the undivided attention of the woman in my life
without as much as asking about what her day was like?

Oh my god!
what about empathy?
have i lost that, too?
would i still understand the pain any woman has to go through
when she has been raped?

Oh my god!
what about the initiative to do the "good little things" i do
for my loved ones

would i not bother to buy a card for those special moments,
cook special meals and do all those actions that speak louder
than words and make a difference?

Oh my god!
i have been there before, i wouldn't leave them to suffer alone!
i know the women folk are overburdened
so please god help me become a better man
and take some of that burden off
or take me back to be a woman!

To Be Nothing Else But a Woman—
To Be a Woman But Nothing Else

—*Bontshetse M. Mazile (Gaborone, Botswana)*

If i was to lose my caring heart and soul
     I would not feel when you silently call for help
     I would not recognise your unspoken need for support
     I would not respond to your heart and soul
If i was to lose my caring heart and soul,
i would cease to be human, i would lose my humanity, i would not
be a woman
I want nothing else but to be a woman, nothing else, nothing else
but a woman.
If i was to lose my compassionate spirit
     I would not sympathise when you are in trouble
     I would not listen when you need to talk
     I would not help your spirit to heal
If i was to lose my compassionate spirit
I would cease to be human, I would lose my humanity
I would not be a woman
I want nothing else but to be a woman, nothing else, nothing else
but a woman
If i was to lose my ability to express love
     I would not be able to laugh with you
     I would not be able to hug and kiss you
     I would not be able to miss your warm company
     I would not be able to smile when i think of you
     I would not be able to forgive you
If i lose my ability to express love
I would cease to be human, i would lose my humanity, i would not
be a woman.
I want nothing else but to be a woman, nothing else, nothing else

but a woman
If i was to lose my ability to express sorrow
    I would not be able to share my sorrow with you my love
    I would isolate you my love
    I would hurt you my love because it hurts not to share what hurts
If I was to lose the ability to express sorrow
I would cease to be human, i would lose my humanity, i would not
be a woman.
I want nothing else but to be a woman, nothing else, nothing else
but a woman.

ANNE: What do you remember about the occasion that gave rise to
    Bontle's and Bontshetse's poems?
MICHELLE: Although I had had occasion to share the Batswana girl
    and boy poems in the U.S.A., Canada, and South Africa, this was
    the first public opportunity for me to share them in Botswana. I
    was bringing them home. This was exciting, but as you know the
    timing wasn't really that great for the group, because they were
    in the midst of writing project proposals and they didn't know we
    had been invited to come and talk about poems. Given that
    impediment, I think it is significant that we had evidence that it
    was a meaningful experience for some of the participants.
ANNE: What was the evidence?
MICHELLE: There were a few people who wanted to come back the
    next day and bring their poems because they wanted advice about
    revising strategies. Bontle seemed very enthusiastic. And yet, she
    was one of the most reluctant people to break away from proposal
    writing. She told you that she had never thought of herself as
    writing poetry. But to her surprise it had been a very engaging and
    useful experience. I remember the next day her meeting with you
    to talk about her poem. You offered things she might think about
    with regard to revising it. And she did revise it.
ANNE: What do you find in Bontle's poem?
MICHELLE: I find there's a lot of energy in her poem. She uses lots of
    questions: What about my compassion? What about
    responsibilities? What about my sincerity? Et cetera. There's
    something about the use of all the questions that's very
    dramatic. I hear in those questions pleading, accusing, and
    worrying. I also read in those questions her celebration of being
    female and woman.
ANNE: What about Bontshetse?

MICHELLE: Bontshetse was clearly excited after our presentation on the use of poetry to represent data. She saw the potential of poetic form for some other data she was working with, on gender issues in Home Economics education.

ANNE: She had not seen data poems before?

MICHELLE: Well, yes, she had because I wrote the poem "Exciting Batswana Women" from interview data she had collected. I guess the broader potential of poetic representation did not click for her until this second experience.

ANNE: What seems important about Bontshetse's poem?

MICHELLE: I'll never forget the way she read it to the group. She enacted the poem with hand gestures and body language and voice. It became a dramatic event. Also I remember liking that she had taken a different approach to writing about gender. Her poem is a refusal of imagining life as a man. It's all about why she would not want to be male, instead of imagining life as a male. She redefined the poetic invitation and delivered this very strong celebration of being "a woman and nothing else." It was so bold.

ANNE: You've used the word "dramatic" in relation to both Bontshetse and Bontle. What is the value or significance of drama in this?

MICHELLE: To me life is full of drama—everyday in small and big ways. So it follows that there should be drama in education. The drama of life should be integrated throughout formal education experiences. This would energize learners and their teachers. Poetic form may be one way to bring more of life's drama into education in classroom settings.

ANNE: What do you see in the thematic concerns of these two poems?

MICHELLE: Responsibility, for one. Women do not perceive men taking responsibility for many things that are relegated to women. Women think men should be taking more responsibility. Women's lives are so often filled with looking after those dependent on them, whereas men are perceived as having more independence to pursue their pleasures or interests or careers. Women being aware of others while men are more aware of themselves.

Michelle's Reflections

One thing I find significant is that the Batswana girl and boy data poems stimulated the writing of experience poems by others. The exciting

Batswana women contributed to the collection of more data when it was used to launch a focus group interview that was audiotaped and transcribed. These data poems are not just outcomes of research. They are also beginnings. They are generative. They have worked in a way that seems unique in comparison to the typical expository informational research article.

It may be clearer to people that a poem should beget an interpretive experience. I think that for most people it is harder to see qualitative and quantitative research texts as open to interpretation. I think there is more freedom to make meaning in response to these poems than I suspect there would be in response to an academic article. The poetic form does not direct the reader's attention to consuming information in the way expository writing does. Poetry has potential for emotional response, in addition to analytic and critical responses.

The brevity of poems seems significant. With a poem you can have an experience in a brief amount time. A poem feels more accessible and less burdensome than other forms of reporting knowledge. A poem says a lot with the fewest words possible. I like the challenge of making a few words do lots of work. It is a kind of word puzzle that depends on developing one's sense of the economy of words. A one-page poem can represent pages and pages of data. There is a prevailing attitude that the more text students read, the more they will be learning. My increasing involvement with poetry has led me to reflect on the misguidedness of that.

I also think it is significant that these poems are about something that everyone can relate to. Everyone in the world is gendered so everyone has experience from which to respond in a personal way, whether they find themselves resonating with or rejecting what is in the poems.

For me, writing data poems has been an important departure from writing linear, rational prose, where you have to fill in all the gaps; where you can't invite as much from the reader; where you're supposed to spell everything out. Writing these poems has not been easy, and the extent to which they might viewed as successful is due in large measure to my collaboration with Anne. She knows poetry. She writes poetry. She studies the art of poetry. She has taught me a lot about revising poems.

I hope that these poems will help to broaden notions of where poetry can come from and what we might do with it. This is a pedagogical strategy that can be used to get people thinking about gender in a different kind of way.

Anne's Reflections

I think these poems take a reader very quickly into the position of educated women in southern Africa at the turn of this century. I find a high degree of consciousness, a vein of resistance, and a celebration of womanhood even from within a social context that is, in many ways, troubling for women. And I think it's important to note that some of these poems could have been written by U.S. women. Issues like "juggling work and home" and fragmentation ("broken thoughts") are highly relevant to women in the United States.

The issues of physical abuse and rape are positioned differently in U.S. culture, but endemic nevertheless. Because there has been no cultural sanction of these behaviors in the U.S., they tend to be buried, hidden in silence. What we have been learning from African men and women is that certain kinds of violence have been traditionally acceptable. Although these traditions are changing, the issues have high visibility. This visibility is represented in the poems above.

As a poet, I find it exciting to see people responding with such energy to a call for poetic expression. I'm always aware when Michelle and I do this kind of work that it elicits a kind of body language and eye contact that's very different from what we usually see in conference or workshop settings. There's something qualitatively different—hard to put a finger on. I think it's a matter both of content, which includes an emotional component, and of form, which heightens the emotional content and brings it into focus alongside conceptual concerns. I remember at Rand Afrikaans University we had a large audience, and in the back of my mind I thought "What if no one wants to do this?" But when we engaged them with the task, they were quiet and visibly engaged. When it was time to invite sharing, I wondered again, "What if nobody wants to?" Hands shot up all over the room. People were eager to share, performed their poems with enthusiasm. I remember a small group of men. They shared their collaboratively constructed poem (I wish we had a copy of it) but it was what they said after they shared that has stuck with me. They said, laughing, that actually, their first response had been "Well, we might as well just be dead." I was struck by how clearly this corresponded to what the Batswana boys had said.

I do have a concern in relation to poetic representation of data. It's not as simple as it may appear. At any rate, it's not easy to do well. Michelle's poems that appear here, for example, have gone though many drafts, in which she invested considerable time and labor, learning the specific craft strategies of revision. She has learned well the art of revising in ways that remain true to the data while using poetic strategies to focus and interpret, rendering in the concrete (rather than the abstract) and bringing a reader into the "lived experience" of gender issues.

I hope that readers of this exploration will be stimulated to think about gender issues in their own lives and that they will guide their students to think about gender issues. I also hope that readers will feel some connection with people of distant nations and cultures, perceiving that while there are differences, there are also commonalities. And I hope it will be evident that poetic form offers a viable strategy for making meaning and for generating dialogue.

Mercy's Reflection

It is so emotionally evocative to read all these poems from different age groups and to pick up the running theme of patriarchal bias that women have had to live with. I am more convinced than ever that poetry is the relevant way of expressing African messages. We are a singing, poetry, and dramatising community. The freedom of expression encapsulated in these subjective data poems is nonetheless based on representative data, case history, and life stories. Poetic expression is beautifully unique and liberating and in step with contemporary thinking that doubts claimed objectivity.

I agree entirely that women and girls do prefer to be women and girls but only if the men can be humane. Females only envy men to the extent that women are suffering under the yoke of singlehanded family responsibility coupled with abuse by men. There is no doubt that women see their role as superior and wish for recognition. Yet they have let patriarchy all these centuries prevail and dominate them in really cruel and sadistic ways.

I, too, am concerned that these poems are not ambidextrous in that they depict the negative only of men and do not portray the gentle and good side that they are capable of. Then again it is captured in subtle ways in some of the poems. I am thinking of the poem that talks about what good comes out of relationships when men do choose to be supportive of their partners to the extent of being mothers so that their wives can go to school. I am also thinking of the last sentence in Thaala's poem. It is an expression of hope for boys that they can or do outgrow the cruel and become men.

I took the poems to my university class. Arbitrarily I gave them out to male and female students, whispering to each that I would be asking him or her to read the poem out loud in class so they should please browse through it in preparation. When we had all settled I reminded the class that our topic for these few sessions was on "A.S.K.," an acronym I fabricated to stand for *attitudes, skills* and *knowledge* that determine effectiveness in counseling and any helping profession. We had already covered the *"A"* and *"S"* and were going to start with these poems to demonstrate some skills and knowledge. Without bother to introduce the poems in any way I asked the first person to read. After all the poems were read I asked, "What are these poems saying to you?" I had to prod a few times before the first response. But after that I simply could not hold the floor for any moment. It was so alive—the best session I had ever had with this class.

Here are some typical responses paraphrased by me: These poems are biased against men. The poems are outdated expressions of a frustrated and angry feminist. These poems are about what used to be but is no more. They depict men as superior and women as trivial. They are about women hating to be women because they feel inferior. Women have no reason to feel inferior because they are merely socially constructed ways of thinking so they need not be permanent. God did not really create man superior and woman inferior. This thinking is the fault of women. The very women who claim that they are abused go ahead and abuse young men. In Botswana there is even legislation that protects girls under a stipulated age from abusive men. Yet there is no law that protects boys from abusive women. We all know that there are female rapists and sexual abusers in this country. These poems are a momentary coping mechanism for the writer who at some point was frustrated but it does not mean that she really feels this way all the time. If a woman is feeling overwhelmed she might wish to be a man just to escape the burdens, but it does not mean she really prefers being a man. Preferring life as a man is just a way of ventilating emotion. One male student said he associates women with everything that is evil and shameful—witchcraft, prostitution, deceit, rape. It is unreal to imagine being the other sex because boys and girls think differently. They are created differently and can never be the same. This is only a fraction of the overwhelming response from a class of fifty students studying to become teachers.

At the end I explained who the poets were and when the poems were written. I explained that two of the poems were data poems and how they were constructed from essays written Batswana youth in 1998. That surprised the class. I told them the reason for my sharing these poems with them was to bring to their attention the importance of having gender knowledge. If the emotive situations from the poems are socially constructed then as professionals we need to develop attitudes, skills, and knowledge to enable us to influence boys and girls as well as other male and female teachers in ways that will ensure positively synergistic outcomes from male/female interactions. I emphasized that these days we talk as if learner-centered teaching methods and mixed sex group activities are educationally effective. So what do we think are the implications of these harbored animosities between the sexes in a country like Botswana where all schools are coeducational?

There is no doubt that the poems generated and lit up the class in a way that far exceeds giving a lecture on gender issues. My plan is to ask these students to join with some of my other students in replicating the other sex essay activity in neighborhood schools. I hope they can get youth to come up with their own ways of free expression. Let's keep enjoying this cross-cultural dialogue. It is indeed mutually fulfilling.

Options for Dialogue

- In small groups, take the perspective of one of the authors and read her reflection about this project. Discuss the poet/authors' reflections. Do you find the same significance in the students' poetry as they do? Report your ideas to your group.
- Brainstorm how you might use a poetry experience such as this one in a classroom situation. Discuss how this activity brings out students' strengths.

References

Commeyras, M., & Montsi, M. (1999). What if I woke up as the other sex: Batswana youth perspectives on gender. Unpublished manuscript.
Sadker, M., & Sadker, D. (1994). *Failing at fairness: How America's schools cheat girls.* New York: Scribner.

Options for Action

- Brainstorm a list of topics that you could use as a basis for interviews with students (children or adults). Choose one topic and create a list of open-ended interview questions. Interview a student or small group of students about the topic. Present the results of your interview in a data poem form using one of Michelle Commeyra's poems as a guide. You might want to ask other group members to take the voices of your interviewees and present this as a reader's theater with music.

CHAPTER SIX

... Creating Dialogue about the Strengths of Families

Family strengths could be used to build curricula that is relevant in many ways, and particularly in the area of language development. Regarding language development, we now know that children at age six have not yet begun to complete full cognitive development in their first language (Collier, 1989). When children's first language development is discontinued before cognition is fully developed, they may experience negative cognitive effects in their second language development; conversely, children who have an opportunity to learn in their native language and learn a second language, reach full cognitive development in two languages and enjoy cognitive advances over monolinguals (Collier, 1989).

Some research discusses the correlation between formal education (a high school diploma) for mothers and school success for their children (Sticht & McDonald, 1989). Other research has begun to question and contradict that information, its assumptions, and its limiting ramifications (Quintero, 1993). Weinstein-Shr (1992) cites research which discusses family strengths. The research indicates that when families participate in a variety of literacy activities, including home language literacy and activities in which children read to parents (Ada, 1988; Tizard, Schofield & Hewison, 1982; Viola, Gray, & Murphy 1986), the literacy development of the children is enhanced.

Related to home language literacy is the issue of home language use and how this affects schooling. Unfortunately, much of the information publicized in the media, both about language and literacy of non-English-speaking people and about the best schooling programs for these students, is false. Students and their families who speak languages other than English can, and should, continue to nurture their home language while their English acquisition is in progress. The languages and literacies enrich each other; they do not prohibit the students' becoming fluent and literate in English. Again, there is no evidence that native language instruction holds students back, as proponents of "US English Only" contend.

In this section, Mary Kay Rummel leads into our thinking about strengths of mothers with her poem, "What Mothers Do." Elizabeth Quintero discusses what she has learned from families participating in family literacy projects. Thomas Peacock, in the short story "Net Menders" makes teaching and learning in an Ojibwa family come alive to the reader and exemplifies the power of storytelling in giving voice to tradition in the lives of young people.

References

Ada, A. F. (1988). The Pajaro Valley experience: Working with Spanish-speaking parents to develop children's reading and writing skills in the home through the use of children's literature. In T. Skutnabb-Kangas & J. Cummins (Eds.), *Minority education: From shame to struggle* (pp. 46–60). Philadelphia, PA: Multilingual Matters.

Collier, V.P. (1989). How long? A synthesis of research on academic achievement in a second language. *TESOL Quarterly, 23* (3), 509–531.

Hakuta, K., & Snow, C. (1996). The role of research in policy decisions about bilingual education. *NABE News, 9* (3), 1, 18–21.

Quintero, E. (1993). Points of power: Mexican children in family literacy. *Review of Education, (15),* 233–249.

Sticht, T. G., & McDonald, B. A. (January 1989). *Making the nation smarter: The intergenerational transfer of cognitive ability.* [Executive Summary] San Diego, CA: Applied Behavioral and Cognitive Sciences, Inc.

Tizard, J., Schofield, W., & Hewison, J. (1992). Symposium: Reading collaboration between teachers and parents in assisting children's reading. *British Journal of Educational Psychology, 52:*89–97.

Viola, M., Gray, A., & Murphy, B. (1986). *Report on the Navajo parent child reading program at the Chinle Primary School.* Chinle School District, AZ.

Weinstein-Shr, G. (1992). Learning lives in the post-island world. *Anthropology and Education Quarterly 23* (2), 160–165.

Mary Kay Rummel, Teacher Educator, Poet, and Author

What Mothers Do

—Mary Kay Rummel

Call her not Noemi that is beautiful
But Mara that is bitter
For the Almighty hath quite
filled her with bitterness . . .
     —Catholic liturgy for stations of the cross

In Guatemala red is Mary's color.
At the side altar in La Iglesia de San Francisco
the Mayan Mary is a shepherdess with long curled hair
skin darkened by sun and time surrounded by three lambs.
Today her gown is plain red velvet, her straw hat embroidered
with bright flowers, the shepherdess before the sorrow,
before the child, and after when he is feeding
from her breast.

In front of her we chant
"Lamb, Lamb, Lamb"

I walk the cobbled courtyard outside the Iglesia
under the spell of Naomi, find her and Mara both
in a young girl who sits and weaves, loom in lap
her finished tapetes arranged carefully behind her.
Her blouse is blue embroidered with red flowers
her arms strong with the push and pull of thread.
She fast talks with silences between words that I
can't hear to her son who sits on a basket
across from her, his brown eyes lost in the distance
or sometimes turned down as he is wound in her words.
She talks in the rhythm of the weave—her voice rising
with teaching, praying, complaining, working
the skeins of her world, the word she is part of.

Lamb, we chant to her,
Lamb, Lamb, Lamb

Elizabeth Quintero, Teacher Educator and Author

Options for Listening

- Think of an experience in which you were unable to understand the language with which someone was attempting to communicate with you. Maybe the language was a different language from one you understand, or maybe the dialect was unfamiliar to you, or maybe the terms used were simply unknown to you. Write about this. What are some specific questions you have about language, culture, and communication?
- In your journal describe an experience you've had with a grandparent or other elder in which that person taught you something. How did this person teach you? What was the process? Did you learn a skill, a craft, or something less tangible? What did you learn about yourself in the process?
- Read the selection, write any questions that you think of, and note any personal connections.

Family Literacy: Lessons from Latino and Hmong Families
—Elizabeth P. Quintero

I would like to propose that we as educators rethink family literacy programs as a way for schools to include families and their strengths in the educational process. I say this not from a negative perspective, but from a positive one. I see a need for educators to think about family literacy as something other than a way to gain parental support for currently existing school curricula and homework tasks. I see a need for educators to use family literacy classes as opportunities to use families' strengths and knowledge to enrich each others lives, as opportunities for families to determine what knowledge they need and how to get that knowledge, and as opportunities for parents to teach educators much knowledge that is not in textbooks. For example, did you know that children from Somalia have vast amounts of knowledge about and interest in camels? I know a Head Start teacher who learned this by accident and proceeded, with the help of students and their parents, to develop a six-week unit based on learning about camels. Did you know that a Hmong woman who does not read or write in English can recite, through traditional storytelling of folktales and legends, 2000 years of the history of her ancestors? She and her women classmates in family literacy are making audio and picture books for their children and grandchildren to document their history.

My experiences working with early childhood staff, children, and parents have given me hope. The hope has revealed itself to me through activist, caring parents and strong, resilient children. The contexts which stand out the most clearly to me have been in critical, family literacy projects which were serving families in multicultural, multilingual communities. By the year 2030 over half of the students in schools in the United States will be students of multicultural and multilingual backgrounds. The two family literacy projects I will discuss are critical family literacy projects in two different geographical locations with two different cultural groups. I will give examples of things learned from these family literacy families that I believe inform us as educators in a rapidly diversifying world.

Who am I and why do I have something to say about rethinking family literacy? The neighborhood children on my street in Mexico labeled me "the woman who speaks strangely" when I spoke to them in my mixture of Cuban and Mexican Spanish as I strolled my baby through their street soccer game. Now, depending on where one sees me, I might be involved in different, but related, tasks. At Copeland Head Start, one might point me out as the teacher from "The U" who's holding one of the Hmong infants (from the family literacy class in the next room) in one arm and bending over talking to Pae, a Hmong four-year-old in Head Start, about the fantastic environment he's made for his collection of toy humpback whales. At the university, one might point me out as "that early childhood faculty person who cares deeply about her issues." My issues revolve around paying attention to parents' and children's strengths. By doing this I believe educators and leaders in all arenas can learn more about how culture, language, and varying concepts of family affect child development, community development, and ultimately our ability to live with each other with respect and peace.

As I journeyed through my collection of planned and serendipitous learning while I began my career (as explained in chapter 1), I observed and reflected about the developing literacies of children and adults. I had the opportunity to work in early education programs and other programs with many parents of young children as we collaborated in the task and pleasure of positively affecting the children's lives. When the children, the parents, and their cultures were valued, great leaps in learning and literacy occurred.

On the other hand, as I worked and raised my own children, I saw first hand how conflicts about traditions, and myths, and lack of cultural sensitivities on the part of educators negatively affect learning. Shortly after moving from Texas to Minnesota, I realized that being a single mother in a small, conservative town provided a number of challenges for me. Several incidents at my oldest son's middle school jolted me into realizing how insensitive educators can be. For example, I was told that my son showed disrespect by breaking eye contact and looking down when being reprimanded by some of his teachers and sometimes not answering when they knew he disagreed with them. I went briefly into the "Human Diversity 101" lecture about cultural differences in terms of eye contact and in terms of whether it is appropriate to outwardly argue with an elder. Then there was the bus incident. Making a very long and painful story short, my son was picked out by a line-up identification procedure and wrongly accused of "gang" activity. When he and I resisted, the dean of his school (herself an Asian) said that essentially, if one is not white, and middle class, in Duluth, one must work harder, dress better, make better grades, and make more money to be equal. I was incredulous. I wanted to make sure that my son knew that her opinions were not acceptable ones for a responsible adult to have—according to my family's value system. So I pushed it. I asked her a few more questions about equality, respect, and dignity. At which point she said, "I know, it's not right. But that's just the way things are, and I don't think we can do anything to change it." Angrily, I asked that if any people have any hopes of affecting change, isn't it we who are in education?

After the anger subsided, after I moved both of my sons to another school after I had two meetings with this administrator to give her information about what I was talking about, it hit me. I had had experiences with parents in family literacy classes that proved in tangible forms how critical literacy and "doing something to change things that are not right" does happen. So, I began to collect stories about activist parents and resilient children in family literacy programs to try to document a different side, a more proactive, participant-driven side to literacy programming and learning.

These varied experiences made me believe that critical participatory literacy programs are worthwhile partners or integral components for all educational programs. This is in part because teachers are able to see what is not now seen; parents and children can show strengths and needs that sometimes aren't obvious in the regular school contexts.

The Family Literacy Projects

The family literacy groups I have been involved with most closely are organized according to a model designed to provide participatory, critical literacy and biliteracy development opportunities for families in diverse communities. One family literacy project was for Mexican and Mexican American families in El Paso, Texas. The other project is called Poj Niam Thiab Meyuam (Mother/Child School) and is ongoing in Duluth, Minnesota, for Hmong women and their infants, toddlers, and preschoolers. The preschoolers and toddlers of these participating groups are in centerbased and homebased Head Start programs. The family literacy staff, teachers and assistants, are Head Start and early childhood family education staff collaborating on the literacy project.

El Paso, Texas

The project involving Mexican, Mexican American, and Chicano parents and their children, Project FIEL: Family Initiative for English Literacy, brought parents and children together once a week after school for approximately an hour of activities. The goals of the family literacy project were (a) to enhance literacy and biliteracy development of the parents and children through a series of participatory intergenerational activities; (b) to provide information regarding the literacy development process in children to the parents and to provide a setting for the parents to utilize the information; (c) to enhance parents' self-confidence to contribute to their children's literacy development through participatory group interaction; and (d) to empower the participants to connect the literacy activities to their own social and cultural situations, thus encouraging their use of literacy for personal, family, and community purposes.

Duluth, Minnesota

The project involving Hmong women and their infants, toddlers, and preschoolers is currently in its sixth year at Copeland Community Center, in Duluth, Minnesota. The program is a collaborative effort of Head Start staff, early childhood family education staff, adult basic education/English as a second language staff, parents, and children. The goals of this project are reflected in the goals of Project FIEL, with one added related goal, to provide a collaboration model of professional and paraprofessional staff working with Asian families in education and social services. This goal was devised to more effectively and efficiently serve the needs of the Asian families consistently from the time a child is born until the child becomes a high school student.

So What? Quick Glimpses of What I Learned

I believe that the most important function of a critical, participatory family literacy project is the service provided for the participating families. It can support the efforts and activities of existing educational programs. The activity of critical, participatory literacy provides to the family participants information about literacy and codes of power

(Delpit, 1988; Reyes, 1993) in the United States in a context where participants are able to explore the relationship that this information (both the literacy and the political aspects) has on their own way of life. In addition, this participatory critical, literacy setting also uses the background knowledge of the participants in a valued, active situation and can provide teachers and staff with concrete examples of sociocultural information and factual information that is necessary in any educational setting—information that is, to a large degree, not available in books or teacher development class content. We can learn from parents about sleeping routines and family roles as we engage in conversation about storytelling and storybook reading at bedtime. I will tell a few brief stories from these two family literacy projects that illustrate the transformative potential and the information potential, in albeit complex ways. Then English teacher Bea Larson from the Minnesota project will tell you more in the next section.

Parents Do Take Transformative Action

I have seen critical literacy in action. While the parents and children in family literacy aren't always directly involved in issues of "power," they have been respected and encouraged to read their "world" (Freire and Macedo, 1987). Often this results in their taking action in various ways that both improve something in their lives and inform us as staff. While many people define "transformative action" in different ways, most would agree that a prime example is a parent doing something to make a situation better for her child.

A few years ago the Hmong women in Duluth, Minnesota, in one of the first family literacy classes, came to class with a critical question. The question was "Why doesn't Lovet School (the elementary school which their older children attended) tell us about parent conferences, send us notification in our language, or provide an interpreter at meetings?" With the interpreter at the family literacy class and the literacy facilitator taking part in the discussion, the women discussed at length how angry they felt when they heard of the teachers' comments about how the Hmong parents just didn't care about their children's education. The staff at the elementary school said this because the Hmong parents never come to parent conferences, PTA meetings, or other school functions. The women commented on how they had been able to be active in Head Start, in part because the staff always made the effort to provide interpreters at meetings, provide information in their language, and respectfully talked to parents about questions regarding their children. After comparing the two situations (Head Start and the elementary school), they decided to take action. They wrote the following letter:

Tus saib xyuas nyob rau hauv tsev kawm ntawv.

Dear Principal,

Peb yog cov ua niam ua txiv muaj me nyuam tuaj kawn ntawv hauv tsev kawn ntawv Lowell School. Peb xav thov kom nej muab cov ntawv xa los tsev txhais ua ntawv Hmoob. Thaum twg nej muaj tej yam uas tseem ceeb nyob rau hauv tsev kawm ntawv los peb thiaj paub tias yog ntawv tseem ceeb thiab.

Ua tsaug ntau koj muab koj lub sij haum los twm peb tsab ntawv no.

As can be seen here in the letter the only English used was the principal's name (changed here to protect the individual's privacy). To paraphrase the letter, the parents asked the principal why they were not notified of school information regarding their children in their language. They stated that they are active parents who care deeply about their children's education, but when information is illegible to them they cannot participate.

The principal responded with a letter, written in Hmong, a week later. Interpreters have been provided at all school functions in which the parents participate, and school notices have been translated into Hmong ever since this incident. And participation by the Hmong parents in school activities has risen to over 90%.

Examples of parent advocacy growing from family literacy can be seen in the El Paso project as well. A family literacy lesson was developed on "School and You: Avenues for Advocacy," because several of the parents had inquired or expressed discontent with specific situations in their children's schools which they had encountered and were frustrated with. The class discussion focused on the different procedures they could use within the school systems to voice their complaints and advocate for change.

Some of the guiding questions of the lesson were: "When you have a question about what is happening in your child's class at school, when and how can you talk to the teacher?" "If you are not happy with what the teacher tells you or if the teacher won't talk to you, what can you do then?" "What are all the avenues you can think of to be an advocate for your children?"

One parent during the class talked about the situation of her child's teacher. The teacher was treating the child in a disrespectful way that, the parent felt, was damaging the child's self-confidence and inhibiting her learning. Her child had entered kindergarten, after the generally supportive context of Head Start, but day after day as she struggled with various writing tasks, her kindergarten teacher consistently reprimanded her for poor performance and grabbed her paper, crumpled it up, and threw it in the trash in front of all the students. After discussing this situation with other parents in the family literacy class, the parent found other parents outside the class who shared similar stories. They all decided they wanted to meet at the school for a parent discussion group to brainstorm how they could deal with "children's abuse by teachers." The parents began to meet regularly together with each other, sometimes with their school administration, and sometimes attended school board meetings to make their concerns known (Quintero & Macías, 1995). They often informed staff about community and family information that they otherwise wouldn't have known.

Learning from the Families: About Cognition, Literacy, and Language

The staff involved with the literacy project in El Paso, Texas, stressed emergent literacy and developmental writing. We were careful to explain the principles behind this way of learning, while adamantly committed to respecting the parent's choice in method of interaction and teaching with her child. Diana, one of the family literacy participants in this project, lived with both her parents in a working class neighborhood. She was an only child. The family spoke only Spanish at home. Diana's mother was adamant about being a direct part of her daughter's education even when she was given information about the importance of her daughter's independence in learning and literacy events.

Diana was just beginning to learn English as the literacy groups started in September. She was in kindergarten. She had not been able to attend Head Start. Diana exhibited familiar patterns of behavior for a five-year-old at the beginning of the literacy sessions. She spoke little at first, mostly in Spanish, often answering the instructor's questions with a "yes," "no," or short phrase. When the teacher asked her a question in English, she did not seem to understand, so she looked to her mother for a translation. She also often seemed to wait for a response from her mother, even when she understood the language used. As the classes progressed, Diana did begin to participate more in class in terms of her oral language.

The teacher noted that Ms. Garcia made constant corrections to her daughter's work and insisted on perfection. The teacher then tactfully told Mrs. Garcia that Diana could write and draw on her own; she said it was not important at this point in Diana's literacy development whether her writing was misspelled, not on the line, or that the letters were not correctly shaped. She also told Ms. Garcia that her constant corrections may make Diana dependent on her for approval of everything she does. The advice, however, had little effect on the mother. She continued to erase portions of her daughter's work that she didn't think were acceptable and made her redo them. This practice certainly is the antithesis of "literacy development" and developmentally appropriate practice

(Bredekamp, 1987) guidelines. Developmentally appropriate practice guidelines fail to take account of cultural differences in childrearing practices, or the negotiation of the tension that results between home/ school disparities. Diana respected her mother's strong personality and interaction style, yet maintained her own willful intentions when it was important to her. The teacher working with this family literacy class expressed frustration with her attempts to convince the mother to give the daughter more "freedom" to do activities in a "developmentally appropriate" way. *However, the literacy staff tried to keep perspective and keep in mind the critically foremost goal of the project, which was to respect the parents as the most important teachers of their children. We began to feel confident that explaining our teaching methods to the parents as collaborators (not directors), that some parents (Ms. García included) felt confident enough to disagree, do some teaching in their own way, and still keep attending classes.*

Regarding the cognitive issue of language development, Ms. García was realistic to insist that her daughter write well and correctly in both her mother tongue and English. She conceivably had had experiences in both Mexican and American society both of which had stressed the relationship between success and hard work to conform to form, in this case, correct English. She was determined to insure that her daughter succeed in her learning of English. Yet, at the same time, she and her family continued to speak only Spanish in the home. Research now shows that their speaking Spanish at home supports the children's English development at school (Cazden, 1981; Cummins, 1989).

Furthermore, parental authority is an important value in Latino culture. Latino parents inculcate in their children a profound respect for teachers and for school. As Reyes (1993) reports, Latinos hold high regard for teachers as authority figures, thus it is her opinion that direct instruction or active, direct interaction from the teacher is expected. This direct interaction does not necessarily have to take away from a goal of learning to be an independent thinker on the part of the child, but the path leading to the goal is more familiar with a respected guide. "Respeto" (respect) is a central cultural value and requires deference to older and more skilled individuals who have a greater command of the skills being learned. Ms. García's story is not told to typecast all Latino families. Her story simply shows the complexities involved in being sensitive to families and building on their strengths.

If this parental authority is a widespread value, it is manifested in different forms of parent/child interactions. In the case of Andre and Ms. Mora, we see a parenting style quite consistent with the practices and assumptions of family literacy. However, working with Andre and his mother caused us to challenge another myth. Some researchers (Stitch & McDonald, 1989) believe that a parent must have a formal education in order to be supportive of her children's academic development. Andre, age five, and his mother, Ms. Mora, attended Project FIEL activities in central El Paso for two semesters. Andre lived with his mother, father, ten-year-old brother, nineteen-year-old sister, and twenty-one-year-old sister. Ms. Mora had only six years of formal schooling in Mexico. Yet, her *biblioteca (library)* in her home, her literacy practices with her children, as well as her own habits show no lack of academic support. Furthermore, the academic success of all four children—those in elementary school and those in high school and the university—contradict the myth that unless mothers obtain a high school diploma, the children will not succeed in school. Weinstein-Shr (1992) cites research which indicates that when families participate in a variety of literacy activities, including home language literacy and activities in which children read to parents (Ada, 1988; Tizard, Schofield, & Hewison, 1982; Viola, Gray, & Murphy, 1986), the literacy development of the children is enhanced.

Ms. Mora also reported that she reads aloud from the Bible daily and that her home is "una biblioteca" (a library). Both Andre and Ms. Mora talked about the two sisters who are honor students at the University of Texas at El Paso. Also, the tradition of literacy in the home and in the family seems to be taking root in Andre and his brother, who are always on the honor roll at their elementary school. Ms. Mora's comments about being an avid reader herself indicate that while she is a monolingual Spanish speaker she is quite literate in her native language. Videotaped interactions of her and her son during the FIEL classes further showed that she is indeed proficient in literacy behaviors as well. That is to say, she calmly and consistently prompted and encouraged Andre and appropriately explained things to him in Spanish. Andre often then explained to the class the issue or story in perfect English (usually his writing was in English). Thus, while Ms. Mora didn't consider herself bilingual or biliterate she was an effective leader of this bilingual, biliterate family team. Examples from field notes and videotaped class sessions showed mother/son interactions which reveal her leadership on both a literacy development level and a social context level. Consequently, Andre at age five was proficiently bilingual and on his way to becoming biliterate.

Likewise, the children in the Minnesota project speak in two languages—Hmong and English. When their mothers join them in the room, they sing and "show off" their English with the storybook reading in one breath and turn to their mothers and elaborate on the description begun about polar bears, in Hmong in a private conversation. Pae, age four, then may turn to one of the teachers and ask in English, "If polar bear fights brown bear who wins?" His cognitive flexibility is not slowing down at all while his two languages develop. The Hmong children in the family literacy project in Minnesota are showing complex cognitive processing and development in spite of language differences. For example, Tong is a child who attends the Head Start classroom in the morning. Here the teaching is done primarily in English, with a multicultural group of children consisting of American Indians, African Americans, European Americans, and Hmong children. In the afternoon, Tong attends family literacy class and extends his learning from the morning. With the assistance of a Hmong speaking assistant, he talks Hmong with his buddies and relatives, sings, draws, discusses, and writes about what he's learned about whales, the moon, fish and sea life, and dinosaurs. He also reads folktales from Africa, Thailand, Laos, and England. These examples of literacy communication in his first and second languages are closely tied to complex cognitive functioning (Quintero, 1986). Cognitive connections, both in terms of factual information and socioemotional relevance to personal life, build strong critical thinkers and students who are successful in school (Cazden, 1981; Cummins, 1989; Freire & Macedo, 1987).

Family Literacy for a New World

Family literacy programs are complex by their very nature, and they differ according to participants' needs and strengths. Yet, it's been my experience that these programs offer more than most parent education programs and more than many tutorial education programs.

All participants collaborate in ways that often "go against the grain" (Cochran-Smith, 1991) of traditional practice. For some of the parent participants, it is a risk to enter a school building in a new country where the expectations are unknown. Almost all parents risk disruptions in already busy and difficult family routines. In addition, for all parents regardless of background the risk of addressing creativity, child development, and learning needs is a struggle. To decide when to help, how to specifically help with a learning task, and when to encourage independence in their children is a challenge. Yet, by working alongside one's child, the task becomes clearer.

Today I'm learning about my children's creativity and understanding and helping them in whatever I can because I like to share the hour with my children . . . Here I feel comfortable and confident (Parent from Project FIEL, El Paso, Texas. Translated from Spanish).

Children show their strengths in family literacy programs. In the excitement of working with parents and elders some children have risked using innovative literacy practices. Some family literacy projects put aside the textbooks, and use elders' storytelling as authentic history lessons. Other literacy projects let go of the "American Way," in which students study the Columbus story of Europeans coming to the Americas and how the United States began with thirteen colonies and then became a republic and so on. Instead teachers encourage children to discuss and value their cultural traditions and family routines. Some family literacy projects leave behind strict adherence to English grammatical rules and formal writing rules and encourage the use of code-switching, in both oral and written form. For example, Delia, a kindergarten student in El Paso, Texas, chattered in writing about the valentine activity done in her family literacy class where code-switching was encouraged.

Voy a mordir a Grandma with the love bug porque le quiero.
(I'm going to bite Grandma with the love bug because I love her.)

She gets to speak from the heart, but she risks forgetting to use only English the next morning in her regular class setting, where she may be admonished for mixing Spanish and English.

Family child-rearing practices must be supported and built upon to enhance social, emotional, cognitive, and physical development. School and parents must together determine appropriate educational programming that recognizes that the school's developmental milestones may be different from those of a cultural group or an individual family. These complex endeavors can happen through family literacy.

References

Ada, A. F. (1988). The Pajaro Valley experience: Working with Spanish-speaking parents to develop children's reading and writing skills in the home through the use of children's literature. In T. Skutnabb-Kangas & J. Cummins (Eds.), *Minority education: From shame to struggle* (pp.70–93), Philadelphia: Multilingual Matters.

Bredekamp, S. (1987). *Developmentally appropriate practice in early childhood programs serving children from birth through age 8*. Washington, DC: National Association for Education of Young Children.

Cazden, C. (1981). *Language in early childhood education.* Washington, DC: NAEYC.

Cochran-Smith, M. (1991). Learning to teach against the grain. *Harvard Education Review, 61* (3), 279–310.

Cummins, J. (1989). *Empowering minority students.* Sacramento, CA: CABE.

Delpit, L. 1988). The silenced dialogue: Power and pedagogy in educating other peoples' children. *Harvard Educational Review, 58* (3), 280–297.

Freire, P. (1994). *Pedagogy of hope*. New York: Continuum.

Freire, P. (1985). *The politics of education*. Granby, MA: Bergin & Garvey.

Freire, P., & Macedo, D. (1987). *Literacy: Reading the word and the world*. South Hadley, MA: Bergin & Garvey.

Quintero, E. P. (1986). Preschool literacy: The effect of sociocultural context. ERIC Document Reproduction Center (ED 282 181).

Quintero, E., & Macías, A. H. (1995). To participate, to speak out. . . : A story from San Elizario, Texas. In Martin, R. (Ed.) *On equal terms: Addressing issues of race, class and gender in higher education* (pp. 237–253). New York: State University of New York Press.

Reyes, M. de la Luz. (1993). Challenging venerable assumptions: Literacy instruction for linguistically different students. *Harvard Educational Review*, 62(4): 427–446.

Sticht, T. G., and McDonald, B. A. (January 1989). *Making the nation smarter: The intergenerational transfer of cognitive ability*. [Executive Summary] San Diego, CA: Applied Behavioral and Cognitive Sciences.

Tizard, J., Schofield, W., & Hewison, J. (1992). Symposium: Reading collaboration between teachers and parents in assisting children's reading. *British Journal of Educational Psychology*, 52: 79–88.

Viola, M., Gray, A., & Murphy, B. (1986). *Report on the Navajo parent child reading program at the Chinle Primary School*. Chinle [AZ] School District.

Weinstein-Shr, G. (1992). Learning lives in the post-island world. *Anthropology and Education Quarterly* 23 (2), 160–165.

Options for Dialogue

- Please discuss with a partner any ways that you see these family literacy experiences differing from more traditional classroom learning experiences.
- Relate any of the aspects of the article to your reflective writings in the Listening section.
- Critical literacy takes much of its rationale and practical activities from the work of Paulo Freire who worked with peasants and working people in Brazil and later, all over the world. He worked to provide opportunities for participants to "read their world." He felt that identity, analysis, and learning for the purpose of transforming difficulties into

more positive living should be the goal of literacy learning. Do you agree? Did your group see any evidence of this in the stories included here about family literacy participants?

Options for Action

- Interview parents about ways they interact with their young children. Ask about talking, storytelling, storybook reading, cooking, repairing the car, going on hikes or camping or to sporting events. What did you learn? Do you find evidence of the "roots of literacy" developing in the children through these activities? How do you know? Report to the class.
- Visit the Website of the Family Literacy Foundation at http://www. read2kids.org/about.htm. Their mission is to facilitate supportive relationships for children through families and friends reading aloud with them. Make a list of the information provided which you think is positive. Make a separate list of critical questions that come to your mind as you browse the site, such as, "Is reading aloud the only activity that promotes literacy?" "If a parent reads to the child, is that child automatically getting the message that she/he is important to the parent?"
- View a film with subtitles, but with a different language from the above film. Repeat the same activity requested above. Were your reactions the same? Why or why not?
- Research the history of attempts to "English Only" legislation in newspaper or congressional archives. Report the findings to your class.
- Visit the Website of The National Center for Family Literacy at http://www.famlit.org/. Do a critical analysis of this site. Do you see evidence of other societal issues in addition to lack of literacy skills as a problem for families? Report to your class.

Thomas Peacock, Teacher Educator and Author

Options for Listening

- Try to remember an incident in your childhood in which a parent or other significant adult was giving you some sort of moral lesson. Were you told something to the effect that you should always do "what you know is the right thing to do" and "know that you are a good person"? What happened? Please summarize the situation, the understandings you had as a child, and your current understandings about what was really going on. Write a letter (real or imaginary) to this adult with questions you have about the incident, their intentions, and your new (or developing) understanding.

- Reflect and write about a group of people whose values and cultural practices may be slightly or vastly different from others in their community.
- Describe an out-of-school educational experience. Where were you? Who, besides yourself, was involved in the teaching and learning? How was this learning experience different from many of your in-school learning experiences?
- Read the selection, write any questions that you think of, and note any personal connections.

Net Menders

— Thomas Peacock

In the time of my Ojibwe grandfathers, education was experiential and done in phases. Young children were first taught by women, usually by their mothers, aunties, and grandmothers, and the teaching was done primarily through stories and songs. As children grew, their education took on new meaning. Not only were skills and knowledge, but the whole of things was taught, and in this way a child's soul also grew. The lessons of life and the values to guide young people were conveyed in subtle and indirect ways. Boys were trained by the men and girls by the women. In the third and final phase, young adults began the search for wisdom, something which can only be found through close examination of life's journey, by searching everything for its simplicity and complexity and for its many layers of meaning. *Wisdom is the whole of these things.* This is the way education was done for many thousands of years.

I.

On an early morning, in a blue sky late summer day, a boy was helping his father mend fish nets. For the most part it was quiet work, because both the boy and the man were quiet by nature. Always, it was necessary work. Nets were in need of inspection and mending after each use. If they became torn and were not quickly mended, they would soon become useless. This was work that strengthened the bonds between the boy and his father, because in the mending of nets the boy got to know his father more deeply and learned the skills of his father. In this way, he heard stories about the big lake, Lake Superior, and he learned about its moods and subtleties and its seasons. He learned about fish and the way of fish. It was a weaving of story and work.

"These nets," said the father, "In so many ways they are like us. If we don't tend to ourselves and each other, we become useless too."

And when he said that, the father was thinking: *If I could tell you directly what I meant, then I would tell you that we need to care for each other as a family in order to be whole, and that we also need to tend to the whole of ourselves—not simply to our physical being, but also to our emotional well-being and to our spiritual needs. I would tell you that if one of those parts is in need of repair, then it affects other parts, and we cannot be whole people. I would say that not mending might destroy us. That is what I wish I could tell you, but you are too young to know what I mean. So I tell you we are like nets.*

The boy was thinking about what his father said, but he was young and did not know what it meant. So he forgot about it and thought of something else instead. "Dad, do you know of any way I could make some extra money for school things? I'd like to get some of my own clothes and stuff."

The father smiled and thought of the boy's question. He continued to work on the net. He was thinking: *Someday I will say something, and maybe it will be just a word or a look, and you will know what I mean. Someday we will be able to communicate in complete silence, and we will both understand the meaning of our silence. That is how I wish to come to know you.*

He told the boy that his Uncle Eddie and he were going to take a week or so off of setting fish nets, because he found some temporary work with the BIA (Bureau of Indian Affairs) road crew. They were fixing some of the roads up at Fond du Lac, and he was planning on traveling with the crew. That would mean staying over at Fond du Lac and coming home on weekends. It would mean extra money, and that money was needed to get ready for winter and to do repairs on their fish boat. Besides, he could make more money on the road crew than setting nets, and Uncle Eddie didn't mind. Eddie always found something to occupy himself when he wasn't fishing. He told the boy that at this time of the year, Eddie was always looking for a partner to go harvesting wild rice.

On this late August day in Red Cliff, Ron's mind was occupied with thoughts of the return to school. He had already traveled once with his mother to Ashland to buy a collection of notebooks, pencils, and pens, knowing in his heart that the notebooks would be used mostly to draw pictures, and that the pens and pencils would quickly become lost in the mysterious black hole where all pens and pencils seem to disappear. He knew those things were mostly to satisfy his mother, to assure her of his commitment to note-taking and doing homework. On this day, they would return to the concrete jungle to buy school clothes.

So later in the morning, after the mending of nets, the journey down Highway 13 began. Because he had also helped his father put a discount brand AM-FM radio in the old truck, one of the first things he did was ask his mother to change the channel from country western to KZIO, a Duluth, Minnesota, rock and roll station. He asked if they could make a quick stop at the Washburn Dairy Queen, famous because it was the only earth-sheltered Dairy Queen in the country. They did, and as the old truck rounded the corner out of Washburn, he began a litany of school clothes requests.

"I'd like a fitted hat. A UNLV one. And a Chicago White Sox starter jacket. And Air Jordan shoes. And I want three pair of jeans. Levi's." He took a big lick out of a dilly bar and continued, not knowing that part of it was stuck to his upper lip and another part had fallen into his lap. "And I want to get my hair cut while we're there. I want a flat top with a tail. And do you think we could get the new Boyz II Men compact disc?"

"Ronnie, you're already up to about $500, and we have $150 to spend on clothes this year." She was laughing, though, trying to wipe the ice cream from his upper lip with a paper napkin while staying on the road at the same time. The laughing way. The laughing way of teaching. Ron would understand it only when he was older.

"Listen to me," his mother asserted, trying to sound serious. "If you want all of that stuff, you're going to have to find some work and get it yourself. There is just no way we can get you all of the things you want. Maybe you should take your dad's advice and ask Uncle Eddie if he has some extra work you can do to make some money. You do that and you can buy your own new threads. Be the coolest dude on the rez bus."

"I'm already the coolest dude on the rez bus." They both laughed.

The clothes shopping trip was another one of life's little reality checks for Ron. He ended up with school clothes, but they were no-name brands from a discount store. His mother gave him a haircut when he got home, as flat as she could cut it. No tail. As she was brushing the hair off his neck, she mentioned the possibility of Ron asking Uncle Eddie about going ricing (harvesting wild rice).

"You could go ricing with Eddie. He's always looking for a partner, but nobody wants to rice anymore. Everyone is too busy working for the rez or at the casino or fishing, and some of 'em are too damn lazy. And the price for green rice is so low that most people don't want to do all that work for so little money. But if you finish it, the tribal council is buying all the finished rice they can at five dollars a pound. I guess they give it as gifts to important white people and other bigwigs who come on the rez. And of course they give some to the elders."

Soon after that was said, Ron was on his bike and down the road to Uncle Eddie's, scratching an itchy neck and thinking about all the money he was going to make. Thinking about Boyz II Men music and Levi 500 jeans. Thinking about starter jackets.

When he arrived at his uncle's house, Eddie was sitting on the porch pulling burrs off his old dog "Chief" and scolding the animal at the same time. "You been out carousing too much, Chief. You're going to end up getting yourself shot or swatted by a bear, or maybe you'll end up getting run over by a great big truck. You should be hanging around here, sunnin' yourself and sleeping 18 hours a day and filling up on leftover government food commodities. You're getting to be too much of an old fuddy dud to be out chasing the ladies."

Chief always listened to what Eddie had to say, but of course one was never sure what exactly he could understand. He always flopped his tail around in acknowledgment and licked at Eddie's hand whenever he was being lectured.

Eddie looked up toward Ron, still working on Chief and chuckling. He began a light teasing with that familiar twinkle in his eye, a look of both mischief and wisdom. "You need any burrs pulled from you?"

He then noticed that Ron was sporting a new haircut. "Geez, Ronnie. Looks like you got your ears lowered. You'll have to wash your ears until your hair grows back. Now we can see all the scars on your head."

Ron just smiled and responded back with an oft-heard contemporary rez reply. "Sad." He then commenced to ask his uncle about going ricing.

It didn't take any deep thinking on Eddie's part to reply an affirmative, and he told the boy they would begin preparations that very day. Eddie told the boy they would have to make a new rice pole and a set of rice knockers, even though he already had several sets of rice knockers and a rice pole. He told him that some repairs were necessary on the old ricing canoe that was resting against Eddie's house. He also told him they would go ricing on the following Saturday.

Ron would not know of the unspoken reasons for Eddie's behavior until he was older and more practiced in the ways of living. Only later would he know that the purpose of making rice knockers and rice poles sometimes had little to do with the need for them. It had to do with teaching the ways of making them, so the skill could be handed down. It had to do with learning the why of making them. It had to do with an uncle spending time with a nephew, of their journey into the woods to gather the materials for these things. It was the whole of these things.

II.

The first task was making a new rice pole, and most of what they needed was right in back of Eddie's house. Eddie went into his old work shed and came out with a hatchet and bow saw. They walked down a path and into the woods behind Eddie's house, as Chief tagged along. Ronnie remembered being much younger and going down the path with his mother and Auntie Sara. In his dreams it was early winter, and they were going out into the woods to collect princess pine for making Christmas wreaths. He remembered they picked several gunny sacks of it.

But this time it was one of those late summer days, with a late summer sky and late summer smells in the air. They walked in silence. After a time, they came to a small grove of maples. Eddie had this look in his eyes, an almost child-like look of wonderment. The leaves of the trees were just beginning to change color, and he was in awe, almost overcome by their beauty. The way they shone against the sky. The way they seemed to dance in the wind. The way they smelled and the sounds they made.

"It's really beautiful today, isn't it, Ronnie?"

"It's awesome, Uncle."

"Need to find a good maple crotch for the pole. What we're looking for is a crotch about two inches or so around and without any knots. Look at it as a giant sling shot crotch," said Uncle Eddie, gazing up into the trees. "See any up there?"

They both looked up into the trees, and soon Uncle Eddie found an acceptable crotch to use as the base of the rice pole. He pointed up at it. "Now I'm not going to climb up there and get it. That's your job. You climb up there and I'll hand you the saw."

So up the tree the boy climbed, and the saw was handed up soon after. The crotch was cut and handed down. Uncle Eddie pulled out a pocket knife and stripped it of its bark. He handed it to the boy.

Ron smelled it and it smelled good. It smelled like future rice pole. It smelled like money. Chief was nosey. He smelled it too. It smelled like tree.

"Now we gotta get the pole part," mused Uncle Eddie.

So off they went, deeper into the woods, until they came to a clearing. And on the other side of the clearing was a stand of tamarack.

"Looks like a whole bunch of rice poles over there. You pick one out, Ronnie. Should be one about two inches around, and good and straight, and not full of knots, and not dead but alive. One about twelve feet tall. You cut it and strip it of all its branches, and then you can use my knife and smooth out all the rough spots."

The boy went about his task, with an uncle looking on. First a tamarack was selected and cut down. It fell softly to the ground, and as it did an uncle was looking at his nephew. In the boy he pictured himself, as he himself was the first time he went hunting for a rice pole with his uncle. He also saw in the boy physical features of Ron's father, and he always had noticed the boy had his grandmother's gentle ways. He was thinking: *This is the circle of things. This is the circle within circles.* And he was thankful and prayed silently because he was given the opportunity to teach his nephew these things, on this day, at this time, and in the way he himself had learned.

"Long time ago, our grandparents used to frame the wigwams with tamarack. If you bend it when it's wet, it'll stay that way once it's dried. Bend it over like this." Uncle Eddie made a sweeping motion with his arms. "Then tie it up at the top."

"Do you know how to do that, Uncle?" the boy asked, looking up while trimming branches from the tree. "I haven't seen a wigwam except in pictures. You see tepees at all the powwows and stuff like that. But wigwams. No way."

The boy finished stripping all the branches from the tree and then used the hatchet to smooth out the knots. He borrowed Eddie's knife to do the finish work, sitting on the ground when doing it. Chief came over and licked him.

"Maybe someday we'll try to make one of them wigwams, just for the hell of it," Uncle Eddie said, almost philosophically. He was thinking he'd have to pretend he knew what he was doing.

After the tamarack was smooth, Uncle Eddie notched the maple crotch and pole so they would fit neatly together. Then he told the boy that after they had dried for a couple of days, they would fasten the pole and crotch together with a couple of bolts and some muffler wire.

"And that's Rice Poles 101," laughed Uncle Eddie, as they walked the path back to his house. He was thinking about a book, Life 101. He had seen it once at a bookstore in Ashland. And he was thinking about his nephew. *Someday, if I have taught you the right way to make these things, and if you think about these things as important in their own way, and if you live your life in such a way, maybe someday when you have nephews you will teach them Rice Poles 101. And someday, if I have taught you how to make a wigwam, even if I don't know how myself, then we both learn how, and from then on, forever, if I have taught you the right way, someone will know how to do these things.*

Down the path they walked toward Uncle Eddie's, and they came out into the clearing of the house and shed, which stood surrounded by a yard decorated in modern reservation art. A boy was carrying a rice pole over his shoulder. An old man was carrying a rice pole crotch. An old black lab named Chief, who was named after Robert Parish, was walking slowly behind the pair. And all of this was mixed with the sounds of hard leaves and crickets and smells of late summer and blue sky and changing leaves.

. . .

The pole was set against Eddie's old house, and the maple crotch was tossed up on the roof. They needed to dry. "Now we gotta find some cedar."

Uncle Eddie went into his work shed and brought out several pair of rice knockers. They were made of cedar, as all rice knockers have been for thousands of years. "You can never have enough rice knockers. Now this pair," he said holding up one set, "is made for green rice. They're a bit heavier than this pair."

He held up a smaller, thinner pair. "You make these about thirty inches long or so and taper them at the end. Just about as round as a broom handle. Fact is, I seen some white guys using broom handles sometimes when they're making rice, but you know, they don't know what the hell they're doing out there anyway. And a couple of years ago, when I made these," he held up a pair, "I got lazy and went down to the lumber yard to get some cedar dowels. And the guy down there tried to talk me into making them out of ponderosa pine."

At that they both started laughing. Who could ever imagine making rice knockers out of ponderosa pine? "Maybe the Cartwright family, but not me."

Eddie motioned to his nephew that he kept some old cedar fence posts out behind the shed, just for making rice knockers, and the boy fetched them. He told the boy where they were by pointing with his lips and reminded him to look for a pole that wasn't full of knots.

"I sometimes go looking for old cedar fence posts. They make for great rice knockers. Hell, I got enough fence posts back there to make a whole pickup load of rice knockers."

With the bow saw, Uncle Eddie cut a section of post about three feet long. He quartered the section with the hatchet and handed the boy two of the sections. "There's your rice knockers and here's mine. Now, take the hatchet and start trimming them down. And be careful not to trim them too much. After they're trimmed down, take a knife and carve them. Taper one of the ends. Not to a point, but rounded a little. Then we'll sand them down so they're smooth."

The uncle and his nephew went to work, carving out this year's set of rice knockers. As they labored, the uncle told the boy the whole story of cedar. He told him the wax part between the bark and wood will stop bleeding of external wounds. "You might need to remember that if that hatchet slips."

He told him how cedar was used in ceremonies. How a cedar tree was used in the old ceremonial wigwams to represent the tree of life. That its presence there represents all the plant beings. That because it was green throughout the year, it represented all the sustenance of life. He told him how the boughs were used in the old 'jeezikays,' the shaking wigwam. How the boughs should be burned in the home to purify it and rid the house of anything bad. How the boughs could be made into a tea for throat congestion. "Just in case you sing too high."

He told the boy to smell it. He told him to think about how old it smelled. That it smelled thousands of years old.

After an hour of trimming with the hatchet and carving and sanding, two sets of rice knockers emerged from former fence posts. A boy and an uncle sat on the porch of an old house, both covered with shavings and sawdust. A dog lay beside them, sunning himself and thinking about eating government commodities.

"And that's Rice Knockers 101," said the uncle, poking his nephew in the ribs with the tapered end of one of their new creations. "Tomorrow you come over and we'll fix up my old ricing canoe."

. . .

So the boy went home and dreamed of cedar, and he returned early the next day to refurbish the canoe. As he tore into his uncle's yard on his bicycle, he saw Uncle Eddie sitting on the porch pulling burrs from Chief. "Chief's been out raising hell again. I might have to tie him up." Chief looked tired but happy.

He finished the task, and they went to the back yard, where the canoe lay resting against the side of the house. It was one of those old handmade, square stern, flat bottom canoes. It was a bit heavy, but they hauled it into the front yard. His uncle got a couple of junk tires that were resting against a dead pickup truck and put them under the upside down canoe.

It was made with one by twelve's and framed with one by two's. The seams were patched with tar. It looked like it needed a lot of work.

"Are you sure this hasn't turned into a submarine, Uncle?"

"We're gonna find out."

The first task was scraping off all the old paint and tar. It didn't appear to have any rotten pieces, so none of them needed to be replaced. A boy on one end. An uncle on the other. Scraping an old canoe. They did that for an hour, and then Uncle Eddie went into his shed and came out with a can of tar to patch the seams. He built a small fire from some of the cedar shavings and heated the can. Soon the canoe seams, an old man, and a boy were covered with tar.

"Need any holes patched on you?" Uncle Eddie mused, holding up the can of tar.

"Sad."

"Now we'll let the tar dry for a day or so, and then I'll fill it up with water to let the seams swell. Then we'll see whether we have a ricing canoe or a submarine. And if we have a ricing canoe, I got a can of paint in the shed, and you can paint it. Then we'll have the fanciest rice boat on the rez. It'll be so shiny we'll blind the other ricers when they look at it."

He also told the boy that someday he would show him how to build one of the old wooden canoes, that they could just borrow someone's aluminum one, but that he liked the old wooden ones better because they sat lower in the water and worked better, especially when in short rice.

Sure enough, the rice canoe was waterproof. Ronnie painted it John Deere green. The pole was fastened to the crotch, and a complete rice pole joined the legions of other rice poles. Uncle Eddie found a couple of feed sacks and they were all set to go ricing.

"And that's Ricing Canoes 101," said an uncle to his nephew.

III.

As he prepared for his first time ricing, Ronnie was reminded by his mother to pick out some old clothes to wear. "Wear the grubbiest clothes you can find. And here," she handed over his father's sunglasses, "wear these. They'll keep the sun out your eyes and keep out the rice hulls. And if you feel one of those get in your eyes, don't rub it. It has a barbed end on it, and you'll end up in the hospital and come home with a patch over your eye. And wear a sweat band." She handed him a red bandanna, and he rolled it up and tied it around his head.

"Geez, Ronnie," she was laughing, "You look just traditional." She was referring to the dress and manner of some of the Indian activists in the community who made a habit of wearing red headbands and sunglasses and wearing their hair in the old way. And sure enough. Ronnie looked in the mirror. Red head band. Sunglasses. Just traditional looking.

"And I packed you two some sandwiches and stuff." Sure enough there was a large sack of bologna sandwiches, a couple of banana splits, and three semi-crushed Little Debbie chocolate flatcakes. She handed the boy his father's thermos. "This is full of tea."

Soon he was headed down the road on his bicycle to his Uncle Eddie's, holding a large bag of bologna sandwiches and munchies in one hand and a thermos of tea in the other. He was wearing a permanently old pair of blue jeans, a stretched out old T-shirt, and one of his father's flannel shirts. Around his head was the cleanest sweat band on the rez and a shiny pair of sunglasses. He raced down the road, and on the way several cars slowed down to wave at him. Some of the occupants were laughing at how he looked. Ronnie didn't care. He was feeling traditional.

When he got to his uncle's, they loaded up the canoe and everything else and headed down the road. After a good hour drive, they pulled into the public landing at Bullhead Lake. There was one other car of ricers at the landing. Eddie recognized them as being from Bad River, and the adults spoke and laughed together in Ojibwe while they unloaded their canoes and put the poles, rice knockers, and provisions in the boats.

"Pretty snazzy rice pole you got there, Neej," one of the Bad Riverites chuckled to Ronnie, as he was loading it on the canoe. Ronnie just smiled. He was too Indianish to reply.

Eddie reminded Ronnie that as poler, Ronnie's job was to keep the canoe in the rice beds, and to pole back and forth through it. He also reminded him that standing up in the canoe and poling it was hard work. "And if you're going to fall in, be sure to fall in all by yourself. Don't take me and all our rice with you."

On that day, Ron found out that being a rice poler was indeed hard work. But it was good work too, because he got to see how good his uncle was at being a rice knocker, the one who knocked the rice into the canoe. He would gracefully bend the rice over into the canoe with one knocker, then tap the rice off the stalks with the other. And as he knocked, his uncle told him stories of when he was young.

"In our grandfather's time, the people used to move into the rice camps in later summer. They would set up camp, and then go out into the lake and tie the rice up, so it could be harvested more easily. They would parch the rice up on the same day (cook it and remove it from the chaff). That's the way. And they lived on that rice all the rest of the year, because without the rice they would have starved. They ate rice with everything. Even dessert. Why they even mixed it up and had blueberries and wild rice."

By this time, Ronnie was sweating profusely. His shirt sleeves were sopped with water, and he was itchy. Ladybugs were crawling all over him. Rice worms were finding nooks and crannies on him that even he didn't know about until they found them. He was having trouble maintaining his balance and was worried about falling in. He was wondering whether if he fell in, would he take his uncle and all the rice with him. He thought about it, and in a way it was funny because he'd never seen his uncle swim before.

"Uncle, if we tipped over right now it would be funnier than hell. I bet you'd look like a muskrat swimming around in the lake." The boy started laughing and almost lost his balance.

"Now when I was young," mused his uncle, "your grandparents would take all of us kids out to the boat landings for the day. And they would go ricing and leave us kids there to play. I remember how much fun that was. We met all kinds of friends that way, because back then everybody on the rez went ricing, and all the kids in the village were there. Us boys would play hide and seek and cowboys and Indians. Nobody ever wanted to be the Indians, because the Indians always lost. And the girls would play dolls and make mud pies. Some of them still do. I met my first girl friend at the Rice Portage landing. She made the best mud pies I've ever seen."

Through most of what he said, he had been smiling or laughing ever so slightly. Then the smile was gone and he continued. "Nowadays, nobody goes ricing anymore. And that's too bad, because it's something that our grandfathers did forever and now it isn't important anymore. They would say the rice is a spirit. But now, you know, all of that has changed."

It was this mix of humor and seriousness that was so much a part of his uncle. This way of teaching. This way of learning these things. The layers of meaning not yet completely understood by a boy dressed up looking just traditional but feeling itchy as hell.

They riced for several hours and in between took bologna sandwich and tea breaks. The Little Debbies disappeared sometime during their second hour on the lake, but they left telltale evidence with crumbs strewn all over the front of the boy's shirt. Uncle Eddie never tired, and Ronnie noticed that. His tired muscles noticed that too.

After four hours out on the lake, they decided to call it a day. Uncle Eddie let his nephew knock rice and did the poling as they returned to shore. Ronnie noticed that his uncle poled from the front rather than the back.

"It's easier once you get use to it. And you can control the canoe better and see the rice better. Only thing is, it's harder to keep your balance. So someday, when you develop your balance, you can try poling from the front."

When they reached the landing, his uncle got out of the canoe and pulled it up on shore. Ronnie got out. It felt really good to be on solid ground. Really good. They cleaned out the few rushes that were in the rice. His uncle was a good knocker, so for the most part the rice was clean.

"Looks like we got about ninety pounds of rice. It'll finish out to about fifty when we're done with it. At five bucks a pound, we'll make over a hundred bucks apiece."

That was enough for a starter jacket, Ronnie was thinking.

They bagged up the rice, and the rice worms, and the ladybugs, and all, and put it in the back of the pickup and headed back to Red Cliff. Ronnie was exhausted and slept all the way back. Too tired to dream. Too tired to scratch his itchy body but tired enough to drool all over the side of his face and shirt.

When they got to Uncle Eddie's, they unloaded everything and his uncle laid out a tarp on the ground. The rice was poured and spread out on the tarp to dry. As they did this, they removed a few blades of rushes.

"What about the bugs, Uncle?"

"Ladybugs and rice worms get parched up with rice, Ronnie. They give the rice that nutty flavor."

When Ron finally went home that day, with instructions to return the next to do the finishing, he was thinking of other ways to spend his money. Maybe he'd get a Boyz II Men compact disc and a fitted hat instead. Maybe he'd get a pair of Levi's and spend the rest at the video arcade. Maybe.

. . .

He slept a full twelve hours that night and awoke the next morning feeling a lot older than sixteen years. Every muscle in his body was aching. His hands were even aching. He got dressed slowly, ate enough for a horse, and headed down the road to his uncle Eddie's.

The old dirt road to the main highway is narrow and overhung with birch and maple and blue spruce. Always, when there is sun, the road wears tree shadows. Trees and shadows little noticed by boys. But on this day, on his way down the road, the boy noticed for the first time the blue of the sky and the way the changing leaves shone against them. He saw the trees and the tree shadows. And he noticed the smells and the wind in his hair and the way it felt against his face. He saw for the first time the shimmer of sun off the big lake and the way the water seemed to sparkle like diamonds, like it was dancing. He saw the whole of these things.

On that day, they finished all of the rice. Uncle Eddie built a fire from dried hardwood and let it die down to almost coals. He fetched an old wash tub and a handmade cedar paddle from the shed. They poured the rice into the tub, and the uncle showed the boy how to parch it, to keep stirring it with the paddle and checking it to see if it was roasting correctly. He showed Ronnie how to rub the rice between his palms to test if it was ready to come off the chaff. And when it did, they dumped the parched rice onto the tarp and loaded the tub with a fresh batch. They did this for hours, and his uncle told the boy more stories about when he was young and about the time of their grandfathers.

When all the rice was parched, his uncle had Ronnie dig a small pit. He lined it with another tarp and put rice into it. Then he went into his house and came out with a pair of moccasins. They were old and smelled of smoke and cedar and many years of dancing.

"Now you put these on, nephew, and you get in that pit and you jig that rice. You dance on it like this," he made a semi-circular motion with the palm of his hand." The boy did as he was directed. He put on the old moccasins.

"My mother made these for me," Uncle Eddie said.

The boy danced the rice. He danced it until the rice became loosened from the chaff. Then they removed it from the pit and set it aside, and then the pit was partially filled with rice again and the process was repeated until all the rice was danced. Then his uncle went in the shed and emerged with an old birch bark winnowing basket. It was ovular, like an old dish pan.

"Now watch this," the old man said. He put some of the parched rice in the basket and tossed it in the air. Each time he tossed it some of the chaff would blow away from the rice. After some time, all the chaff had blown away and only rice remained in the basket.

"Now you try it," he said. The boy did, and it was hard, but soon he too was winnowing the rice. They would take turns, and after a while all the rice was finished.

Before he left his uncle's house that day, they cooked up a small portion to taste test. It tasted great. They put a couple of pounds in an old grocery bag, and the uncle told the boy to take it up to his mother, and the boy did as he was directed. The remainder of the rice was taken to the tribal council and sold. The money was evenly divided.

On the way home, Ron stopped his bicycle and put his hands in the bag to feel the rice. He put it between his hands and it felt warm. He picked some up and smelled it. It smelled old. It smelled thousands of years old. And his hand went into his pocket, and he pulled out one hundred and ten dollars, his share of the ricing proceeds. He smelled it. It smelled like money.

All night, he thought about how he was going to spend the money, and when he went to sleep he dreamed of himself with a pair of headphones on, listening to music and wearing a starter jacket. He dreamed about how popular he would be with the girls at school.

IV.

He awoke on that Sunday to find his mother on the phone. She had a worried look on her face. His father stood beside her. His hand was on her shoulder. "When did it happen? Do you think he will be okay? Oh no. Maybe you should take him into Ashland."

Ron knew something was wrong. What was wrong? Did something happen? Was Uncle Eddie sick? "What's wrong mom?" said Ron, as soon as his mother got off the phone.

His mother replied, "Chief got beat up by a pack of dogs. He's all tore up, and Uncle Eddie is saying that he might have to shoot him. I feel just awful. That dog means the world to Eddie. He's had it forever. Raised it from a pup. And Sara gave him that dog. I remember she got it at a yard sale."

Ron didn't know what to do. He felt so bad for Chief and his uncle. But he was awkward with his emotions and didn't feel comfortable in talking to or seeing his uncle at this time.

His mother looked toward his father. Her quiet and gentle voice was a mix of hurt and love and pain. "Eddie can't really afford to bring that dog into a vet. He has a tough time just surviving' himself. And Eddie can't shoot it himself. He could never do that. You're going to have to go down there and do it for him." The house fell silent. Death and impending death have their dark and silent ways. Ways no words can cleave. The man went to a closet. He took out a cased rifle and got a box of shells from the cupboard. His face was ashen, and he moved with a heavy heart. And a boy was crying on the inside.

"Dad, don't do that. Not yet. Here." He took a roll of money from his pants pocket. "Take this and give it to Uncle. Tell him to take Chief to a vet."

. . .

On a blue sky late summer day, an old dog lay on a porch, and an old man patted him on the head. Every once in a while, the dog would look up at the man and lick his hand. The old man would pet the dog on its side, carefully so as not to touch fresh stitches. Up the road, a young man was helping his father mend fishing nets.

Options for Dialogue

- Discuss with a partner what stands out for you as the strengths of Ron and Uncle Eddie. What were each character's barriers?
- Discuss in what ways Ron and Uncle Eddie are similar to and different from a sixteen-year-old whom you know and one of your relatives.
- Discuss ways Uncle Eddie carried out his teachings.

Options for Action

- Interview an American Indian person who has learned about the history of ricing through family teaching and experience or research the history in the library. If you have the good fortune to be able to interview an American Indian person, ask that person whether or not they believe a tradition such as ricing can, in fact, be researched in a library. Why or why not? What do you learn? Relate what you learn to the story and report to your class.
- Reread the comments by Uncle Eddie about Life 101. What is he talking about? Write a short essay about this using examples from your own life.
- Read one of the following books or one with a related theme:

Danticat, Edwidge. (1994). *Eyes, Breath, Memory*. New York: Soho Press. This novel is set in Haiti and New York. Sophie Caco, the narrator, a child of rape, comes to the United States at the age of twelve to join her immigrant mother, whom she had never known.
Danticat, Edwidge. (1995). *Krik? Krak!* New York: Soho Press.

This is a collection of short stories about life in contemporary Haiti and Haitian refugees in the United States.

Erdrich, Louise. (1986). *The Beet Queen*. New York: Henry Holt and Company. A tough yet empathetic novel exposes the loneliness and craving that keep people separate even when their lives intersect.

García, Cristina. (1992). *Dreaming in Cuban*. New York: Ballantine. This novel is about Cuba, García's native country, and three generations of del Pino women who are seeking spiritual homes for their passionate, often troubled souls.

Høeg, Peter. (1994). *Smilla's Sense of Snow*. New York: Dell. This is a mystery novel on one level and at the same time very much a story about relationships, multicultural issues, and science.

Matthiessen, Peter. (1991). *In the Spirit of Crazy Horse*. New York: Viking. A solidly documented history of the United States government's oppression of American Indians. The account brings in issues from the early 19th century and weaves in modern events leading to the fighting at Pine Ridge Reservation and the trial of Leonard Peltier.

Northrup, Jim. (1993). *Walking the Rez Road*. Stillwater, MN: Voyageur Press. This is a book of short stories by an Ojibwe writer.

Urquhart, Jane. (1994). *Away*. New York: Viking. This is a novel from an Irish family's memory storehouse of politics and nation, myth and artifact, dreams and losses.

Vizenor, Gerald. (1990). *Interior Landscapes*. Minneapolis: University of Minnesota Press. Gerald Vizenor writes about his experiences as a tribal mixed blood in the new world of simulations; the themes in his autobiographical stories are lost memories, and a "remembrance past the barriers."

CHAPTER SEVEN

... Creating Dialogue about Strengths of Communities

Personal history and current lifestyles affect students' approaches to learning and needs for information. Americans travel widely to the far reaches of the globe, but often the histories underlying beliefs of the people they meet are unknown. The philosophies and beliefs that influence education in other countries and cultures affect education in the United States of America, both indirectly and directly. By building upon. . . .

One school district's approach to building upon community and cultural strengths shows possible ways to use diverse learners' strengths and serve their needs. In 1997, in an urban school district in Minnesota, there were 7,537 students classified as Limited English Proficiency (LEP), with the majority (71%) speaking Hmong. To address the specific needs of children learning English as a second language, an innovative transitional bilingual/whole language program was developed. This program, supported by Title VII funding, spanned a two-year period, and its effectiveness was evaluated at the end of its second year. The overarching philosophy of the school district is that every student can learn. It is a special challenge to provide opportunities for success for children who come to school with limited English proficiency and, in some cases, with minimal formal education. The goal of this bilingual program was "to provide opportunities for success through the presentation of concepts and the development of skills in a language which they fully understand, and in a manner sensitive to the cultural values and behavioral patterns with which they are familiar."

As collaborators involved in the evaluation at one school, the authors found that the complete evaluation documented a strong educational program that values bilingual, multilingual children's language process and sociolinguistic skills and the resulting interpretations of their worlds. The program supports the sociocultural relationship between family, community, and child and especially applauds the contributions of caring, active parents. The program, and others like it, are models in which the participants have taken risks to cross academic and funding lines and form links between child and adult programs, schools and community agencies, elders and children, practitioners and researchers. The programs rely on the participants' strengths and their own creative ability and tenacity in the learning process.

Some aspects of the evaluation show directly the important ways schools can support community strengths in the schools. For example, during the project evaluation, every parent interviewed in the experimental group was happy that the children were being taught to read and write Hmong and were being encouraged to speak Hmong for part of their day, every day, at school. A few comments in the parents' words reflected these thoughts (translated from Hmong):

> *My daughter speaks both Hmong and English to me, but I am happy to see that the Hmong language has been taught in the public school systems. Yes, I am happy. It will be useful to her and she will have a sense of culture.*

> *All persons in the home speak Hmong. Their writing and reading of Hmong is fair but progressing. I am only happy for them because it can only help them to read and write Hmong.*

The parents also acknowledged wanting their children to study and learn English. They commented:

> *They both are very enthusiastic about their work and I am sure their English skills are great. But they speak only Hmong in the home. They can speak fine to Americans.*

> *Learning English is good for job to help their future.*

Every parent interviewed stated that one of the most important goals they have for their children is that they be successful in school. Some of their words relating to this goal were:

> *I want him to continue with education throughout college.*

School is the only thing that no one can take away from them (an education).

We have dreams of giving our children a good education so they will live better than we did.

Many of the parents seemed to feel connected to the school. About half of the parents interviewed said that they had been to parent/teacher conferences and over half of the parents interviewed reported that they had had telephone conversations with the children's teachers or educational assistants.

As a parent so poignantly said:

School is the only thing that no one can take away from them (an education).

On a more general note, David Haynes, educator and novelist, believes that imagination transforms and guides not only his writing but his belief in his students.

> *I think that part of what you need to do to be a good teacher is to be able to imagine the lives of your students and to respond compassionately to that and through that compassionate response make a decision that they are worth while and that they are bringing something to the experience and that you as the teacher have an important role in shaping them.* (Haynes in Rummel and Quintero, 1997, p. 59)

Haynes, through his writings, through his stories, through his interactions with students—all unabashedly drawing on his imagination—transforms situations, places, even people as he goes through his life. One of his short story characters, LaDonna, illustrates what can be done with imagination.

> *LaDonna knew their problem. These girls lacked dignity and self respect. They had never been allowed to achieve their full potential. They had never unleashed the goddesses within themselves. That's why she was developing Madame LaDonna's Herbal Beauty Care Products.* (Haynes, 1997, p. 12)

Haynes believes in strengths. He joins Beth Swadener and others who insist upon naming children and families "At Promise" rather than "At Risk" (Swadener and Lubeck, 1995). Visionary teachers live what writer Audre Lorde metaphorically describes:

> *It is learning how to take our differences and make them strengths. For the master's tools will never dismantle the master's house. They may allow us temporarily to beat him at his own game, but they will never enable us to bring about change.* (Lorde, 1984)

The following selections exemplify the strengths of two communities of learners, one in a nontraditional educational setting and the other in a high school. Bea Larson tells the story of *Hmong Roots,* a bilingual book designed and written by a community of Hmong refugee women in Duluth, Minnesota. *Theater of the Absurd,* by Pat Barone, is a short story about a teacher learning through literature to be personally and politically involved in her classroom community and beyond.

References

Haynes, D. (1997). *Steps to a new and more wonderful you.* Minneapolis: New Rivers Press.

Greene, M. (1995). Notes on the search for coherence. In Beane, J. (Ed.) *ASCD Yearbook.* pp. 139–145. Alexandria, VA: ASCD.

Greene, M. (1999). Presentation at National Council of Teachers of English, Denver, CO.

Lorde, A. (1984). *Sister outsider.* Freedom, CA: The Crossing Press.

Rummel, M. K., & Quintero, E. P. (1997). *Teachers' reading/ Teachers' lives.* Albany: State University of New York.

Rummel, M. K., & Quintero, E. P. (2002). In Mirochnik, E., & Sherman, D. (Eds). *Passion and pedagogy: Relation, creation and transformation in teaching.* New York: Peter Lang.

Swadener, B. & Lubeck, S. (Eds) (1995). *Children and families "at promise": Deconstructing the discourse of risk.* Albany: State University of New York Press.

Bea Larson, English as a Second Language Teacher

Options for Listening

- Write about an experience in which you were introduced to a person, or group of people, from a place and a culture unfamiliar to you. How did you find out about the culture while you were building a relationship with the person or group?

- What family stories do you remember your elder relatives telling you when you were a child? Write about one story you remember.
- For those of you whose families speak languages other than English, what examples of the languages do you see (or did you see when you were a child) around the home? Write about the print sources of languages you can remember seeing there—a religious text, a recipe for cooking, a storybook for children, a love letter?
- Listen to Bea Larson describe her bilingual storytelling literacy project and how she learned about Hmong culture and made new friends:

I began teaching adult basic education/English as a second language classes in Duluth, Minnesota in the winter of 1984. I was immediately intrigued by the people I met who had come from all around the world. There was such a wealth of culture and diversity in my classroom compared to my childhood in a small town in western Minnesota where there was very little diversity of culture, color, tradition, or language.

Slowly, as I listened to my students share personal stories and cultural information, I became more and more astounded by the experiences of the Hmong of Laos, and I set out to learn as much as I could about them so that I could better help them adjust to the American culture that circumstances had flung them into so suddenly. All of my students, from whatever country or culture they have come, have had very compelling stories, but I decided to focus my own personal learning more on the Hmong because they appeared to me to face the greatest challenges in adapting to modern America.

Essential to working effectively with a culture like the Hmong is a relationship of trust. Respect was no problem for me, because from the very first personal experience story that I had heard, I was hooked. From there, I spent a great deal of time learning, mostly by listening and participating whenever I could, about the folks I was working with, their culture, their values, their families, their barriers to success in America, and their paths to success.

After several years of having Hmong students in my class, I was given the opportunity to be the ESL teacher for a class of Hmong women who had had little or no formal education or access to

English instruction. By this time, I knew most of these women, had worked with many of their husbands and older children, had attended family celebrations and traditional observances in their homes, and had often been at the airport when their families arrived from the refugee camps in Thailand, so it was with great joy that I accepted the assignment. The job site was in a collaborative program with Early Childhood/Family Education, Headstart, Learning Readiness, and Family Literacy being partners with Adult Basic Education, so that the women had on-site programming for their children concurrent with their English instruction in a neighborhood community center. It was, in short, an ideal situation for these clients. I began to picture a nontraditional, naturalistic research project with its beginnings in this adult basic education (ABE)/English as a second language (ESL) literacy class of Hmong women who had had little or no access to formal education in their lives. This was especially interesting to me because the Hmong culture is historically an oral culture; this is the first generation of Hmong who are using printed materials as a way to learn. I began working toward developing this project.

At the end of the first year of being their ESL teacher, I told the women that I would be their teacher again in the fall, and I asked about what their personal needs and issues were. After a discussion, we decided that it would be interesting to try to record their experiences and write them in English as a way to preserve and document them for future generations, as well as to improve their understanding of English. During that summer, I went to every Hmong event I was invited to, and I spent as much time as I could talking about what we were thinking about doing with the husbands of the women in the class as well as the women. I wanted the men to be familiar with the project and comfortable with it, so the women would feel free to be frank and open with their stories. This was very important to the success of the project.

- Now read about the process of the literacy class and developing relationships that produced Hmong Roots Project. As you read, take note of evidence you see of not only how this teacher was learning about a new culture, but also about what happened so that the learners trusted both the teacher and the learning situation.

Hmong Roots: Hmong Women Refugees in Minnesota Tell Their Stories
—Bea Larson

In the fall, I opened the women's literacy class with the primary goal of the women participants achieving functional literacy and survival English skills for empowerment so that they could participate within the mainstream culture in our community. The Hmong women participants had had little or no access to formal education and English instruction. Their age range was sixteen to fifties. Some were pre-literate.

Our related objectives were to establish camaraderie within the group, provide access to group problem-solving skills, increase participants' comfort level with American people/culture/institutions, preserve, honor, and respect the Hmong culture, preserve the Hmong oral and written language for future generations, understand the current generation of children, and to deal effectively with cultural, generational issues.

As a way to achieve our objectives, we decided to spend the year creating a personal history of each of the students. The stories began with earliest memories. (Some remembered homes in Laos; others remembered the refugee camps.) We chose topics to write about together, and then each woman ended her entry with her hopes for her children and grandchildren. The text was written in both English and Hmong for all the women. (By the time we finished collecting and organizing materials, our original objectives changed a little to become a composite story—this was at the women's request because they wanted what each other could tell as part of their own collections.)

The women were unsure of how to begin and what would be interesting, so I suggested some broad topics and had them translated into their language by the class member who became our interpreter. These were the suggestions:

1. First memory—*thawj yam ua yus nco thaum yus tseem me me tuaj*
2. Coming to the USA—*tuaj nyob rau teb chaws USA*
3. Traditional stories—*cov dab neeg thaum ub*
4. Traditional celebrations—*noj tsiab peb caug*
5. Courtship, marriage, child birth—*ua nkauj ua nraug, kev sib yuav, kev yug me nyuam*
6. Medical care—*kev ua neeb ua yaig*
7. Hmong history—*Hmoob lub neeg puag thaum ub*
8. Hopes for children, grandchildren—*xav kom tej xeem ntxhwv nco qab ntsoov tias lawv yog leej twh thiab nyob qhov twg tuaj*

We next began to build an atmosphere that was encouraging and comfortable for the twelve class members who were involved in the project. I was concerned because I am not always comfortable sharing very personal experiences in a group, and I didn't know how my students would do. My concerns proved to be largely unfounded, however, as the Hmong women have been sharing stories and experiences orally in groups for as long as they have been able to meet together. We settled into a routine that included a snack on storytelling day and complete openness. Stories were audiotaped for reference and the women were free to tell their stories in their native language. (Again, the women were not at all reluctant to be audiotaped because they frequently communicated with relatives this way.) A casual observer might have thought we were a group of good friends having a coffee party.

Key to the success of this project was the participation of a group member who could translate and provide a sort of cultural bridge between the Hmong and American cultures. Yee Moua, who agreed to serve in this role, is extraordinarily gifted in her ability to effectively fill this difficult position. Any problem or question that the participants had, they were always comfortable bringing up because they were free to talk to Yee in Hmong and she then either translated or helped communicate the issues in English. Without Yee's facilitation, this could not have happened. Even though she is one of the younger group members, her skills at respecting her own cultural heritage, combined with her obvious intelligence and ability to adapt in American culture, made her a natural facilitator for this project.

Meanwhile the group developed an extraordinary closeness. It's difficult to separate what happened as a result of the class and collaborative program from what happened as a result of the storytelling, but clearly there was bonding, support, and affirmation going on that were beyond the depth of what usually occurs in a class of this type. The women no longer seemed so isolated and powerless to participate in our culture. They were becoming very comfortable with talking about their tradional beliefs, culture, and some cultural conflicts that were difficult for them.

My original plan was to write a short, personal experience story for each of the women and get the stories written bilingually, but as the once-a-week storytelling sessions progressed, a very different outcome began to suggest itself. The women soon began making suggestions and requests about how the stories they were telling could be used and who they would like to have access to them. From there, I suggested that we compile them into a book that would be a group-composed story of the experiences of this generation of Hmong women. We also needed to include a chapter of the wonderful traditional folktales they were generating; the women decided that this seemed to be the place to add the written Hmong so that they would all, even those who were not literate in Hmong, have a sample of their written language for future generations.

I was struggling with how to get that written Hmong to be accurate; I didn't want a re-translation of the adapted story that I had written in English for fear that it wouldn't even resemble the original folktale. As I worried over this issue with the students, they quickly came up with the obvious solution; have my Hmong translator listen to the original audiotapes and write the Hmong version from them. I had to find a Hmong translator, however, who was not only skilled in writing the Hmong language, but willing to write the stories the way the women had told them. I eventually located a college student, whose mother was in the class, who was highly skilled in written Hmong and readily understood why we wanted the stories the way the women told them. He even agreed to make oral tapes of the Hmong version of the folktales for us.

Options for Dialogue

- Have you ever experienced a learning situation in which the relationship of participants became one of such trust that very personal stories were shared? What was the situation? What do you think helped the atmosphere develop in such a way? Please discuss this.
- Discuss what you believe the author was getting at above when she talked about needing a translator who was not only skilled in the Hmong language, but who would also write the stories "the way the women had told them." What do you think she meant?
- Continue reading and stop to discuss with your group at any point you have questions or comments.

From there we progressed to choosing a name, *Hmong Roots*, and went about selecting, organizing, and editing what the women were willing to have available for public use. At this point, they could clearly see that we collectively could produce something that could be used as a tool for teaching others about them and the Hmong culture. Soon, I brought a proposed title page for the book that listed the name of the book, the names of the storytellers as authors, the translator's name, and my name at the bottom of the page as merely a collector of the stories and writer of the English; I had made it clear that the stories were theirs. They were very excited to see this initial page.

Already I could see the women changing their feelings about their culture/themselves as they interacted more with American culture. In the beginning of this project, not a single woman was telling her children about her childhood; now several of them regularly reported telling their children about the stories they had told in class, and they were always proud when they talked about them. I'd had some of their older children asking me when the next stories would be ready for them to read. (We edited and sent home bits and pieces when we could.) The women had listed other human services providers they interacted with whom they would like to have read these materials when they'd finished. Many other members of the local Hmong community had asked to follow the development of the project and offered assistance. Some of the fathers thanked me for doing this. But foremost in the minds of the women was the fact that these were their stories, they were the authors, and total control of what would be printed belonged to them. This seemed to have been very empowering to them and to have freed them to be very open and frank. They surprised me with their ability to participate in the organizing and handling of the materials, even though their literacy and experience with print were very limited.

Throughout the writing of their stories, I brought the process to the class members. I initially told them that I had never written a "book" before, so that we would be learning how to do this together. The management of the materials was always their responsibility, and I was continually surprised by their level of input and ability to manage the materials to create a cohesive collection. Late in the process, we talked about what we had and organized it into chapters. We chose these titles for the chapters:

1. The Early Hmong—Hmong Immigrants to the USA
2. Traditional Hmong Homes and Family Life in Laos
3. Children in the Midst of War
4. Living in the Refugee Camps of Thailand
5. Changes and Challenges: Living in the USA
6. Traditional Folktales Written in English and Hmong

What Developed

With the collaboration of Yee Moua and the permission of the participants in the class, we completed this project with a compilation that provides a contemporary social history of the experience of Hmong women who immigrated to America as refugees from the war in Vietnam toward the end of the twentieth century. It is a composite story that begins in Laos, travels through the war years, journeys through the refugee camps of Thailand, and ends in America. We also included a chapter of traditional folktales. We were able to locate resources to have the folktales written and recorded in Hmong and to get copies of the collection printed for all the participating families and their relatives in addition to making copies available to local human service providers who serve Hmong clients. Feedback on the collection has been positive and exciting for the women who shared their stories.

Options for Action

- Read Ms. Larson's description of Phoua Lee, one of the authors of *Hmong Roots* and some of Mrs. Lee's stories.

Phoua Lee is a most remarkable woman. She lived in the refugee camps of Thailand (and raised her family there) until she came to Duluth, Minnesota, as a refugee to join her son shortly before her 54th birthday and after having become a widow. She enjoys when I introduce her as "a remarkable woman who first met a pencil when she was almost 54." She joined the class when the storytelling was well underway, but quickly was a popular contributor. Following are some excerpts from some of her stories.

> *The early Hmong people came from the part of China called Mongolia. For many years they fought until they were finally driven south out of China into the mountains of northern Laos by the Chinese. The Green and Blue Hmong came first and the White Hmong came later. The Chinese used the words Meo or Miao for the Hmong people. This is a derogatory name that means 'savage' or 'barbarian.' The word Hmong means 'a free people.'*
>
> *Once there were two brothers whose parents were Chinese. One of the brothers married a Chinese girl and the other brother married a Hmong girl and became Hmong. A few generations later, a daughter of the Chinese family was asked to marry the Hmong leader's son so that she could spy on the Hmong because the Chinese were afraid that the Hmong people were becoming too strong.*
>
> *With their spy in place, the Chinese knew everything about the Hmong. They plotted to kill the Hmong leader to make the Hmong people weak. The plan was discovered so the Hmong leader hid in the temple, but the Chinese soldiers knew where the Hmong leader's house was. The Chinese soldiers went there and tricked the Hmong soldiers guarding the Hmong leader into believing that the Chinese were afraid to fight the stronger*

Hmong. The Chinese asked to talk to the Hmong leader about surrendering, but it was a trick. When he came outside, the Chinese killed him with a bow and arrow.

Without a leader, the Hmong had many troubles. Eventually the Green Hmong went to Laos. The Chinese attacked anyone they saw whose clothes identified them as Hmong, so the White Hmong people turned their clothes inside out to make them look Chinese. If they fooled the Chinese soldiers with their clothes, they weren't bothered.

When Hmong people died while fleeing from the Chinese, their families buried them in the traditional Hmong way. But the Chinese dug up their graves and destroyed their bodies. So the Hmong people buried their dead the same as the Chinese did so their bodies wouldn't be disturbed. Since we lost our country, we have lost many things.

Mrs. Lee later told a story about history and art as seen reflected in Hmong traditional embroidery.

My parents had nine children—seven girls and two boys. I was the oldest girl in my family. My mom knew I was good at weaving, so I stayed home and did that instead of going to the fields to work with the rest of the children. We believed that it was good luck to have the person doing the weaving be someone who was good at it.

During the weaving of the hemp threads into cloth, it was important that no man, boy, or dog interrupted the work, or it would have to be started all over again. One day when I was weaving with my mother-in-law, we told all the men to go to the fields so we could work. My husband came home about 4: oo P.M. and said, 'Aren't you done yet?' and we had to start all over again!

• Read Bea Larson's final reflections about the bilingual storytelling project and the following folktale. Reflect on your learnings, as a group or individually, from this chapter and have a brainstorming session about how teachers and schools could use this type of project and information to learn about and support immigrants in our communities.

Stories like these gave us Americans a real firsthand glimpse into the traditional culture of the Hmong and some of the challenges they faced. Their personal experience stories also often dictated the curriculum for the other days of class, because they often talked about what was difficult for them here, and those topics became the issues we worked on. This project also gave the participants a different understanding of what a "book" really is and how books can be used. I was able to teach the moms how to help their children study their school books even before the moms had the literacy in English to read their children's books. It seemed like "writing a book" made this an easier concept for them to understand.

There were some important resources that were necessary to complete a project of this scope. Since I know no Hmong, I needed an interpreter for the story—telling; that role was ably filled by one of the participants, Yee Moua. However, Yee had neither the time to donate nor the literacy skills to provide the written Hmong, so I was able to obtain a small grant that allowed me to hire a college work-study student (Yang Vang) who was highly skilled in written Hmong and very excited to help put this together. That grant also paid to have copies of the book made in the school district print shop when the book was finished. Other important resources were an inexhaustible supply of tissues for the times when we all grieved together and support from a psychiatrist friend who specializes in treating post traumatic stress disorder, especially in victims of war. Debriefing with him was an invaluable help. I also cannot understate the importance of having the entire local Hmong community, especially the elders, informed about and included in the writing of these stories. They were always kind enough to help me in any way they could and to answer all of my questions.

Hmong Roots Stories told by Sae Yang, Feng Her, Yee Moua, Youa Her, Cher Xiong, Yer Yang, Ai Lee, Nhia Vang, Mai Vue, Bee Yang, Sue Yang, and Phoua Lee. Translated to English by Yee Moua. Stories collected and written in English by Bea Larson. Hmong version of folktales adapted and written by Yang Vang

Patricia Barone, Writer and Health Professional

Options for Listening

- What have you heard or read about the events of 1968–1969 in the United States regarding the conflicts that arose on college campuses as a result of differing political beliefs and agendas? Write about what you remember.

- Write about whether or not you believe political events and issues should be a part of the day-to-day teaching and learning in the educational community.
- This is a story about high school students in the United States in the 1960s who are faced with momentous historical events that affect their lives. As you read the story think about (and note) these students, their communities, and the events in their lives that influenced them.

Theater of the Absurd

—*Patricia Barone*

In August of 1969, I moved to New Orleans after my divorce and fell in love with an Irishman two weeks after I arrived. I had a new job teaching English and dramatics at a posh private school on Napoleon Avenue called Socrates Hall (Socks for short). There I was, a first-time teacher at the age of thirty-nine.

The Irishman parked a U-Haul in the driveway and said as I opened the door, "Well, here we are—myself, Malachy Harney, and the last of the earthly possessions you left with that cretinous rascal, my cousin—blind into the bargain to have let you go." Within ten minutes, he'd confided that only seven years ago he'd been a priest, and had been no further from Ireland in 45 years than Scotland. He was a kindred soul—I'd been living in a small river town 1,000 miles upstream from New Orleans, moored in a somnolent marriage for almost twenty years, until I woke up and traveled on. Malachy, losing no more time, had a 3-month tour of the USA until his Greyhound pass ran out, and he remembered his cousin in Minnesota. It was a good deal for them both. Malachy had a trip to New Orleans on Vincent's dime, and Vincent had a cheaper option than shipping the rest of my belongings.

"On sabbatical, I am!" he said, congratulating himself. "That is, from my job as a librarian in a Londonderry community college," he explained, "but while I stay here, I'll be working on my novel about a nineteenth-century Irish immigrant." (And he said this all on one breath.) Though it was the very first time he'd met me, within an hour it was, "Mary, acushula!" (whatever that meant—later I discovered it was an endearment), "it seems I've come to the perfect fair place," he said. His deep-set eyes were an improbable blue and his long upper lip gave a humorous caste to his mouth, which saved him from mere handsomeness. I tell you all this so you'll get the picture. I had my reasons, or unreasons—you see, his chin was slightly pugnacious. Because I was so taken with him, it didn't hit me that I didn't know him at all until I brought him that evening to the first faculty party of the year where I didn't know anyone else either. Going around meeting people, smiling until my cheeks hurt, I was about to introduce Malachy to the headmaster when I realized that, at some point, he'd left me. I recognized his laugh even though I'd never heard it before. There he was under a palm tree with the music department.

"Oh, I love your brogue!" The senior high choir teacher, a blonde with long straight hair and a speaking voice like elevator music, was leaning toward him. "Why don't we put on some more recent American music for Malachy!" Soon Simon and Garfunkel's "Bridge Over Troubled Water" crossed the patch of lantern-ringed sky above the patio. The aspic shivered on the buffet table and we had a rendezvous by the stuffed crab and shrimp remoulade.

The months of September and October I spent my days trying to impress the school with my energy and enthusiasm, and my evenings trying to impress Malachy Harney. We talked over Ramos gin fizzes at the Napoleon House and all through the seven-course Creole meal at Tujaques. I soon decided he was more than charming. "Teaching!" he said, "I miss it, Gaelic and history it was, my third formers with pimply faces, but I don't miss the slums of Belfast, coward that I am." I think it was his honesty that got me—though I didn't believe he was a coward. At almost 40, you feel guilty about having a compromised life. He eased me.

At lunch time in the oak-paneled faculty lounge, the faculty gossiped about everything and everyone as long as it made for a good story—it was the New Orleans way. There was many a teasing conjecture about Malachy in my life, but I just smiled and asked a question about one of my students. I learned that Soozu Lions, the best actress in the school, was at Sock's Hall on scholarship. This tidbit I gathered as I sampled one of Dorothy's pecan sugar cookies. (The school actually had an elderly black maid who also prepared strong chicory coffee in a little kitchen off the lounge.) Stevie Newton's father was a law professor at Loyola. Because Stevie was such an analytical girl, everyone agreed that the intuition and feeling in the drama class would challenge her. "Stevie said she was glad I wasn't artsy," I told my colleagues, and everyone chuckled. It was my mission, they told me, to provide a cultural outlet for some of the best students in the school. Okey dokey, I thought, but being a new teacher was a strain.

In the beginning, the kids sort of laughed at me, though not, I thought, unkindly. Mike Fine was typical of my kids—neither a jock nor a spirit, a bit of a loner in middle school, he'd finally made friends who didn't think it was nerdy to like Bella Lugosi movies and single-frame animation. These were the kids with big brains who also liked to make things. So in my first enthusiasm, I found myself giving a bunch of hall passes—Mike, Marcus, and Dan off scrounging paint and plywood from the custodian for the sets, Soozoo and Stevie off practicing their lines in the senior rec room. How was I going to explain that to the headmaster if he met them wandering about the school? So then I had the dramatics class sit in their desks and work on essays about George Bernard Shaw's *Man and Superman.*

On the very first day of that new regimen, Mike, looking bored, raised his hand and waved it back and forth. "Mary? Excuse me—Mrs. Harney. Did the headmaster and the principal tell you to stop letting us have so much fun?" I felt my smile wavering on and off my face. Fun—it wasn't something you were supposed to allow too much of, if you had discipline, was it? "Why can't things go on the way they were," he said, "you could call this class a play workshop." That was how most of my classes turned into workshops. Because new methods of education, like open classrooms with everyone sitting on the floor in a circle, were the rage back then, I got away with it.

When Malachy came to speak to my honors English class about Yeats' Ireland and his lesser known political poetry, he was charismatic as I suspected he would be, especially when he strayed off the subject. "The world is a terrible place just now," he told them. "My country is struggling with its division. The British try—they will not succeed—to keep an unjust rule in Northern Ireland. And your country is involved in the most damaging of wars in Vietnam. Also unjust, if you will permit an outsider to say so. The native Irish, like the Vietnamese, were and are victimized by a colonial power, England. Other colonial powers, the United States and the western nations that join it in Vietnam, use fire from heaven against living people in Southeast Asia." Malachy cleared his throat, took a sip of water, and the class was very quiet, in the sort of delight that is typical of kids, not heartless but loving the gravity of conflict.

Then Jacques Faradeaux, who always sat in the first row and would surely be valedictorian for the class of '71, raised his hand. "Excuse me, sir, but I think that the communists are also colonial powers."

Malachy smiled. "It's a valid point you're making. It's an argument you see in the newspapers, one proposed by men older and more experienced than yourself. The only problem with that point of view is its sheer wrongheadedness. I'll show you why." Malachy drew on the black board, in rather accurate perspective, a series of three-dimensional, rectangles, adding dots. "The famous dominoes," he said, "According to the theory, they will all fall down if the U.S. of A. doesn't prevent the first one from falling. But the big hand—that's the States" (drawing a recognizable hand, fingers knobby, wrist hairy)— "the big hand keeps picking up the first piece and putting it into position, so it can fall again. That's the hand that keeps the game going, and the pieces falling. For every dot on the domino, a thousand people die. Vietnamese, and Americans."

I let out a breath I hadn't realized I'd been holding. The class was quiet until Jacques said, "If we leave, then the big hand will be the hand of Russia, or China!"

"Isn't that giving too little credit to the people?" Malachy said, still smiling at him.

Then we all went to lunch and I wished I could eavesdrop on what the students said about him over their brown bags in the patio. As it turned out, Stevie told me everything after school. "A table of senior guys behind them was getting pretty worked up," she said, "Jacques especially, he said that the Irish guy was full of it! And then Dan got into it, and he said Mr. Harney made good sense, and Jacques's big problem was he didn't question the military. Oh, then Mrs. H., it was a low blow, Dan said Jacques might want to go to West Point—as it ran in the family and all." (I can still picture Stevie, headband over long straight hair, peasant dress, earnest eyes magnified by granny glasses.) Then Jacques said that has nothing to do with what I think about communism, and Dan said, "Tell it like it is, Faradeaux, I say you're the privileged class."

I have to smile now, thinking how bemused I felt as I listened to Stevie describe their argument. Dan wore his black hair in a pony tail. Jacques's hair was so short it looked freshly mowed. Liberal or conservative—people of all ages took a stand back then, and it wasn't easy for an apolitical person like me, someone with mildly liberal inclinations.

Well, I finally couldn't stand it, "Excuse me, Dan," I said, "I don't see why you are picking on Jacques. The senior guys might as well apply for a group deferment! None of you will go to Vietnam unless you want to. You've all been on a different track since your parents first sent you to our Montessori preschool!"

"Come on, you're exaggerating," Dan said, and he got all red. "I know a recent Socks graduate who had a low number and went to Nam!" I was chuckling inside.

Stevie said, "It's hard to get a rise out of Dan. He pretended to be nonchalant, blew up his lunch bag and popped it between his hands. Of course, he had to admit, and only when I reminded him, Mrs. H., he knew a few people who managed to get into the National Guard. That's my point, connections."

"Okay, maybe I shouldn't have singled out Jacques," Dan said. "Forget all of us! It's the war itself that's stupid and wrong."

"Then Marcus Boccage said, 'It's stupid and wrong who's doing the fighting' which shut everybody up, Stevie said with an air of great satisfaction. Marcus was our one upper school black, and what he implied was true—a disproportional number of blacks fought that awful war. And for all the talk in the faculty lounge about tutoring in the projects, we had only two black kids in the middle school and three or four in the lower school. Stevie said it was pretty ironic what Marcus said, because he'd probably get an easy deferment too. His family, creoles of color—New Orleans black society—had great connections. His uncle was president of Dillard University.

It was Marcus and Soozu who suggested we put on Samuel Beckett's play *Waiting for Godot*. Marcus's parents had taken him to see it at the New Orleans Repertory, and Soozu's drama camp—where she'd spent a scholarship month every summer since she was ten—staged it.

But Stevie, Dan, and Mike were a little wary. "What's it all about?" Stevie demanded after she read the script. "It looks to me like these two guys just standing around bullshitting, excuse me, Mrs. H."

I laughed and said, "Who else had a chance to read it? We need a longer plot summary, though the plot is not the point." I waited. "Soozu?"

"OK, these two tramps, Vladimir and Estragon, who call each other DiDi and GoGo, have been traveling together forever. They come to a place with a rock and a bare tree to wait for this guy named Godot. We don't know who Godot is and we never find out who he is, and he probably never comes, but then again, maybe he does."

"I'm fascinated," Dan said. He yawned and put his head on his desk. "So when do we come to the climax, the crisis, the catharsis—in other words, the action?" Soozu poked him in the ribs. "Wake up! I'm getting there. This play is just so beautiful, I feel real inadequate or something that I can't explain why I love it."

I felt the same—I loved the poignant music of Beckett's writing, though maybe you had to be older—hurt, laugh, and cry for longer. I didn't know how to help them feel it and watched as Soozu stood, unselfconsciously, her long neck arched, looking at the ceiling. OK, so then while they're waiting," she said, "Pozzo comes in with his slave, Lucky, who has a rope around his neck, and Pozzo treats him like an animal . . ."

"By the beginning of Act 2, though, Pozzo becomes blind," Marcus said. "The biggest puzzle in the play is why, when this bully Pozzo has been weakened, his slave still follows his commands, and still hands Pozzo the whip."

"That's good—a puzzle," Soozu said, and smiled at Marcus, a pulse beat in his temple as he leaned toward her. "I like it how this play doesn't tell you for sure," she went on, "what's happening or how to think about it— it's about trying to make sense out of life."

"And about people trying to survive in a violent world," Marcus said, "it's all about what people do when they see other people getting beat up."

Mike, Dan, and Stevie were quiet and looked glum. Marcus shook his head. "Now I feel like you said, Soozu—they're not getting it 'cause I'm not giving it. . . . I know. I'll read from my script, now where is . . . OK, Vladimir says, 'To all mankind, they were addressed, these cries for help still ringing in our ears! But at this place, at this moment of time, all mankind is us, whether we like it or not.' "

"Oh, so it's idealistic, about social justice," Mike said, "Well, cool, good, but will people be entertained? I hate to sound crass, but—you know. "

"Wait!" I said, "There are no fine attitudes in this play; as soon as someone makes a noble speech, someone else undercuts it by doing or saying something funny, absurd, cruel. Sometimes all at once. For instance, Estragon calls Lucky a brute because he hurts his toe kicking Lucky in the face and crotch." "Good example, Mrs. H!" Marcus said, "Right after Vladimir talks about listening to cries for help, he himself goes over and kicks Pozzo in the balls—oops, sorry Mrs. H."

"I don't know," Stevie said, "That's a theme I don't particularly warm up to. Maybe we should stick to kicking people in the shins; anyway, *Waiting for Godot* is depressing."

"It's a tragicomedy, you can play it for laughs," I said. "Really! In an absurd world, everything is turned upside down and this play is the opposite of corny. "

Stevie leaned forward in her chair, and Mike grinned. At last they were beginning to see it. I told the cast how Beckett wrote *Waiting for Godot*. "After being assaulted by a stranger, and incapacitated for a long time, he went to the prison and asked the criminal why he had attacked him. The theater of the absurd came into being because the prisoner said he didn't know why," I said. Then, at last, the cast was enthusiastic. Not, I thought, because Soozu, Marcus, and I had been so persuasive, but because the kids loved the idea of being absurd.

"That's it, that's us!" Dan shouted, "we're absurd, we're cool."

"But not cruel," Stevie said.

"So we'll rock this school," Mike said, and everyone groaned.

"All the better," I said. At the right moment, I planned tell the cast what Malachy told me—that the play was the most important religious play of our age, that in *Waiting for Godot*, they wait for God. Maybe not— a depressing thought, though Malachy didn't seem to find it so.

The evening before the first cast read-through, I suddenly remembered I hadn't directed a play since I graduated from college in 1951, and Malachy laughed at me. Was this the first time it hit me I'd been acting all along? And now I might as well act the part of the director. What else was teaching but acting, then directing, or both at once, he said, and giving some shape to the risk?

Only because he asked, I decided to give Marcus the part of Lucky. "But Marcus," I'd said when he first suggested it, "I thought of Estragon for you. I was shocked he chose to be Lucky, a slave with a rope around his neck." "No, Lucky's better for me," he said, "it's all in how I play it, Mrs. H." Soozu made a good Estragon with her pouty whine, talking about leaving Vladimir, but then, the little hedonist was willing to be entertained. Perhaps he could dance first, Estragon said of Lucky, and think afterwards if it isn't too much to ask. She was delighted when everyone laughed at her. At first, Stevie had played Vladimir with too much consistency. "He's this intellectual, someone who can't see the nose in front of his face," she said.

"Well . . . true," I said. "Still people have shadings and contradictions." Then Stevie added a manic note or two to her portrayal, and Vladimir came to life. With Mike, who was already making sketches and planning circuits, in charge of lighting, sound, and set, we would have a professional-looking production.

So the play began for me and my students, and it was a good beginning. But a chapter ended in the maybe romance of Malachy and Mary, who happened to have the same last name, though mine was borrowed and I'd thought of getting back my own until I met him. You see, Malachy had to fly home because his father was seriously ill. But he also spoke of some mysterious other business at home, something he could do for the Irish cause. "Ah, don't look so worried, Mary, it's a small thing, but we all play some small part in history." I knew he was afraid for his family, for Northern Ireland, and I was afraid for him. He promised to return, he had research to do on his novel after all, and in the mean time there were letters, he said. You'll get the picture if I give you a few excerpts from our weekly letters—and no, I didn't edit out the really juicy parts. There weren't any.

November 2, 1969

Dear Mary,

So Dan is playing Pozzo as a cigar-smoking capitalist. You asked if I sometimes felt that God might not exist or might be leaving us to the Pozzos of this world. I just left the priesthood, not my faith. I think it's up to us not to turn God into Pozzo. Not in N. Ireland under Macmillan's boot, or in America under Nixon. Mary, you would be chilled to see how like the Klu Klux Klan they are—these Orangemen parading. The Brits are truly racist in the way they regard us. And, like the blacks in your country and South Africa, any attempts by the native Irish to come together and resist have been met with force. . .

Your friend,
Malachy

December 14

Dear Malachy,

I wish you could have seen the way Soozu helped Marcus choreograph the dance that Pozzo makes him do. She has him turn stiffly at first like a robot with his arms and hands still in the position they were when he was carrying that burdensome basket for Pozzo, then he winds down like clockwork, and stands as children do when they are caught playing statues. Do Irish children play that game? And Dan actually brings out something human and pathetic in Pozzo, who forgets his worldly position and becomes like anyone else for a moment, watching his slave, and saying: The Net. He thinks he's entangled in a net.

Your friend,
Mary

January 6, 1970

Mary, My Dear Idiot,

And no, I've not been arrested yet. Were you joking? I hope so, but what made you ask me that—you knowing where I've been these past years? Do you suspect me of smuggling arms to the IRA? My cousin Breda in Belfast has been arrested for working with a resistance group, and is the brave one of our family. There's something I have to say. Behind your joke about Bernadette Devlin luring me away from the monastery is, I think, a question. Why did I stop being a priest and start being—whoever I am now? It's easier to write it than say it. Breda was caught with a fellow known by the Tommies to be with the IRA. She was interned (meaning, at best, interrogated and arrested, at worst, tortured). She was thrown against a wall, spread-eagled, strip-searched and as a result she lost her baby at 5 months. She is strong and is going on.

I'm very cowardly in many ways. (For instance, I've only kissed you twice. I think of more, but am, most likely, as unwillingly prudish as any Irishman can be. It comes naturally to men on this priest-ridden island to make jokes instead of love.)

When I read this, I tried not to think of more—the breeze through the back door carried the vanilla scent of magnolia.

Mary, I need to see your sweet face. I love the way your child-like upper teeth show, slightly, beneath your upper lip when you're wondering. Now don't take this wrong because I smile and think how pretty you are, how funny—you look for all the world like a surprised rabbit. Think of me from time to time as you enjoy New Orleans. (This is not sarcasm. I do love your happy nature.)

Affectionately,
Malachy

January 31, 1970

Dear Malachy,

Oh, I am so sorry for what happened to your cousin, how horrifying, how sad. She must be bitter, I know I'd be. Thank you for telling me. It does help me understand you better.

Fondly,
Mary

By March 3, on my 40th birthday, I couldn't stand his absence because I didn't know if and when he'd return. I read and reread his letters. Did he really love my happy nature? If so, I'd better control my crying. I'd never been a crier, so it alarmed me. If he would have been here, I would have confessed how I couldn't think of weighty matters—for longing. And how, until recently, I'd forgotten how to make the good things happen in my life. In the middle of the night, I wrote:

Dear Malachy,

If you were here you would advise me. I want to help, everyone makes history, but I don't feel it. I'm watching a play. I watch and wonder, and love to play, but I feel insubstantial. I love Soozu and Marcus, seeing the way they each smile when the other one collaborates with a thought, not a thought but a feeling, an image. They are colleagues, so quick and subtle, making sets and scenes with their gestures, that they've left the others behind. But I'm afraid for them. All forms of love are dangerous— even if not politically dangerous. Maybe I'm afraid for myself. You write me about a large life—mine is small. I want to help, but my feelings are small. I wonder, I laugh, and people are dying in the world. I'm at a play, I care, but I clap. What will happen next with the two of us? That's almost all I care about.

And here is the letter I could send him:

April 8, 1970

Dear Malachy,

Despite my frivolous life in New Orleans, I follow the tense situation in your country with concern. I can't imagine what it would be like to live in an occupied country, but Marcus knows what that's like. This is true despite Marcus being upper class, which has only made him feel guilty. Because he's light skinned, he said he has nowhere he really belongs, not with other blacks, and not with whites. He told Soozu (and Soozu told Stevie and Stevie told me) that he feels lonely almost all of the time unless he's acting.

The headmaster, who dropped by one of our rehearsals, said the way
Marcus played the slave was a powerful piece of protest. Marcus told the
cast he's glad it came over that way, but it's also very sad, Marcus said,
and if the headmaster didn't get that part, he needed to show, in his
acting, how Lucky has learned to be help

Yours,
Mary

In Ireland, it always was raining, and raining in all ways, Malachy wrote.
In New Orleans, April frivolity continued into May, the air perfumed with
expensive flowers growing in courtyards behind high brick walls. Then
came the fourth of May. It was almost seven minutes past the start of class
and there were no students, then Soozu ran into the classroom. They
opened fire on the students, she cried, just opened fire! Who opened fire? I
said to her back as she turned, and I ran through the door after her. Here? I
asked, at Sock Hall? Did we need, I thought as I panted after her, to take
cover? At Kent State University, she said over her shoulder, I think it's
somewhere in the Midwest, the National Guard killed some students, and
everyone is in the Lecture Hall looking at the news.

On the TV: a hill, a body, a girl kneeling by the body, her arm
outstretched, her mouth a scream; then reeling backward—helmeted
guardsmen in a line, milling students. Four dead the voice said, nine
wounded. After the broadcast, one of the teachers clicked off the TV, and
everyone just sat there. Then everyone began to talk at once, especially
my students. One at a time! the upper school principal boomed.

"I don't believe it," Stevie said, "How could they fire on unarmed
students!"

"They were armed with stones," Jacques said, and he folded his arms
across his chest.

"That's the biggest pile of—that's outrageous. Dan's face was red and he
shouted. "That's like saying the students deserved to be killed!"

"Besides it's not true," Soozu said, "that they were throwing stones—
on the news last night, a commentator was saying how the students were
there as nonviolent protestors, so Nixon would stop bombing Cambodia."

"Students are not, by definition, nonviolent!" Jacques stared at Soozu
and Dan, and then looked around the room. "Look at Berkeley! Look at
the Weatherman bomb factory blow-up! And some famous college
dropouts graduated to the SDS, real scum—only good for destroying our
whole society."

"Yeah, Jacques is right!" The captain of the football team addressed his
remarks to the upper school principal. "If students keep protesting the
war, then they'll close down the colleges and universities and we'll all get
drafted." He shifted in his chair and looked at the students behind him.

"I think you're forgetting four people are dead," Marcus said in a low but carrying voice, his eyes downcast. He raised his head and said more loudly, "Four brave white students. Still, college boys, especially if they're white, can always find some way to avoid that war in Vietnam. But there's no way, no way poor black men can avoid that war or the one we're fighting here at home." Nobody had anything to say after that. Marcus was the first one to head for the door where he paused, and said, "that's how it is on this bitch of an earth." The rest of the cast followed him out the door. It wasn't his line, Lucky's line, it belonged to Pozzo, Dan, Lucky's slave-master, but from then on, it was the cast's byword.

May 6, 1970

My Mary,

I am appalled by the Kent State massacre. It reminds me of the way young students at Queens University in Belfast were brutally beaten by the police as they marched across the Burtollet Bridge over the river Faughan. I've been following the activities of the Berrigan brothers and their comrades. I have only respect for them, but I saw in the Irish Times, *from the protest rally in D.C. following Kent State, this photo of a large cross, a body on it. Must the nonviolent be crucified? Enough of my ravings. I'm coming back to the States sooner than I'd thought. My father is doing well. Then it is on the 17th I see you, a few days after you get this letter.*

Fondly,
Malachy

The next day was only a month before the opening, and I had the kids arrive at six in the morning so they'd have a two-hour block of time for play practice. They gobbled the beignets I brought them, and they got to work. The blocking went well—Beckett's directions for movement were so telling, especially in the scene where Lucky comes in trailing a long rope and disappears stage right followed by Pozzo, who, according to Dan, was the sort of jerk who made a pile of money in armaments.

Vladimir: You want to get rid of him?" (pointing to Lucky.)

Pozzo: I do. But instead of driving him away as I might have done, I mean instead of simply kicking him out on his arse, in the goodness of my heart, I am bringing him to the fair, where I hope to get a good price for him. The truth is you can't drive such creatures away. The best thing would be to kill them. Lucky is supposed to weep here, Marcus said, but couldn't he strangle Pozzo instead? Everyone laughed and so did I, but then I shivered.

Estragon: He's crying! And indeed Marcus had come up with a blood curdling sound, a cross between a strangle and a sob.

Pozzo: Old dogs have more dignity. He offered his handkerchief to

Estragon. Comfort him since you pity him. Soozu did a Charlie Chaplin imitation that was perfect, leaning back on her heels away from Lucky. Pozzo growled, Come on! Wipe away his tears, he'll feel less forsaken, Pozzo said. Estragon lowered his head to his chest.

Vladimir: Here, give it to me, I'll do it. Estragon snatched the hanky, hugging it, shuffling away from Vladmir's reach with quick little steps, sticking out his tongue and waggling his fingers on his nose. "Good, Soozu!" I cried out, and clapped my hand over my mouth.

Pozzo: Make haste, before he stops. Estragon tiptoed toward Lucky and poked the hanky at his eyes. Lucky proceeded to kick Estragon in the shin, but stopped just short of Soozu's leg. Estragon staggered around the stage, howling and holding his leg.

Pozzo: I told you he didn't like strangers.

Vladimir: Show. Estragon shows his leg. Vladimir turns to confront Pozzo. He's bleeding!

Pozzo: It's a good sign. Estragon is hopping on one leg: I'll never walk again! Vladimir: I'll carry you! Stevie made her voice yearning, then, said gruffly, If necessary. I hugged myself, this play was going to be very good.

Pozzo: He's stopped crying. Pozzo strolled over to Estragon, beaming. You have replaced him as it were. His voice rose: The tears of the world are a constant quantity. For each one who begins to weep, somewhere else another stops . . . Dan paused and looked at the back of the auditorium.

As the heavy metal auditorium door creaked open, I glanced at my watch. Almost eight already, and that would be Gervais come to shoo us out. I turned around and it was Malachy.

"Please!" he called down to us, "don't stop on my account. It's my very favorite play and I'll just sit here in the back until you finish." "Malachy!" I said, and immediately hoped I hadn't sounded too happy in front of the kids. "We have to stop now in any event," I said and forced myself to walk calmly toward him. I took both his hands to forestall a hug, and turned back to the kids: "It's going very well! Tomorrow at six again!"

"Mary, it's so good to see you, but I just now heard some really terrible news on the taxi radio—It's happened again—at Jackson State University."

"What's happened?" Mike asked. The others, heading for the door on the way to their first hour classes, paused.

"Two students dead and ten injured. Police shooting into a dormitory. One coed they interviewed was crying" and said, "they came here to kill all of us!"

"And they did, too!" Marcus yelled. "First it's Kent State, and then only four days ago they killed six and wounded sixty in Augusta! Someone has got to stop those red neck pigs!"

"I feel really scared," Soozu said. "I feel like I could explode," Marcus said and he shoved against the door with his shoulder, but feebly, and it didn't open. "I'm sorry," Marcus said. Dan put a hand on his shoulder.

"Man, we're your friends. Why shouldn't you be mad? I'm mad too!"

"I'm scared and mad," Soozu said.

Malachy put his arm around my shoulder.

"Want me to cry?" Marcus asked me. "I just think I might be able to manage it now." He sat down in the last row, his head bowed in his hands. Mike squeezed his shoulder as he went by. Stevie bent to hug him. Soozu sat next to him after the others left.

Malachy and I lingered in the door. "How about I write hall passes for you both?" I asked.

"Yes, Mary," Soozu said, "thank you."

"You cry like you did before," I told Marcus, "it was angry crying." We closed the door.

Talk is the great weakness of the Irish—my weakness anyway. "It's my way of making things pretty," Malachy said, "but, ah, how we need, each and every one of us, to talk."

Options for Dialogue

- Discuss how the different students react to the shootings on campuses. What role did their backgrounds play in these reactions? Relate this to different reactions to a recent political event. Why do individuals in the same community react differently?
- Compare these events to what was happening in Malachy's Ireland. What was similar, what was different?
- How did Beckett's play help the students work through their complex feelings about all the things that had been happening?
- What beliefs do you see in the characters of this story? How does this story relate to a study of education? Make a Venn diagram showing the beliefs, national and international events, and education in this story.

Options for Action

- Read the play discussed in the story or another by Beckett. Compare your reactions to the reactions of the students in the story. What evidence of existentialism do you see in the play? Tell your class about this using either a skit or reader's theater.
- Attend a play and analyze what set of beliefs you see represented in the play. Report to your class.

- Read one of the articles presented in *The Zinn Reader: Writings on Disobedience and Democracy* (New York: Seven Stories Press, 1997). The essays are categorized by titles: Race, Class, War, Law, Means and Ends, and many in each section deal with historical events during and leading up to this turbulent time in the sixties. Report what you learn to the class.

CHAPTER EIGHT

How Do Educators Become Agents of Social Change?

In the following poem, Declan Collinge gives those who work with children reason to be activists.

After-image
—*Declan Collinge*

*(To Claire Gallagher
blinded in the Omagh bombing,
August 1998 and to all
the Omagh bomb victims)*

Against the hellish blast
The smiling faces of friends
Imposed their after-image.

Now, in your dark confusion
The after-image pains and
   comforts,
Informs your dreams

Beyond the riotous collage
Of thirty years depravity
And peace beyond our fingertips,

Through the blindness of hate,
Across distances that burn
And chill the young,

Iar-íomhá
Déaglán Collinge, Eanáir 1999.

*(Do Claire Gallagher a dalladh
I bpléasc Oméigh Lúnasa 1998)*

I mbéal na pléisce damanta
Mhair mionghéire do chaired
Mar iar-íomhá ar d'aigne.

Mar láchrann trí do mhearbhall
Is ábhar sóláis is céasta ar aon
An iar-íomhá a scairteann ar do
   bhrionglóid.

I bhfad ó chollage fuilteach
Tríocha bliain de thruaillíocht
Is an tsíochain fad ár méire uainn,

I bhfad ó dhaille dearg-ghrânach,
Thar achair a dhónn
Is an reonn an óige,

Your waif voice touches us Like Gloucester or Lear himself, Tearing at our hearts:	Cloisimid do ghlór síofra, Mar ghlór Gloucester nó Lear é féin, Ag réabadh ár gcroíthe:

Child of Omagh's Gethsemane
We move as one to take your
  hand
Guiding you gently to the
  keys.
	A chailín Gethsemane Óméigh,
	Bogaimid uile I do threo dod
	  bhreith
	Ar láimh leat chuig na méara bright
	  geala.

Listening to Personal Experience:
Activist Educators Tell Their Stories

We begin this chapter with stories from two community educators who have devoted their lives to social action. It is from them that we learn how to "locate your deepest private thoughts—your morality, your spirituality—you live them with a minimum amount of compromise" to be a whole, human person (Davidov, 1999). We end the section with a report of a primary school teacher, Kristen Palm, about how she activiely approached the subject of "peace" with her students.

Marv Davidov participated in The Freedom Rides to Jackson, Mississippi during the civil rights movement in 1961. He later founded the Honeywell Project in 1968 and Minnesota Institute for Social Transformation (MIST) in 1991. MIST stems from the 1968–1991 Honeywell Project, an organization that brought attention to the nuclear and conventional arms trade in its local manifestation at Honeywell Corporation, and its aftermath in Laos and elsewhere. MIST is one of the most active groups in the world (in terms of direct action) on the International Land Mine Campaign; currently, at weekly vigils, MIST points to the company's continued production of indiscriminate weapons and rocket motors for virtually every missile in the United States arsenal.

Marv Davidov currently teaches revolutionary nonviolence at St. Thomas University, Carleton College, Metropolitan State College, and St. Cloud State College, all in Minnesota. He is a powerful educator and coalition builder who has been arrested dozens of times for justice and peace. In an interview with the authors he describes events in his life that have influenced his work.

Marv Davidov's Personal History

I grew up in a Jewish working-class family in Detroit. My mother, who is 98, reminded me recently that when I was a kid babysitting in the neighborhood, I had a sliding scale for fees based on income at about age 11. So I was a Marxist at 11 and didn't know it.

We moved here in 1949. My mother's family was here so she'd always wanted to be with them. I went to Macalester and got drafted my senior year—a week after the Korean War ended. And I was a Democratic Farm Labor liberal at the time. I'd never met a radical, though they existed here—but, I'd never come across them. There weren't many at Macalester in the early '50s. There are now and we're in contact with them.

Experiences That Led to Commitment and Action

In the army I had problems. For example, . . . in the summer of 1953, I was in basic training at Ft. Riley, Kansas. Sixteen weeks' infantry basic training and I'd never fired a gun. My father didn't hunt. It was all new to me. Kind of interesting. I remember the first time on the rifle range. You've got to be in a prone position with the M16 with the strap around your elbow and around the shoulder to steady the gun. I couldn't quite get my elbow directly beneath the gun. A sergeant came by numerous times and kicked my elbow with his boot. My elbow was bleeding right through the fatigue jacket. Finally an officer saw that and stopped him from doing it. That's typical shit—indoctrination shit.

About the sixth week, they sent a guy named Anderson into our platoon. That afternoon in training, Anderson was in the barracks and our sergeant, who had fought in Korea and was rather young, said to our platoon, "We put a guy named Anderson into the barracks. He missed fighting the gooks in Korea, so I want you to beat the shit out of him tonight."

I went back to the barracks. I was 21 at the time, a little older than the others—many of them juvenile delinquents from Chicago who had been given a choice by a juvenile judge—reform school or the army. So they chose one prison over the other. And everybody got on the top floor of the barracks with Anderson alone downstairs. And they all said let's go beat him up. And of course when the sergeant said gooks, that stuck with me right away. And I thought he must think of me as a Kike and blacks as Niggers. I looked around, being a liberal, waiting to see if anyone would object and when I realized they were gonna go beat this kid, I said, "Wait a minute. Do you remember we were in the post theater and the general in charge said to us we're gonna make you trained killers who will obey every order without thinking?" And I said "I'm Jewish and because so many Germans, French, Ukrainian zealots obeyed the orders, six million of my people went to the gas chambers." And I knew enough to say the gypsies of Europe, the artists, writers, gay and lesbian people, people who had polio [were killed too]. "So I don't think we should do that. I think we should go downstairs and ask this kid why he jumped the boat and missed going to Korea. He's come out of the stockade. He's been punished. Maybe he had a good reason."

Well, they went downstairs, put a blanket on his head, shoved him down a gauntlet, and punched and kicked him. Then they took the GI brushes which we used to clean the barracks and bloodied up his skin. Blanket still on his head so he couldn't see who did it. Then they went upstairs. Friends of mine told me what they did. I couldn't sleep that night. Next morning we were changing sheets and before going out to training again, I went in to the guys on my floor and said "You're a bunch of fucking cowards and so am I. I should've been down there standing next to him. I'm ashamed of myself. And don't you know what you've done to yourselves by beating him?"

Then I turned around to fix my bunk and suddenly there's a blanket on my head, two guys holding me, somebody punching me in the face. That radicalized the shit out of me.

As we talked more with Marv, he told us about other personal experiences in which he saw grave injustices and had to act. He told us about a close friend and his experiences:

My friend is Black. He's a painter, an artist. We lived together. We were supposed to have an art show in our apartment, one summer night in 1956 or so. He is dark skinned, really muscular. A really compassionate guy for everyone. He was punctual and he wasn't there. I knew something had happened. I got a call from jail. I said, "What the fuck are you doing in jail?" He said, "Do you have twenty-five bucks?" I said, "I'll be right down."

He'd been standing outside our apartment drinking a can of beer. Two white cops came around the corner. He said he ducked behind a bush. I said, "Why the hell'd you duck?" He said, "Because I'm Black." They then picked him up on suspicion, punched him around and took him downtown. So, we talked all night.

White guys standing out—a man or a woman—in front of their house in Edina, Minnesota the cops may just wave.

Then Marv told us about participating in the Civil Rights movement in the 1960s.

So I went on the freedom rides. I knew by then, you got to walk it, not just talk it like . . . many do. They talk it and don't walk it in any profound sense.

So I had a profound experience like everybody else who was in Parchman Penitentiary—a maximum security. First night in a small cell—my roommate was a Quaker from Ohio. Stokely Carmichael was down the way. Incredible people we met—John Lewis, Diane Lewis, many others. First night at Parchman, people were singing freedom songs. They did what they called devotional when there was a minister or a rabbi . . . then sing. The Student Nonviolent Coordinating Committee Freedom Singers came out of Parchman in the movement.

And they're singing the songs and I'm lying on my bunk crying, and (I tell this to my students, and anyone who was there will tell you the same thing) thinking there's no other place I should be on earth but right here in this cell with these people—most of whom I'd never met. It was like a mountain top experience and now I know what I'll do the rest of my life—look for this feeling of blessed human feeling of solidarity. Everybody felt it.

You could ask any white kids who went to Mississippi. In the summer of '64 knowing that Schwerner, Chaney, and Goodman were missing and probably murdered—they'd say the same thing. Despite all the bullshit . . . I also want to tell the kids . . . it ain't all noble and glorious. There are sharks in the movement. We're not all that different from the general population. Perhaps a little more enlightened. You got to resist it.

But that was a moment beyond belief. When people say, "Why do you do it?" I say, "I'm looking for that feeling again." I've met the most incredible people in the world.

And then closer to home in Minnesota, Marv told us what he and others learned from Clancey Segal.

Clancey Segal . . . When we brought him here to Minneapolis/St. Paul in 1961. He was so tough. When we picked him up from the bus . . . he'd come from Detroit on the bus because he wanted to be with the working people in the Greyhound and talked with people about what's going on in their lives . . . we picked him up. Driving across one of the bridges in town we saw this down-and-out looking woman with a baby in a buggy and two other kids. He said where and how in this town do they get the help they need to live? No one knew. He said, "And you call yourselves radical? What the fuck's wrong with you?" Wherever he went he hit people so hard. He said, "You locate your deepest private thoughts about justice, peace, who you are, and attempt to live those out in a commensurate way in public with a minimum of compromise." ALL my friends that I've met—most of them are doing it. So that you're not schizophrenic. In this capitalist society . . . we grow up schizophrenic. This culture is so dysfunctional that almost every family in it is dysfunctional.

He elaborated about how the complexity of what he calls schizo-phrenia, believing in one way and acting in another, intersects with politics and economics and how it cannot be discussed in public media.

And that accounts for school killings and the rest of it. What can't be brought up on the tube. Chomsky's right. The indoctrination system is almost complete in this country. Thought control is what exists in democratic capitalism to keep people in line. Even the best of people don't grasp it because they're indoctrinated.

Hope for the Future

Marv was instrumental in planning and implementing the 1999 Commitment to Peace Conference in St. Paul, Minnesota in Octo-ber, 1999. He explains:

Our conference is to build a mass movement. And get a lot of kids in-volved. When college and high school students have opportunities to have experiences with these people, they choose to be involved. Par-ents can plant seeds through their actions and their stories. Teachers too. People love stories.

He goes on to tell us that in his university class, which focuses on nonviolent civic action, he always asks on the first day, "Who are you? Why are your here? Have you ever been arrested? If you want to do crime, do political crime so it means something."

He then tells us how over the years he has become convinced that by using films, music, and poetry—all the arts—students are more able to understand the complexities that influence all our lives.

It became clear as we watched Marv interact with students at the conference that what we were seeing was the actualization of the comment by Rita McDonald, another activist: "A good teacher in-structs, a great teacher inspires." Marv inspires young people with whom he works not only by his teaching, but by his life. "If we are in one aspect of human struggle we are in the whole thing. Touch-ing human life in one way, we touch all of life" (Berrigan, 1999).

Educators both in and out of classrooms who do this are people we can learn from. At this same Commitment to Peace Conference, Elizabeth Martinez, Chicana activist, talked about building bridges between the different political groups working for social change. She explained connections between the Student Nonviolent Coor-dinating Committee and the Chicano Movement. She also pointed out that one of the reasons we don't understand these connections is that there is not much information published or spoken about these links. She explained that race relations in the past were most often defined in black and white terms, while in reality, struggles of many of the activist groups are struggles against colonialization. Martinez urged the audience to "Hang on to what was gained in the past." She pointed out that a whole new labor movement is developing because organized labor finally realized that organizing immigrants is worthwhile. Martinez believes that it is important in social justice struggles that we build solidarity among different groups working for change. She gave an example of a letter that Subcomandante Marcos, the leader of the indignous people's struggle in Chiapas, Mexico, wrote to Mounia, an African American activist who is in prison and the focus of a strong amnesty movement.

Marcos, Jan 1, 1994

Señor Mounia,

   We have nothing big to give you. It is poor and little. It is an embrace from all of us. We hope that when you are free again you will visit us and we will give you a party. There will be dancing and singing. And people of all colors will come together. We will build bridges where all peoples will walk toward tomorrow (quoted by Martinez, 1999).

Eugene Jax's Personal History

The next person interviewed, Gene Jax (1999), is an activist social worker who has been involved with education in communities for his whole career. Most recently he works with people who are homeless through the Alliance of the Streets in St. Paul, Minnesota. His story is an example of the profound effect that the philosophy and work of an inspirational teacher can have on others. Gene talks about the influence of Brazilian philosopher and educator Paulo Freire on his life and work. The influence was so profound it is important to give a brief abstract of Freire's work before including Gene's interview.

   Brazilian philosopher and educator Paulo Freire, who was born in Brazil in 1921 and died of heart failure in Sao Paulo on May 2, 1997, inspired a whole generation of critical educators. He was an educator who expanded many people's perceptions of the world, encouraged their efforts, and enlightened their awareness of the causes and consequences of human suffering. He believed we must develop an ethical and utopian pedagogy for social change.

Freire worked in adult education and workers' training, and became the first director of the department of cultural extension of the University of Recife (1961–1964). He quickly gained international recognition for his experiences in literacy training in the Brazilian Northeast, particularly the experience of literacy training in Angicos, Rio Grande do Norte, that led the populist government of Joao Goulart to appoint him in 1963 as President of the National Commission on Popular Culture. After the military coup d'etat of 1964, he was considered a dangerous political pedagogue, was put in jail for seventy days, and was later forced into a fifteen-year exile. He then went to Chile where he spent five years working for international organizations in the context of the Christian Democratic Agrarian Reform movement. After a short stint teaching at Harvard in 1969, Paulo Freire moved to Geneva to be an special educational adviser to the World Congress of Churches. He worked in Geneva for a decade and finally returned to Brazil in 1979 when the Brazilian military government lifted his travel restrictions.

In addition to this description of his life, it is important to understand Freire's political philosophy of education and his lifetime obsession with integrating theory, research and praxis. Freire argued that few human encounters are exempt from oppression of one kind or another because of race, class, or gender, and that people tend to be victims and/or perpetrators of oppression. The theoretical and practical framework based on Freire's work is called critical theory.

Gene Jax's work is a dynamic example of critical pedagogy in a community setting. Gene Jax tells his story:

> What led me to Freire and social work? It's a very odd thing, because I knew in high school that I wanted to be a social worker but I'd never met one. So I don't know how it got in there. I suspect I was raised with a fair amount of liberty and freedom, so that I liked that a lot. I grew up in high school during the McCarthy era. (During the 1950s Joseph McCarthy spearheaded the oppression of intellectuals and artists in the United States of America in the name of anticommunism. His persuasive influence affected the education of young people all over the country.)
>
> I can remember in a civics class, we were doing a discussion—this was in Wisconsin—and I was really against McCarthy. There was a

*lot of support for him (he was from Wisconsin). I remember my
father asking me to please not discuss McCarthy with the people
who were coming for his poker game. McCarthy was a very strong influence at that time. I worked at the mall. I was paid to talk
McCarthy. I went to Madison. Madison was the most liberal school
at the time and because McCarthy was from Wisconsin, they weren't
afraid of him there.*

Gene continues:

*The Rogerian influence had something to do with it too. I would seek
educational sources. I suspect that's what most people do—follow
those leaders that fit the things you're interested in at the time.*

Gene tells how his experiences with a paternalistic social service system lead him to seek leaders in the field who were more
egalitarian.

Social work has a great risk of paternalism. Programs in the past
have been conservative and paternalistic. He quotes an Archbishop
from Brazil. "If people come to violence because violence is done to
them, then one must consider forgiving them." Another Bishop
from Brazil said, "If the poor people are stealing from the ware-
houses it's not a sin."

Experiences That Led to Commitment and Action

Gene contacted Paulo Freire and told him that he used Freire's
methods of problem-posing and cultural circles in his work with
homeless people. Freire returned the correspondence and when
Freire came to New York, Gene telephoned him.

Freire said, "We must talk. You must come to New York. Now.
You must come to New York now."

So Gene traveled from Minnesota to New York and phoned Freire
from the airport.

"I called him at 9:30 when we arrived, and he said 'I think we
could come together at 9:45!'"

Then they met and Gene explained,

We went over the whole thing. He said "It's (Gene's work) very different
from the work that I have done."
I told him about that, that I'd run across his written work in Mexico . . .
that I'd been to Mexico and then come back. I wanted to apply his

thinking to my work with the poor, and people said it couldn't be done—
that's only in poor countries. And he said, "Ah! Of course, the capitalists!
The colonialists! They all say that!"

He said what I'm doing was very different, but it was very interesting to
him and that he was willing to work with me. We could work together
and learn from each other. We talked about the homeless . . . he had seen
the homeless in California and was very sympathetic. And he said if I
could do something before I die I'd be very happy.

I was really ecstatic—it was Good Friday. . . . I had been going through
some heart tests and then right away I had to go in for surgery and after 3
days I was leaving the hospital. A friend of mine, who'd also followed
Freire's work, told me he'd died that day. It was so odd . . . both of us had
been talking there in New York and both of us with heart trouble and
neither of us had said anything.

Then afterwards I had to write to see what else was available and so I
finally got all the arrangements in order to go down there (San Paulo). I
went down a year ago last August and spent a month there. I decided to do
a memorial tour type of thing and meet with as many people as I could
with whom he'd worked and to follow the areas that he'd been in. I spent
time at the Paulo Freire Center and in his library and that was
wonderful—I made lists of all the things he'd been reading.

There are two libraries: One from when he was a student and his more
modern library which I was more interested in. I was very surprised to
find that he had a fair amount of Carl Rogers literature. He mentioned
Carl Rogers in his work. That surprised me because Carl Rogers was at
Wisconsin when I was there—and he was so safe. Young beginning
counselors, now therapists, could use it without damaging anyone. I can
see where it fits into Freire's thinking too. Ownership of what happens,
allowing the person to set their own (goals) . . . not saying you must talk of
this or of that. Erich Fromm was the other one. I can understand that too
because of his liberation theory. William Glasser—I used Freire and
Glasser combined. Freire was always and totally for democracy. A person
is to be the subject and not the object.

Freire was so big on definition. One of the largest things about human
beings is their capacity to name things . . . Glasser also. Define "what is,"
never accepting what's put out there. I've worked with elderly. I've
worked with children. I've worked with homeless. You have to ask, "What
is homeless, what is poverty, define mental illness, what is it?" It happens
with so much of Freire's stuff—you get in trouble. It's so much against the
status quo.

Then Gene Jax gave specific examples of how he uses Freire's
methodology in meetings he holds with homeless people through
the Alliance of the Streets in St. Paul, Minnesota.

What is it—mental illness? Who makes money from mental illness: People who are outside institutions are passive. Often women who come there feel that they are not respected. It's kind of difficult because homeless people are different. There's a huge amount of alcoholism, drug addiction. They can't drink there but they can come drunk or on drugs as long as they're quiet. I never thought I could do this but it's been going on for years now. I never thought I could run a meeting where someone's hallucinating. And I just have to ask them to hallucinate more quietly.

The issues get touchy when some get work and others don't (some people in the meetings are hired by the Alliance). The others say that there's been favoritism. Then we'll try to get an idea of "work." That's another thing that was very interesting that came out a couple of years ago. I think that when you do things like this—when you work with populations different from yourself you always go in with certain assumptions and some of the assumptions . . . are so approved of by the general population itself that the people themselves go into this culture of silence and one of them was "work." It is real fortunate that work has been so good lately that unemployment (is down). Everybody asks "why very poor people aren't working if they don't have young children to take care of? It's been more difficult to say I've been discriminated against. I won't be hired. Then after a number of meetings around the concept of work, it becomes clear people are not desiring any kind of regular full time jobs. It's seen as not fitting them. The ideal is like 15–30 hours a week. Then you don't have to show up at the same time every day. The actual work program has been more difficult. The idea that it's not desired is very good for me to know and many of them are not employable because of their addictions. It's very hard for them to go through the systems to help them get disability, etc. But you have to be able to go through the system to be able to cooperate.

When asked whether or not the situation for poor people he works with has gotten worse over the years, he said:

It's gotten worse. Yes, on an objective level, it's gotten worse because before we had general assistance. People were on disability and social security and then these people lost that disability (disability for addiction, for example, was cut off) at the federal level for many of the people who were chemically dependent. On a state level general assistance is only given to those who can prove a grave inability to work.

Every year is rich for a definition of addiction . . . what is addiction? What does it mean? The people who've been through treatment have formulas that they tell, and then someone asks "Is that right?" "How come someone who's been through treatment 20 times (has to go again)?

Another interesting one: Is addiction an illness? What is it? Some say yes, some say no, it's will. What is "will"? The way thc meeting (Freire's method) is structured . . . there's a meeting, then there's a meal. If you don't come to the meeting, you don't get the meal. There's many who don't want the meeting—they dislike the meeting—there's an antagonism, but they're interesting, they're worthwhile.

I don't know how much change takes place. What I see is—what I do at the meeting is, everyone goes around and gives their first name. And that was very different at first. People would say, "Why should I do that—why do you want my name?" I say, "For god's sake so we can know each other."

Where do you come from . . . that was very rich. Once we did a discussion on friendship. That was very surprising to me. Almost to the person, they did not believe they had any friends. They had acquaintances. One person said, "My only friend is my mother."

Hope for the Future

Gene believes that education, both in and out of school, is the hope for the future.

> *Education is really paternalistic—heavy on one person knowing more than the other the thought of really wanting people to be in charge of. There's no trust that children will come to good.*

Yet, Gene does believe in the ultimate good of human beings.

> *One thing that Freire (has taught) is that identity is so important. When he talks of being in identity with people we're working with I suspect it means giving up a fair amount of yourself to do that. Your ideals of superiority. I don't know if service work is necessary or not for students to do. I think it's good to see and actually know that things exist. I think people will eventually reach out if they find a purpose. If you can get them to do an analysis to go further and further into their humanistic experiences . . . allow answers to come and not insert yourself.*

In fact, Gene's words mirror our hopes for this book:

> *Historical analysis . . . taking a look at the past. Freire was always and totally for democracy. The person should be subject not object. Freire was big on definitions (Glasser too)—never accept what's given—put it out there for the group.*

Speak loud
Tell the truth
Face the devil
Let's Get Free
—Rabelais

References

Berrigan, D. (1999, October) Address at the Commitment to Peace
    Conference, St. Paul, Minnesota.
Davidov, M. (1999, October). Address at the Commitment to Peace
    Conference, St. Paul, Minnesota.
Jax, G. (1999, September). Interview, St. Paul, Minnesota.
Martinez, E. (1999, October). Address at Commitment to Peace
    Conference, St. Paul, Minnesota.

Kristen Palm, Elementary Teacher

Options for Listening

- Many people question the ability of young children to understand difficult issues such as peace and conflict resolution.
  However, many teachers know that young children can
  understand and do important work in these areas. Kristen
  Palm is one such teacher. Listen to her thoughts about peace.

Negotiating Peace
—*Kristen Palm*

Peace comes with a calm heart.
Ask your neighbor, ask your partner, ask your
enemy, ask your friend,
Ask them!
Ask why they did it, and how they see and
what they want and when you
can agree.

Listen, then clearly speak.
Employ respect,
be responsible,

work together.
Ideas must fly and then
Compromise.
Try it.
Try again. Try again.
Find Peace.

• Now listen to Palm explain how she acted upon her convictions by choosing her teaching activities with sixth grade students.

Peace Education with Elementary Students

—Kristen Palm

This project was developed to introduce and expand on elementary students' knowledge of peacemaking concepts such as: different visions of peace; famous peacemakers and peace organizations; empathy with others; peaceful negotiating strategies; and international goals for peace. I selected the subject of peace because I believe it is important for children to have good examples and positive role models to encourage constructive actions and solutions in their daily encounters. My intent is to empower children with the knowledge and tools of peacemaking with the hopes that they will come to believe that they are capable of making a positive impact within themselves, their families, community, and world.

Poetry was chosen as the main literary means of expression, because it is through writing poetry that a student is required to find the most effective words to convey their ideas. The poet is compelled to evoke emotions with a clarity of descriptions and concise definition. When reading and reviewing the students' poems, I stressed authenticity to true emotions, honest expression, specific applications of the assignment, and creativity.

I initially collected poems written primarily by children from a variety of countries around the world. Then we began with looking at the wide range of definitions of peace, and then, we spent time thinking about one's personal concept of peace. Next we explored the lives of others and their view of peace, including famous people and organizations working for peace and concluding with a personal commitment to action.

I was delighted to be able to teach this unit to a group of 25 sixth grade students in a public school in Duluth, Minnesota. The students were respectful, responsive, and happy to participate. They showed a willingness to listen to and interpret the poems I shared as well as an eagerness to write their own poetry. After the first session of writing poems individually, I realized a review of the basic structure and conventions of poetry was needed. I brought in poems for examples and we critiqued student work. One student, inspired by the topic of "peace with nature," took the initiative to write a poem independently after the class went on an all-day outing to a local nature reserve. I noticed a great improvement in the content of the poems as students shifted from cliche and somewhat shallow definitions of peace to an in-depth look at their own lives and empathy for the lives and needs of others. We learned that peacemaking is not often a passive activity, and chose to put our talents into action by writing a poem as a gift to a specific person.

- Write about any poems you have read about peace, or famous people you have heard making quotable comments about peace. Kristen Palm shared these, in addition to the poems she mentioned, with her students.

  Peace is a daily, a weekly, a monthly process,
  gradually changing opinions,
  slowly eroding old barriers,
  quietly building new structures.
  —J. F. Kennedy

  For it isn't enough to talk about peace.
  One must believe in it. And it isn't enough
  to believe in it. One must work at it.
  —Eleanor Roosevelt

  I wondered why somebody didn't do something for peace.
  Then I realized that I am somebody.
  —Anonymous

Options for Dialogue

- Discuss this teacher's idea for teaching about peacemaking. Do you think it is a good idea? Would you teach about peacemaking this way? Could you?
- Brainstorm with the group about different definitions of peace, and then break the definitions into broad categories such as: peace with self, family, community, nature, among nations, generations, genders, and so on. Work together to write a poem on one of the topics. Share the poems with the class and display them in the room when written. Here

are a few samples from Ms. Palm's students doing this
same activity:

Peace with Yourself

I can't do anything right
nobody likes me
everybody hates me
Why don't I go—
to a peaceful area
apologize
help someone
play basketball
take a nap
work it out
talk it over
be honest
be kind
trust others
stop drop and think about it
do this and call me
tomorrow
and hopefully I'll have
peace with myself

Peace with Community

Peace is working together, and helping others.
Peace is having friendship with others.
Peace is family.
Peace is a dove flying in the air.
Peace is happiness with others.
Peace is having peace.

Peace with Nature

If you cut down even one tree,
the world wouldn't be
as beautiful as it used to be.

If you see some litter by the lake,
pick it up for nature's sake.
If all the animals were in danger,
help them out, don't be a stranger.

Peace of the World

If the world is filled with all kinds of different animals
that are in other countries,
If we don't do something soon
these animals will come to an end.
We need to save places like Europe and Asia.
And if it comes to be hard,
It would be pointless to send a card.
PEACE
Make Peace in the World!

Friendship

Friendship is two people who get
along like peanut butter and jelly,
Like the sun and the moon,
Like the stars in the sky,
Like salt and pepper,
Like silver and gold
Friendship makes a peaceful world.

You and Me

You and me are always fighting,
You and I, we just don't click.
How can we solve this stupid
conflict?

We could
talk it over
listen to each other,
compromise

We could
think about it

So let's work it out and see
what comes out.

- Kristen Palm reported that the focus then shifted from defining peace in general categories, to a personal definition
of peace, to looking at the lives of others and empathizing
with their situation. The last part of her teaching unit deals
with recognizing that we are all unique individuals, celebrating our differences, and learning how to employ peaceful negotiations.

Options for Action

- Now look at what the sixth grade students wrote, and then
compare their ideas with what you were saying in your group
discussions.

Solving Arguments

When you're in an argument talk it out,
don't blow your spout.

When you're getting mad,
don't feel so bad.

If you can find a solution,
there will be less bad pollution.

So think it over, then
talk it over.

If you get in a fight
just don't bite and use all your might.

Peace with Compromise

When you disagree
Go over the steps.
Calm yourself
know your view
listen carefully

speak clearly
brainstorm
compromise
make a plan
meet.
If all else fails, just repeat!

- Go back to Marv Davidov's discussion of the role of teachers
  at the beginning of this chapter. Relate his ideas to the work
  of Kristen Palm.

CHAPTER NINE

. . . Creating Dialogue about Social Change: The Personal

The authors, through our study of critical literacy in a global context, have learned much about social change on the personal level from individual teachers. We have learned that there is a relationship among teaching and learning and the political, social, historical strengths and tensions, and funds of local knowledge of all cultures and the ways in which policy and practice play out.

We have a perspective about literacies which frames the ways we work. We research issues of writing, language and critical literacy in the context of home culture and culture of learners' learning environments in both schools and communities. We look at local knowledge and politicize reading and writing in the classroom. These critical issues affect Hmong immigrant learners in U.S. schools, Chicanos in California schools, Turkish students in Eastern Europe and Central Asia, Welsh and Irish students in England, Black South Africans in newly created, post-apartheid schools, and many other learners. These issues influence how we use, learn, and teach literacy in many languages in many forms of media. We believe this is why literacy must be taught with a critical framework. We believe critical literacy is one important avenue for social change on the personal level.

We define critical literacy as a *process of constructing meaning and critically using language (oral and written) as a means of expression, interpretation and/or transformation through literacies of our lives and the lives of those around us*. All scholars and teachers do not agree about what critical literacy is. The need for the plural form—"critical literacies"—suggests, rather, that a diversity of curriculum interventions are in theoretical, practical and political contest with one another (Luke & Freebody 1996). Yet, Comber (1998) believes it is possible to identify some shared assumptions about critical literacy:

- that literacy is a social and cultural construction,
- that its functions and uses are never neutral or innocent,
- that the meanings constructed in text are ideological and involved in producing, reproducing and maintaining arrangements of power which are unequal.

What does personal history mean when studying literacy? Critical literacy is a process of both reading history (the world) and creating history (what do you believe is important?). No one develops literacy out of the context of family, community, country, world at the present time, or without a connection to the past—the stories of those who have gone before. Literacy develops among particularities, among persons and objects in families and communities. It is an example of the large sweeps of history taking meaning from the small. For hundreds of years manuscripts were illuminated, embellished with luminous color with either literal or symbolic decoration to help with the layout or reading. In modern times this oneness of the written with the visual was lost except in books for children or more recently in conceptual art. The written and visual are moving together again this new graphic age and so literacy has to be intertextual. A literate person must be able to read between and within these different texts. Writing is central to this intertextual literacy. "Writing is not just a mopping up activity at the end of a research project . . . (it) is also a way of knowing . . . a method of inquiry" (Richardson, 1994, p. 516).

Writing and reading can be transforming on a personal level. As children read and write, they change. A child's writing can tell us much about her/his personal, family and community contexts. It is a way of nurturing the ability to summon up an "as if," as Maxine Greene calls it (1992), a sense of "what is out there, what I can reach if I try." It is a way of doing what Maxine Greene suggests, "helping students find language to bring dreams into being, language that introduces them to the experience of going beyond. . . ." We believe that education must support students to become effective writers, readers, and participants in literacy.

In this chapter, Mary Kay Rummel, in *Class for Beginners*, begins with the languages of the poet, the English speaker, learning Spanish, the person reflecting upon her past and present life and the personal choices she makes. Karen Soul presents a critical, multi-genre case study which details the journey of a student who has obvious personal strengths and yet many barriers in school. Ms. Soul, as teacher, uses the power of imaginative genres of writing to voice to the issues critical for change.

Finally, *Aikido: Personal Change* is a creative self-help way to be an agent of change. We believe all these contributions and the thoughts they conjure up relate to the thinking and actions of a responsible teacher.

References

Comber B. (1998) *Coming, ready or not: Changing what counts as early literacy.* Keynote address to the Seventh Australia and New Zealand Conference on the First Years of School.

Greene, M. (1992). Imagination and breakthroughs in the unexpected. Unpublished paper presented to the Association of Supervision and Curriculum Development. New Orleans.

Luke, A., & Freebody, P. (1996). Critical literacy and the question of normativity: An introduction. In S. Muspratt, A. Luke, P. Freebody, (11996) *Constructing critical literacies: Teaching and learning textual practice,* pp. 1–13. Creskill, NJ: Hampton Press.

Richardson, L. (1994). Writing, A method of inquiry. In N. Denzin and Y. Lincoln (Eds.), pp. 516–529, *Handbook of qualitative research.* Thousand Oaks, CA: Sage.

Mary Kay Rummel, Poet and Educator

Options for Listening

- Reflect for a few moments about a personal experience or one of someone close to you in which you felt discriminated against. What was the situation? What did you do about it in order to try to make a change? Did you do something overtly or more subtly? Was your "action" related to politics, economics, family dynamics, all of the above? Write about this.
- Read the following poem.

Class for Beginners

—*Mary Kay Rummel*

> *In spite of the repression, which is as fierce and remorseless today as it ever was, the Guatemalans lead lives of great dignity, maintaining as best they can their cultural traditions, worshipping nature in a very real sense, and making beautiful things.*
> —Jessye Norman, 1992 in *Guatemala, Burden of Paradise*

René the van driver tells us about
"La mitad la naranja"
meaning, my spouse, my other half
He wants us to stop halfway
between Panajachel and Antigua to shop
at Paulina's, a trap for tourists
where we buy bright serapes
that we will never wear in public
but they bring us the comfort of the sixties
and we know René gets a cut from the sale.

> *Seeking a way to be closer to the world*
> *and be less a part of it*

My mother used to say,
"See how the other half lives,"
meaning those who are not poor
Now, mother, I live in the other half
but I am finding it is no half
only the tiniest tip of the orange
and all the rest are poor.
I like having money
can you tell me how to live my life?

> *I am searching for "la mitad"*
> *the middle ground of guilt*

When I was sixteen
I worked part time at the dime store
with Rosita who worked full time
and was in charge of yard goods,
all day cutting and measuring cloth.
I went to her house to play cards
in the West side neighborhood,

poorer than mine on West Seventh,
Her husband swore in every sentence
Jesus and Jesus and Jesus.

René is a teacher but
makes more driving
for tourists—one thousand
quetzals a month (120 dollars).
On the road from Atitlan
he teaches us Spanish
he's good at saying
"no es correcto"
gives us declensions.
When I ask, "What is a llano?"
he thinks it is "yawn"
and we learn
yo bostizo
ella bosteze
nosotros bostezamos

> *Seeking a way to be closer to the world*
> *and be less a part of it*

I wanted to be like Jesus
was already poor
had nothing to give away
so joined the convent
and made a vow to own nothing
even the toothbrush was "ours."
We were given two habits to wear
but we were not hungry.
Poverty was the easiest vow.

> *Searching for "la mitad"*
> *the middle ground of guilt.*

A gift to be able to visit the home of Zoila,
the weaver, in her Mayan village.
She shows us how to make tortillas
over the open fire and eat them hot and fresh.
When we walk up mountain with the girls
Lilian Maribel, Astri Sofilia and Arelisa,
they point out fields of squash, cilantro, beans.

Boys come down the path
wood stacked high on their backs.
Buenas Tardes, Buenas Tardes
Farmers work on the mountain so steep
they are tied to their small fields so they won't fall.

The girls go to school in the morning.
Afternoons other students go because
there are not enough schools, few books.
Later, they sit at the newly acquired table
and read to each other in the fading light.

> *Seeing the beauty, learning to see*
> *the world in which it lives*

The table reminds me of childhood dinners
the same dark wood, my brothers fighting,
my father silent, my mother mad,
all beneath a picture of Jesus in Agony.

When I was a young woman
I wanted to come to Guatemala
to teach in the mountains
in my black veil and heavy shoes.
When I left the convent I said
I'd never again wear those black shoes
but here I am moving into the time
called old, walking the cobbled streets
of La Antigua wearing nun shoes
on my sore feet, the learner, not the teacher.
I am watching the hands of weavers,
trying to reach them across the cloth.

> *Seeing the beauty, learning to see*
> *the world in which it lives*

> *La Antigua, Guatemala*

Options for Dialogue

- As you read the poem, did you relate to any of the poet's issues?
- Discuss choices you make in your daily life that "take a stand."

- Brainstorm with your group ways the different "choices" we all make influence teaching and learning.

Options for Action

- Go to the Website for The Resource Center of the Americas *http://www.americas.org/.* This is a Minneapolis-based non-profit publisher of AMERICAS.ORG which is devoted to the notion that every person in this world is entitled to the same fundamental human rights. Its starting point for promoting these rights is learning and teaching about the peoples and countries of the Americas—their history, culture and politics. Read one or more of the articles and relate the information to the poem.

Karen Soul, Educator

Options for Listening

- Have you ever kept a journal or a diary? What was the situation? What did you like about the process of keeping a journal? What did you not like about it? Look around the room and choose a person to write about. Write a short paragraph about that person from the point of view of an adoring parent.
- Listen to Karen Soul, an elementary school teacher in Austin, Texas, discuss some of her reasons for keeping a journal, and then read the multi-genre case study.

Teacher Journal and Process Documentation

I am a "new teacher" again. Isn't that interesting how when a teacher transfers or accepts a new position, they are "new teachers" all over again? Of course, I do feel new. New city, new school, new curriculum, new students, new everything. How do I cope with all this newness? I started my journal last week. I keep a journal of my teaching experiences. Not a "today we learned-the-letter-'p' journal." No, I try to keep a journal that captures the essence of my classroom, my students, and myself as we all change and develop. I begin by writing my own feelings and experiences and then shift into the students' voices, trying to illustrate how they might perceive the classroom and events in it. Eventually, I will probably choose two or three students on which to focus and use them to help me better understand, teach, and learn. What I hope that my journal really becomes is case studies.

Composing case studies has been viewed as a sort of "reflection" for teachers.

Wassermann (1993), speaking of herself and other teachers, says:

> Developing habits of thinking about classroom events frees us from the need to judge and act impulsively. We allow ourselves time for reflection, time to make sense of what is happening at deeper levels, and consequently, to respond in more thoughtful, reasonable ways ... Writing gives us distance from the event and allows for new perspectives ... In the process, we learn to see ourselves more objectively and learn more about ourselves as teachers. (pp. 194–195)

Spurred by the case study approach that was utilized in my college education and yearning to find ways to use my reflective writing from my journal to learn more about teaching, my students, and myself, I completed a research project in 1998 that I called "Multi-Genre Case Studies."

I used different types of writing genres to develop case studies of students that were multilayered and gave information about educational and social contexts from the perspective of the students and their teacher. I found that through this project traditionally unseen aspects of both teacher and student came to surface and that this experience became the catalyst in sustaining my personal growth and passion for teaching.

The student participants I chose represented children with normal problems and issues in school today. Three cases evolved from the research: Crystal, a seventh grade student; Jesse, a sixth grade student; and myself, their teacher. Each case is unique unto itself and is composed of poetry, narratives, character sketches, research and literature reviews, dialogues, and more. The case included here is Crystal. While I cannot include the full case here, I have tried to choose excerpts that glimpse significant changes in the participants and their perspectives. The multigenre aspect of this article is the use of a variety of genres such as poetry, essay, dialogue, and stream-of-consciousness documentation to provide information to the reader.

As I made my observations, recordings, and writings, certain issues relating to the participants emerged. These "themes" seemed to surface again and again during the course of the project and run throughout the cases. Some of the themes, such as "at risk," are readily associated with educational settings and will come as little surprise to the reader, while other themes, such as "grief," are rarely discussed in schools. Presentation of the themes within the cases is meant to evoke and inspire readers to ponder, question, and discuss how and why each theme is related to the participants and what effect the themes have on the participants and their future. Although there are endless lists of issues relating to students, teachers, and education, five themes emerged solidly for me: at risk, emotional and behavioral disorders (E/BD), school suspension and effectiveness, grief, and chemicals and teens.

Crystal: Multigenre Case Study

—*Karen Covington Soul*

Crystal was a seventh grade female student with a history of school and personal difficulties. Crystal began school as an average, well-functioning child; educational and developmental concerns began in third grade, and by fourth grade, Crystal was referred for Special Education assessment. She did not qualify for services, but was again referred in fifth grade and sixth grade. By seventh grade, concerns for Crystal ranged from low educational ability to low self-concept and negative social interactions.

On the outside, Crystal was a not quite normal looking teenager. With her bleached blonde hair, sometimes sexy clothes, and mature body, she often appeared much older than her thirteen years. In other ways, Crystal was a very normal teenager, listening to popular music, writing notes to friends during class, and experiencing the growing pains of peer pressure, social circles, parental strife, and increasing homework.

In looking through my journal notes one day, I realized that Crystal's eye glasses, or lack thereof, were mentioned many times.

"A New Pair of Glasses"

A pair of glasses. Could a seemingly so insignificant object like a pair of glasses predict academic success or failure? Obviously, a student must be able to see, to view clearly—the chalkboard, books, worksheets—in order to learn in a regular classroom.

Teachers know that when they see a student squinting to view the overhead or chalkboard from the back of the room to automatically move that student to the front of the room and contact the school nurse for a vision check. This is routine; it happens all the time.

But what about when a student already has glasses and chooses when, or when not, to wear them? This can be quite common in middle school, when students are most conscious of physical appearance. After all, glasses are ugly; they are geeky, retarded, nerdy, and stupid. It is preferable, especially for girls, to simply struggle, no matter how hard, to see the chalkboard, rather than pull out glasses.

It became apparent in watching Crystal that her glasses were at school only when her mind was at school. She felt good about wearing them only when she felt good about herself. She chose to put them on when she chose to succeed. From this, I have watched other students—especially girls—in the same dilemma. I am amazed at the correspondence.

"Glasses On"

glasses on
book open
notebook out
she's working on geography

glasses on
worksheet out
hand up
she asks for help

glasses on
eyes up
mouth closed
she's taking notes

glasses on
book closed
wide smile
she finished the assignment

glasses on
pretty smile
clear eyes
she's with us today

glasses on
teachers' eyes
look upon
a great student

"Glasses Off"

Crystal was taken out of science class because she failed too many grading periods to pass and placed in study hall in the In School

Suspension (ISS) room to, hopefully, catch up on missing work. On a day when I was absent, Crystal received a behavior referral from the substitute teacher.

The referral was number 22 for Crystal and the substitute's comments read, "Student would not stop talking in ISS. Asked several times. Was rude and disrespectful to teacher—called teacher a 'bitch'."

Today, Crystal is pale, ghostly. Pewter circles frame her eyes. Unkempt, unwashed hair drifts across her face. She is wearing a dirty hooded sweatshirt, one she borrowed from Eddie in first hour. From the large front pocket, she pulls a pencil and a clear rubber ball. These are her materials for class. She bounces the ball—*ka-wip*—and a red strobe light flashes instantly inside the ball from impact.

A discussion takes place:
ka-wip ka-wip
"The substitute left me a note about yesterday." I begin. "I'd like to know what happened."
"She's a bitch."
ka-wip
"That's not what I'm interested in. I know what she thinks happened. I'd like to know what you think happened. And I would appreciate it if you could tell me without name calling."
ka-wip, snatch, eye contact.
Crystal always wants to tell her side of the story.
Crystal explains, "Well, she didn't know I was in here for study hall. She thought I got a referral, so she started trying to tell me what to do. She was rude. I even told her to call the counselor to see that I have study hall in here. She just told me to be quiet, so I called her a 'bitch'."
ka-wip
"I see." And I do. "Well, I understand her mistake. I will be sure to leave in my lesson plans next time that you are in here for study hall. I apologize for the mistake. I can't take the referral off because of the name calling. Next time, if that happens, just get out your books and work quietly and independently. Do you think you can do that?"
"Yeah, I guess."
ka-wip
"Do you have any work today?"
"Yeah."
ka-wip ka-wip
"Where is it?"
"I dunno."
ka-wip
"Where's your backpack?"
"I dunno."

"Do you have your books or anything?"
ka-wip
"No. I left them all, but I dunno what house."
"Well," *ka-wip* "whose house are you staying at?"
"I been staying at my aunt's, but sometimes I stay at my granma's or just friends'."
"What about your mom?" *ka-wip*
"She went" *ka-wip* "outta town."
"Without you?"
ka-wip
"Yeah, she does all the time."
"Who" *ka-wip* "do you stay with?"
"Me." *ka-wip ka-wip*
"Alone?"
ka-wip
"Yeah."
"Are you scared?"
"No." *ka-wip ka-wip ka-wip* "I love this ball."
"Do you have" *ka-wip* "relatives you can stay with?"
"No, they're all in Grand Martus." *ka-wip* "It's not a big deal."
ka-wip "I've stayed by myself since I was eight."
ka-wip ka-wip
"Look at this. I love that strobe." *ka-wip* "Isn't it awesome?"
ka-wip
"It's cool. Just don't bounce it in class." *ka-wip*
"I know. They'll take it."
"I don't" *ka-wip* "blame them—it is pretty distracting."
ka-wip
"Yeah, but I love it."
love that ball—amusing diversion
love that friend—approving companion
love that shirt—revealing distraction
love that show—shocking action
love that song—frightening lamentation
love that boy—confusing attraction
as intense as that red strobe

hate this school—stifling institution
hate my mom—lying custodian
hate all teachers—harassing instruction
hate my hair—annoying distinction
hate my life—terrifying alienation
hate myself—revolting creation
as intense as that red strobe

"Crystal, do you have your glasses?"
"Naw, I lost them."
ka-wip

"Glasses On"

students helping students (peer tutoring)
   I watched Crystal spend an entire class period helping a younger
student with a science assignment. I was the "teacher" in the classroom,
but was committed to taking care of a problem that had arisen. Crystal
took it upon herself to help another student. I never would have thought
to ask.

students helping
students helping
students helping
themselves

        at risk students helping
        at risk students helping
        lower students helping
        lower students helping
        higher students helping
        higher students helping
        lower students helping
        at risk students helping
        each other

                teachers helping
                students helping
                students helping
                teachers helping
                teachers

                        we all need to help
                        we all need help
                        we all need
                        we all do

Theme: At Risk

I have often heard and even used the term "at risk" to describe certain students. It is not a new term to me or my colleagues. In fact,

"since 1989, over 2,500 articles and conference papers have been focused on this topic [at risk]" (Fine, 1995, p. 1). To my fellow middle school teachers and myself, at risk students were those students who were at risk of academic failure, were not responding to typical intervention strategies, and might exhibit disruptive or inappropriate behavior in or out of school, including juvenile delinquency, truancy, chemical issues, and/or other social problems.

In reflecting, I determined that it was not acceptable for me to label a student without first learning more of what the label signifies for the student, teacher, school, family, and community.

In the literature I reviewed, I found that the term "at risk" is used to describe students who are at risk of dropping out of school, leaving school without necessary knowledge and skills, using drugs, getting pregnant, and/or being abused by family members or others. Specific factors associated with at risk students may "include membership in a racial or ethnic minority, low socioeconomic status, a single parent in the home, and low educational attainment by one or both parent(s)" (Pallas, Natriello, & McDill, 1989, p. 9). It is estimated that "by the year 2020, the majority of students in America's public schools will be living in circumstances traditionally regarded as placing them at risk for educational failure" (Rossi & Stringfield, 1995, paragraph 2).

The term is a widely accepted one, with most research concentrating not on the label "at risk," but on what to do about those students who fall under the label. However, Swadener and Lubeck (1995) chose to take a long, hard look at both the label and the student, submitting that "the generalized use of the 'at risk' label is highly problematic and implicitly racist, classist, sexist, and a 1990s version of the cultural deficit model which locates problems or 'pathologies' in individuals, families, and communities rather than in institutional structures that create and maintain inequality" (Lubeck & Garrett, 1990, p. 3). This premise leads to many questions. For middle-class America and educational professionals, does the term "at risk" provide comfort because it not only separates "us" from "them," but also gives us cause why we cannot seem to educate those students? Does the label place blame on the student and allow teachers, schools, and society to remain complacent? There appear to be two distinct consequences of the label. As mentioned above, it could do more harm than good, allowing institutions to remain static and ineffective. Or, Fine (1995) suggests, the possibility of the "benevolent consequence"—that the at risk students' needs will be attended to through identification (p. 88). The majority of the literature tends to focus on the latter postulate.

The following is Ms. Soul's multi-genre response regarding these issues and this particular student.

"Through Her Glasses"

This passage is based on a quote made by the assistant principal concerning Crystal's insider knowledge of the "troubled" children and their doings in our school:

The assistant principal said, "If I knew half of what Crystal knows, I could really clean things up around here."

The counselor said, "If I knew half of what Crystal knows, I could get her into a rehab program."

The social worker said, "If I knew half of what Crystal knows, I could get her social services."

The boy said, "If I knew half of what Crystal knows, I would be sat-is-fied."

Her friend said, "If I knew half of what Crystal knows, I would be as popular as she is."

The teacher said, "Crystal? What does Crystal know?"

Her mother said, "If I knew half of what Crystal knew, I would be disgusted."

I say, "If we took the time to listen, we might know what Crystal knows."

Crystal says, "If you knew half of what I know, you wouldn't look at me like that, would you?"

"Glasses Off"

after the holidays

Most students come back to school after the winter holidays refreshed, cheery, excited to share events experienced and new things obtained. Not

Crystal. She's cut and dyed her hair over the holidays—a short, bleached, dirty, tangled mess, and her puffy red eyes, pallid complexion, and grimace make her look more like a sick Scrooge than a rested student.

7:45. . . Crystal makes it to class just as the bell rings, slouches to her chair and drops into it. 7:48. . . She slumps over her desk, rests her head in her arm, sighs, and rolls her eyes. 7:52. . . Attendance has been taken and instructions given to get out goal sheets for the new year. 7:56. . . Crystal's head is completely down now, eyes closed. 7:58. . . The teacher instructs Crystal to please sit up and follow instructions. 7:59. . ."What instructions?" Crystal interjects. "I didn't hear anything." 8:00. . . Instructions are repeated for Crystal's benefit. 8:04. . . Crystal's head is down again, eyes closed. She makes no movement to follow the lesson. 8:07. . . The teacher, obviously perturbed, instructs Crystal again to raise her head and join the lesson. The teacher moves closer to Crystal to emphasize seriousness and action. 8:09. . . Crystal sits up with her eyes half open. Still she does not make an effort to find her goal sheets. She does not yet have a pencil out. 8:12. . . The teacher has the other students working independently by now. She walks over to Crystal's desk and sits in a chair next to her. She quietly asks, "What's the problem today? Why aren't you working with us?" 8:13. . . In a loud voice Crystal responds, "Because I don't want to. I don't feel like it. I feel sick. I sat up, didn't I?" 8:15. . . The teacher writes a pass for Crystal to go to the nurse. 8:22. . . Crystal returns from the nurse. Her mother is not home. There is nothing the nurse can do; Crystal will have to stay in class. 8:25. . . Crystal's head is back down, eyes closed. The teacher makes no effort to revive her; she ponders whether Crystal is really sick or not, but has seventeen other EXCEL students just as needy as Crystal who are ready to work. 8:32. . . Bell rings. Crystal shoots up and out the door. 8:47. . . Crystal is seen at the vending machines in the hall laughing and goofing with friends.

"Glasses Off"

ru·mor (rú:mer) n. an unauthenticated story or report put into circulation

"You know, I've had rumors told about me my whole life: Where I came from; why I don't have a dad; why my mom is so young; why I dress the way I do; why I dye my hair; why I do those things with boys; why I don't do good in school; why I get in trouble. Sometimes they're true and sometimes they're not. Sometimes I care and sometimes I don't. There's a rumor going around right now. The rumor is that last weekend my mom took me to the casino and I stayed there way past midnight and that I got really drunk. My friends think it's pretty cool and so does Shawn and he's really cool. I won't tell you if it's true or not. It doesn't really matter anyway—it's a rumor."

The school student study team got wind of this rumor in December.

They immediately referred Crystal to the chemical specialist in the school and reviewed the planned documented interventions that teachers had implemented since November. They felt that the interventions had not been successful and that an assessment should be done as soon as possible for an Emotional/Behavior Disorder.

Options for Dialogue

- Please discuss: What did you learn about Crystal? How would you describe her as an individual? As a student? As a teacher, how would you deal with Crystal? What would you do to "get her to put her glasses on" and participate in school? What would you do if she reacted belligerently toward you? What kind of discipline do you think would work best with Crystal? Do you think Crystal has an Emotional/Behavioral Disorder? What evidence supports/disputes such a diagnosis? How might a substance abuse problem affect Crystal's behavior and actions in school? Does she display any of the signs/symptoms of a substance abuse problem?
- What are Crystal's strengths? What are her coping skills? What do you think would make her education a happier experience? A more successful experience?
- Discuss how the format Ms. Soul uses gives you a picture of the student.

Options for Action

- Go back to the paragraph you wrote in the Listening activity about a person in the class. Continue to write about that person from the point of view of their strengths or their weaknesses. Your writing could take the form of poetry, prose, a play, free-style rap or another creative format.
- Read one of the articles in Swadener and Lubeck. Write a brief summary of the article and also write a brief personal essay in which you deconstruct the term "at risk."

Epilogue: Crystal

Crystal was assessed and qualified for Emotional/Behavioral Disorder in May 1998. Crystal began working with an E/BD specialist during study hall and when she was sent out of regular classrooms with discipline referrals. The month before school ended, Crystal's behavior worsened. She became aggressively disruptive in class and at school events, overtly confrontational with teachers, and compulsively tormenting and threatening toward peers.

References

Fine, M. (1995). The Politics of Who's "at Risk." In B. B. Swadener & S. Lubeck, *Children and Families "At Promise"* (pp. 76–96). Albany: State University of New York Press.

Lubeck and Garrett (1990).

Pallas, A. M., Natriello, G., & McDill, E. L. (1989). The changing nature of the disadvantaged population: Current dimensions and future trends. *Educational Researcher, 18:* 16–22.

Rossi, R., & Stringfield, S. (1995). What we must do for students placed at risk. *Phi Delta Kappan,* 77 (1): 73–76.

Swadener, B. & S. Lubeck. (1995). *Children and Families "At Promise."* Albany: State University of New York Press.

Wassermann, S. (1993). *Getting Down to Cases.* New York: Teachers College Press.

Frank Guldbrandsen, Teacher Educator

Options for Listening

- Do you or anyone you know practice one of the martial arts? If so, write about this in your journal. If not, write what you know about one of the martial arts either from reading or from a film.
- If you have participated in any sort of athletic endeavors, write about what your coaches and mentors told you about a mind-body connection in terms of being successful at what you were attempting.

Aikido: Personal Change

—*Frank Guldbrandsen*

I was looking to find something where I could be a student again, something that kept me out of the front of the room and in control. I saw a note posted at the university where I teach that Aikido class was beginning at the YMCA and figured this might be my chance. I talked it over with a running buddy and we both decided to go for it.

We had heard some things about Aikido. We were told that it was considered by many to be the most sophisticated of the martial arts. Aikido was said to be nonagressive; whereas so many of the fighting arts were based on strikes and kicks, Aikido was based on blends and unbalancing the opponent, using their force to render them harmless. Great strength was not required. One need not be gymnastic or nasty, but rather, open to "the force." We heard that the character Yoda from Star Wars was based on the founder of Aikido, Morehei Ueshiba.

There were eight or ten of us there the first night. We learned that the teacher had just moved up from Austin, Texas. He was dressed in a judo uniform with a black skirt which he called a hakema. He moved with great fluidity, reminding me of the nuns in elementary school who we thought might be on roller skates beneath their habits. He said that Aikido was about learning to harmonize with whatever came your way, learning to roll with the punches.

That evening we literally began learning to roll, to be spherical as we went forward and backward on the gymnastics mats. That first night was enough for my buddy. Next day he informed me that he was sore all over and hated the thought of beginning anew in some physical activity that he felt very awkward at. He would stick to running. I was excited and could hardly wait for the next class.

That was fourteen years ago. During that time, I have moved, from being the rank beginner in the back of the room to the beginner in the front of the room, teaching Aikido classes in addition to my regular load of education classes each semester. I find that Aikido has entered my daily life as a college professor and has transformed my thinking about teaching and learning.

Get Off the Line of Attack

In Aikido we learn that there is an attack angle, and that if we move off from it, if only a small amount, we gain an advantage from our attacker as we are no longer in a position of their greatest strength and our greatest vulnerability. Countless times in the classroom and in faculty meetings I envision these attack angles as someone is trying to win an arguing point from another, as situations are set up to be win/lose. We are told in Aikido that even if we accomplish little else, if we are off the line, we protect ourselves from the full force of aggressive energy. How often do we think that there is no alternative but to meet aggression with counteraggression? After all, they asked for it.

You just walked into your dorm room and your new roommate starts screaming about what a slob you are. You were born a slob and will die that way. Your first reaction is to counter with asking whether anal retentive is spelled with or without a hyphen, but instead, you move off the line.

Make Contact

As I move safely off the line of attack and harm's immediate way, almost counterintuitively, I move toward my opponent and make contact, just touching. It is important to be close to my opponent, often turning a half revolution so that I see the world as they do. In my regular college classes, making contact plays such an important role. To the extent that I am the other to them, that I separate myself from my students, I cannot know their world, what is important to them, how they view their lives or what we are studying together. But I find that if I am able to make that half turn, to stand close by, just touching their world, then things become visible that had been invisible. I know better what to say and to do. I see the world, though darkly, as they do.

Instead of nailing your roommate with a zingy witticism, you respond by saying, "You must really be miffed at me." You've made contact.

Take Your Opponent's Posture

If a person who is attacking has strong balance, they are more dangerous and are more likely to do harm. It is important in Aikido that once I have moved off the line of attack I make contact with my opponent, then take their posture by extending them beyond their optimal range of effectiveness. I put them off balance as I operate well within my range of effectiveness.

There is the moment of surprise when, in a classroom, the teacher does not respond as the student expects, does not meet force with force, negativity with negativity. In the faculty room or the dean's office, this unexpected response means to become like the fog, to give no resistance when pushed against, to melt away from where you have been, only to reemerge standing alongside and taking the balance of the other through nonaggression. There is delight in discovering harmony where there was dissonance.

Having gotten off the line and made contact, your roommate responds with, "You bet I'm miffed. I can't stand it any more." You realize your job is to take their posture, to lead them outside their range of effectiveness. You respond by saying, "You're absolutely right. And if you moved out, I'd understand it completely."

Find a Technique

A master Aikidoist never enters a situation of conflict with a particular resolution in mind. The situation itself will present the resolution as long as the Aikidoist's mind is open to the moment. Calmness in action is what is sought, without an opinion as to what is happening. It is neither good nor bad, up nor down, sweet nor sour, hot nor cold. What is, is. As we move off the line of attack, make contact, and take the posture of the opponent, a technique right for the moment will present itself. It is imperative that we have trained long and hard for this moment so that we have a number of alternative movements in our repertoire of possible actions. With that, we can trust that a technique will present itself unique to our opponent's aggression. We literally "find" the right technique out of all the possible techniques we might use.

In the classroom, the quote attributed to Churchill often comes to my mind. "Plans are worthless. Planning is invaluable." More and more, things rarely seem to go as I have planned them; and less and less am I inclined to attempt to force my plans into the evolving structure of the class. I "find a technique" that presents itself in the uniqueness of the moment. What is called for, what is demanded by the situation? If I am sensitive enough to know to know that, and skilled enough to provide what is needed, then I am rewarded with the exquisite realization that what is happening is exactly what should be happening given these exact circumstances.

You are somewhat surprised when they inform you that they would really rather stay, but things need to change. Your technique presents itself. In Aikido it is known as makiotoshj, body wrap/down. You totally agree with their point of view, that things do need to change.

Give Your Opponent a Place to Fall

On the Aikido mat we learn that two masses cannot occupy the same spot at the same time and retain any sense of harmony. Often an opponent seems to want the place that we are occupying, and so we move and give them that, and rather than fighting for that space, we blend with the energy of our opponent. If we have successfully moved off the line of attack, made initial contact, taken their posture, and then found a technique, then we are ready to invite them to the mat. Aikido energy is in most cases centrifugal, spherical energy responding to centripetal, linear energy. The result of the meeting of these two forces is the redirection of the linear energy down and into the mat. Being conscious of the fact that two forces cannot occupy the same space at the same time, we make room for our opponents to fall, rendering their aggression less dangerous and harmful in the moment. I use the term "invite them to the mat" because in a real sense we do not throw our opponents. The redirection of linear energy down will, most often, cause the loss of balance; and then it takes very little effort to continue that energy to the mat.

In the classroom I find that I can often successfully redirect a student's energy without taking their dignity. If I am able to listen deeply enough to their words, though they may be directing their thoughts to a conclusion of conflict and disharmony, I find that with only minute redirection, no harm is done. "Oh I see, what you are really saying is. . . . It sounded at first that you meant this, but I see that where you are going with the thought is. . . . Is that right?" "Yes." With the agreement that things need to change, you are in a perfect position to propose the very things you were already thinking about in order for you to be better organized for the new semester coming up. Your roommate is satisfied that they were heard and their wishes were honored. You are pleased because rather than there being another uproar, you are moving in the direction that you want to go, and you are on the road to becoming a black belt martial artist.

The colleague who is intent on winning an argument in the faculty meeting, rather than finding active resistance, is met with understanding and a sense of being heard. It takes a level of skill and practice then to "find a technique" that will not allow harm to occur, that "lets them down easy." It is important to emphasize that to the skilled Aikidoist, there is no desire to win while the other loses. Truly the goal is harmony while first protecting self, then protecting the other. So the colleague senses no outrage when they discover what "really" has happened.

After that initial meeting of the Aikido club those many years ago, I had no idea of the power that it would carry in my understanding of daily life. My classroom has subtly and ineluctably taken on the atmosphere of a place visited from time to time by Yoda. I understand more than ever that there are warring forces vying for prominence in the galaxy. I train so that the force may be with me and may it be with you.

Options for Dialogue

- In small groups, using Dr. Guldbrandsen, subheadings, re-view his interpretation of the meaning of that idea under each heading, and then try to give an example from your life:

Get Off the Line of Attack
Make Contact
Take Your Opponent's Posture
Find a Technique
Give Your Opponent a Place to Fall

Options for Action

- Read a book about aikido, jujitsu, judo, or another martial art. Relate what you learn to both the beliefs and histories you have been studying in this class. Present what you learn to your class in an oral presentation.
- Visit the Website *http://www.aikiweb.com.* This site is Aiki Web, one of the many sources of information for aikido on the Internet. Now go to one of the search engines on the Internet and look up information about one of the other martial arts. Compare some of the information you learn about the two different forms and report to your class.
- Read *Autumn Lightning* by Dave Lowry, Shambhala Publications, 1995. Report what you learn to your class.
- Read *The Shambhala Guide to Yoga* by G. Feverstein, Shambhala Publications, 1996. Relate this information to this short essay presented here and report.
- Visit the web site *http://www.fightingfilms.com.* This is an organization based in London with many types of information about martial arts and many sources available for finding information. It is reported to be the only accredited supplier of judo videos for the International Judo Federation.

CHAPTER TEN

... Creating Dialogue about Social Change: The Institutional

How do educators maintain their commitment to change in organizations which in today's political and educational climate do not encourage change? A wise Anishinabe woman once advised activists in the Minnesota community where she had lived and worked for decades, "I just have to wake up each morning and tell myself that I'm going to do the best I can to make one small change for the better for my people. And I vow not to let society take the sparkle out of my grandchildren's eyes." This seems to describe the work of outstanding educators. We have found in interviewing them that the path that leads from the school into the broader community flows directly from lives enriched by critical literacy, action and art (in a broad sense). "It takes imagination to engage with literature and other art forms," Maxine Greene (1995) tells us. "Encounters of this sort push back the boundaries . . . They locate learners in a wider world, even as they bring them in closer touch with their own actualities." In this introduction we share some of the stories told by exemplary teachers whom we've met.

An interview with Bill Simpson, a special education teacher in Minnesota, provides an example of this. The connections between his reading for self-nurturance, his adventuring and his work for children become global:

We started a sister city in Ginger, Uganda with Stillwater. Then we started a special school project with our school and a school in Uganda. There are three thousand students in this school and no books. So a friend of mine started this program. This month the community and schools in Stillwater are bringing in their favorite new books. And also fifty cents for postage. And then we are shipping them to Africa. So my goal is to go over there and visit this school. It would be nice to set up some kind of exchange program with students. (Rummel & Quintero, 1997, p. 47)

Bill now leads adventure treks in which participants donate money to this and other programs.

Other teachers talk about reading and art in ways that clearly convey their nurturing power. Their words also illuminate the spirituality that underlies their literate, artistic and teaching lives. It is the life of the spirit (not necessarily connected to formal religion) which they describe. Mary Tacheny, a primary teacher, talked about connecting stories her students are reading "to a meaning or value." As she described reading to connect herself to worlds beyond, she also talked about reading to her children, and thus her teaching is nurturance, connected to worlds beyond.

I like to read books with a message. I hate stupid books. I try to connect the stories to a meaning or value. I often try to have students discuss by using their personal experience . . . I read a lot of spiritual books that have had an influence on my life . . . I read to connect myself to a world beyond. . . . Over the years I think I've learned a great deal from children. . . . (Rummel & Quintero, 1997. p. 152)

As explained earlier, our interviews showed us that exemplary teachers had some common approaches to pedagogy consistent with and expanding upon the characteristics of "teacher as artisan" (Casey, 1993). They all exhibited a belief that it is their responsibility to find ways of engaging all their students in learning activity. They accept responsibility for making the classroom an interesting, engaging place. They persist in trying to meet the individual needs of the children in their classes, searching for what works best for each student. Their basic stance is a continual search for better ways of doing things. An example of this continual search is the involvement of students in learning that transcends curriculum, textbooks (often) and achievement tests. None of them talked about testing as a measure of success. They have a predisposition to emphasize students' efforts in defining success. These teachers see protecting and enhancing students' involvement in learning activities as their highest priority. If they run into a problem in doing this they find ways around it. They are able to generate practical, specific applications of theories and philosophies; at the same time, they are able to see the whole picture. Day by day, these teachers are working hard to make schools better.

Support of colleagues is important to sustain these teachers both professionally and personally. Vicki Brathwaite, a teacher in Brooklyn, New York seems especially sensitive to the cycles of literacy describing her reading club called "Brown Women." Vicki provides an example of the wide breadth of the reading of the teachers in this study. It is characterized by the absence of a negative, limiting "political correctness." Our interviews tell us much about what makes strong teachers in a diverse society. The strengths found in these teachers has little to do with admissions test scores and more to do with an expansive, creative approach to both life and teaching as well as a strong inner life of mind and spirit. One of the teachers described this quality as the "creative teacher's love of play."

As Haberman (1995) found in his study, *Star teachers of children in poverty*, the best teachers live what they believe. It is not possible to talk about beliefs and commitments apart from behaviors. The reading selections in this chapter represent many genres and look at individual responses to institutions as well as how changes in political climate change institutions.

In the first selection is a poem by Norbert Hirschhorn, a public health physician who has spent much time working in Lebanon. His poem is a response to conflict in the Middle East. Bob O'Brien, a teacher educator in New Zealand, documents governmental efforts to create institutional change and teacher responses to government- induced change. In a follow-up essay he records how a change in government can affect educational programs. Next is a poem by Neil Shepard which is set in the South Pacific and has implications relating to Dr. O'Brien's information. Carol Master's story, "Count Time" takes place in a different institution, a U.S. prison. It is about the complexities in the life of a woman who is imprisoned because of critical actions against government policies. Finally, John Mayer speaks to the wider implications of pedagogical movements and the connections between political and educational institutions.

References

Casey, K. (1993). *I answer with my life: Life histories of women teachers working for social change*. New York: Routledge Press.

Greene, M. (1995). Notes on the search for coherence. Beane, J. (Ed). *Toward a coherent curriculum: The 1995 ASCD yearbook*. Alexandria, VA: ASCD.

Haberman, M. (1995). *Star teachers of children in poverty*. West Lafayette, IN: Kappa Delta Pi.

Rummel, M. K., & Quintero, E. P. (1997). *Teachers' reading/ Teachers' lives*. Albany, NY: State University of New York Press.

Norbert Hirschhorn, Poet and Public Health Physician

Options for Listening

- Have you ever been involved in an institutional effort to make social change? What was the process? What did you think about? Please explain these feelings in writing.
- Read the following poem and discuss who is speaking in the poem. What are the ways in which the conflict in the poem relates to political conflicts around the world?

I Will Allow Myself Just One Political Poem

—*Norbert Hirschhorn*

I will ravage your trees, the ones your father planted,
    and their fathers before them,
      so your children must sit in the boiling sun,
      so I may listen to them thirst.

I will smash your houses, scatter gas and glass
    into your eyes, blind you in my rage.

I will hunt you down:
      in your bed, at your table, in your fields.
      Your children will fall in strange streets,
      their mothers keen over empty coffins.

I will choke your nightingales.

I will poison your doves.

My David to your Goliath! I will crush your head
    with missiles, like an egg shattered on rocks.

I will destroy your name. You have no name.
    I alone will name you. No one shall know you.
    You shall be a roach unto nations.

I will beat you and burn you and beat you
    until you stop hating me.

        Now let grief consume our trees—
        we shall instead plant dead bodies,
        and eat of them their fruit.

Options for Action

- Visit a museum, if possible in your community, if not possible, on the Internet. Find examples of art that document institutional social change. Report to your class.

Robert O'Brien, Teacher Educator and Biographer

Options for Listening

- Write about any way your family has been directly affected by a law or policy made by the government. Did you have to change residences or neighborhoods? Did you have to change schools? Did you have to change where you bought necessities? Did you loose or gain access to work or recreational facilities?
- Think back to what you were taught in history classes about public policy. How do you see the past alive in the present (in terms of history, politics, and education)? What historical events have affected your geographic region in ways that are still evident today?
- Read the following article by Bob O'Brien. He is giving information about the situation in New Zealand, in particular as education relates to the indigenous Maori people. As you read, journal about ways you see the information relating to your current or future teaching situation even though initially, on the surface, the situations may seem very different.

· · ·

Due to the amount of very important information and length of presentation, the essay that follows is interspersed with Dialogue Questions for discussion as the readers journey through the reading.

Migration Patterns and Teacher Readiness to Respond:
The New Zealand Experience 1840–1996
—Robert O'Brien

Aotearoa in Polynesia

The islands of Aotearoa/New Zealand in the South Pacific Ocean have been inhabited by Polynesians for at least a thousand years. They lie between 33 and 50 degrees south latitude and represent one of a triangular area of sea and islands that the Polynesians have traditionally occupied. Easter Island and the Hawaiian archipelago are markers too. The indigenous people of these atolls and volcanic peaks have been profoundly affected by the diseases and cultures of invading and colonising Europeans. Any attempt to understand their contemporary situation is likely to be distorted unless some examination is made of the causes and patterns of the impact of the arrival in the Pacific of steadily increasing number of European-descended people after the seventeenth century. This paper will draw on New Zealand examples but the generality extends to all other parts of Polynesia, Melanesia and Micronesia.

European sea-rafters and traders were usually the first to make contact with the people of Polynesia. Self-seeking and greedy for profit, they learnt sufficient native society and culture to suit their own ends, but by introducing what later became labeled as a cargo-cult driven economy they began the steady disruption of traditional lifestyles, values, and customs. Those who chose to settle in some particular part of the "South Seas" of romance and legend learnt the language, complied with some of the mores, often married into important families, thereby acquiring property rights, and accepted that any offspring would be educated after the manner of the other children of the island. The concept of whanautanga (the obligations of the extended family) had helped in the maintenance of each island's heritage over the centuries, in spite of natural disasters (volcanic eruptions, hurricanes, droughts and tidal waves) and the often bitter and bloody rivalries between groups which led to enslavement, revenge, warfare and cannibalism. The pakeha (European) traders accepted this and saw possible profit by supplying new means (arms and liquor particularly) for advancing the cause of one group over another.

Early in the nineteenth century the Christian missionaries, their wives, and children, mainly born in the Pacific, began arriving with proselytising zeal. What they saw as heathenism, superstition, barbarism, and licentiousness among "the natives" had to be combated vigorously so that Christian (i.e. pakeha) enlightenment could replace the deplorable ways of the past.

Colonisation from Britain

As colonisation, mainly from Britain, gathered momentum in New Zealand after 1840 the provision of elementary education was accepted as a responsibility of, firstly, provincial authorities and, after 1877, central government. Rudimentary systems, derived from the British Isles, were put in place so that the children of the immigrants could have some opportunity to become literate and more socialised. Those in power acknowledged that an educated population would be needed if their vision of a flourishing economy and civilised society were to be realised. Even though there was compliance with some aspects of the 1840 (Treaty of Waitangi) understanding between the British Crown and the apparent leadership of Maori communities in many parts of the country, the relative and actual decline in the Maori population meant that little attention was paid to the needs of the indigenous people. Some Maori village schools were opened and the state accepted that it had a responsibility to supply teachers for both Maori and pakeha. Teacher training programmes were established along with an infrastructure (developed and managed by the Department of Education) which attempted to deliver a national curriculum to urban and rural communities and eke out the resources supplied by governments in Wellington.

Dialogue questions for discussion

What similarities do you see between what you know about ways history affected education in your state and country and what Dr. O'Brien describes?

Reversal of Maori Decline

Assimilationist policies lost support quite rapidly. The Maori population increased. Maori political activism intensified, stimulated by the mounting radicalism of a small number of younger leaders who had, in the main, acquired their knowledge and skills from the increasingly

maligned education system. There was increasing evidence from research
of social and economic indicators that, in spite of the undertakings
implicit in the Treaty of Waitangi, the indigenous people of New Zealand
had not enjoyed the full benefits that had accrued to many pakeha through
the previous century. The need for redress of past injustices was
acknowledged by successive governments and the acceptance of the need
to honour henceforth the principles of the treaty was reaffirmed by
legislation.

Thus it came about that teacher educators were called upon to provide
pre- and in-service training for student teachers and practising teachers.
Teachers were encouraged to introduce in as many curriculum areas as
possible tam Maori (a Maori dimension) to their schemes of work.
Examination prescriptions were revised and the teaching of te reo (the
language) was promoted. Maori language tests (nga kohanga reo) for
preschool-age children proliferated and were seen as having the potential
to provide the renaissance needed if te reo was to survive. By the time of
the next major review of the country's education service (1983–88) the
need for changes and improved outcomes in education for Maori was
widely recognised and the teachers colleges had adjusted their curricula
accordingly.

Multiculturalism Acknowledged

Other ethnic minorities remained unrecognised by the education
service until a series of reports published in the late 1970s began to draw
attention to what was to grow into a sustained debate about the priorities
for New Zealand society: Should the state education system be
emphasising the bicultural or multicultural dimension of the population?
Census information helps to show why some teachers were supportive of
a multicultural rather than a bicultural dimension to the curriculum that
they offered their pupils. The growth in the Maori population was
paralleled by an increase in the number of non-European immigrants after
World War II.

Meeting the Needs of Ethnic Minorities

Although many provisions were made to help ethnic minorities meet
their needs, few attempts were made to help European pupils and staff
understand other cultures. Less than half the schools had a Maori or
Polynesian Club and in those that did, fewer than 20 percent of European
pupils belonged to them. While half the schools had introduced special
programmes to foster knowledge and appreciation of the Maori culture,

only 12 percent had similar programmes about other Polynesian or minority ethnic groups. To bring their pupils into contact with pupils of different ethnic backgrounds, 50 schools had established sporting and social relationships with the schools whose pupils were of different ethnic origin.

Classes in Maori language were available to non-Maori pupils in about half the schools, but in most of them under 20 percent of the pupils took such classes. Form 3–7 girls' schools had the highest average number of non-Maori pupils learning some elements of Maori language. The lowest average numbers were recorded in district high and area schools.

New Zealand teacher educators were stretched to meet the growing needs of beginning and practising teachers in a situation where curriculum change had become more structured and more frequent, and rapidly changing social expectations were creating new challenges for schools and other sectors of the education service. The passage of legislation, firstly giving status to te reo as an official language, and later making it mandatory for all schools to meet the obligations arising from the Treaty of Waitangi, added to the pressure on the teacher educators to modify their courses of pre-service training to meet the new situation. But even as the primacy of concern for the well-being of the indigenous culture was being affirmed, the increasing inward migration of refugees and others from Southeast Asia and the islands of the Pacific gave impetus to the debate about the needs of these newly arriving children in the school system. In recent years, schools have enrolled increasing numbers of children fluent in languages other than English. They have come mainly from the Pacific, Europe, and since 1977, from Southeast Asia. Their previous educational backgrounds are as varied as the teaching and learning styles of their cultures.

Advice such as this and the regular publication of material to support the learning needs of most of the most numerous non-pakeha ethnic groups, became increasingly common as teacher educators responded to the changing nature of their professional direction, but the failure to recruit teachers from the small, but growing, group of qualified Maori hindered the achievement of an improvement in general Maori educational outcomes. During a time of considerable economic and social change, where unemployment forced an acceleration of internal migration to the Greater Auckland area in particular, the sections of society which were most disadvantaged were those with limited education and few of the skills needed in a competitive work environment. Many such disadvantaged citizens came from within the ethnic minority groups. The education service, itself under stress from reforms in administration, qualifications, and curriculum, found itself often without the resources needed to respond to the now quite clearly defined needs of its diverse range of students.

Dialogue questions for discussion

The section you just read, in fact, relates strongly to multicultural education and issues regarding language use in schools and in learning in the United States also. Make a list of all the examples you can think of that reading this account reminds you of. For example, do you think of English Only Initiatives or schools for single ethnic groups? What else?

An International Perspective

Concurrently with these social dynamics, geopolitical decisions underpinned other changes to the population structure and attitudes of New Zealanders. The old white, Anglo-Saxon Commonwealth partners no longer dominated policy making; new alliances, primarily based on the nature of a state's trade needs, began to be formed. As a very small nation New Zealand increasingly began to use the United Nations Organisation to express its viewpoint about political, social, and economic issues. In the second half of the twentieth century New Zealand began to assert its own autonomy as the traditional ties to "the Old Country/Home" (i.e. the United Kingdom) came to be seen as fragile, remote, and unsustainable.

The content of the school curriculum reflected the nation's slow reaction to its changed and changing status. The teacher training courses prepared people to work in a climate of change. Teaching resources became more diversified and transient. New technologies were introduced and teachers often found themselves less adept in their use than were the children whom they "taught." Increasing numbers of students chose to stay at school until an age well past that specified in the successive Education Acts. This had the consequence of creating a demand for amendment to the structure, organization, and objectives of secondary school education, in particular. Teacher educators, teachers, administrators, and the general public entered into deliberations about the nature of the reforms from the late 1970s onwards. Now, two decades on, the process has been greatly advanced but remains incomplete.

Tomorrow's Schools

The challenge for teacher educators now will be for them to come to terms with the continued repositioning and restructuring that is a current feature of tertiary education in New Zealand as elsewhere, while at the same time renewing their efforts to pick up with improved diligence recruitment policies which will succeed in attracting into teacher training adequate numbers of applicants from many of the ethnic groups now found in the New Zealand population. A long-held goal has been to have the ethnicity of the total teaching force match the patterns of the wider society so that young people can be influenced by role models whom they can more readily identify with. The small advances that were made towards achieving this goal were halted by the reforms in tertiary study provisions made by the state and the sustained attacks upon the teaching profession by the protagonists of the appreciable economic changes being introduced to the country as a response to some of the geopolitical forces referred to above. At present it seems that few able students of any ethnic background in their midteenage years seriously contemplate a career in teaching. Given the projected growing shortage in the supply of teachers in the immediate period ahead, there will need to be a considerable change of outlook needed if the agreed principles of the Curriculum Framework are to be carried over into the practices of the New Zealand classroom by a talented, committed, and internationally oriented teaching force.

Dialogue questions for discussion

What can educators in other countries learn from the experiences of New Zealand educators' curriculum revisions? Why is it important that teachers in the classroom reflect the ethnicity and language of the population of students with whom they work?

· · ·

At an international education conference in 1999, Bob O'Brien gave an update of the educational situation in New Zealand. His report documented in particular how the developments were progressing in terms of Maori education and also how closely tied are sociopolitical events, educational policy, and implementation.

Maori Education:
An Update (New Zealand 1991–98)
—*Robert O'Brien*

The outcomes of the education of the indigenous people of Aotearoa-New Zealand continue to be an issue facing teacher educators and others in that country. It seems appropriate that I review again the opportunities and contradictions that now exist for Maori, unquestionably a society at risk.

Mereana Selby, a teacher educator who has been closely associated with the establishment and development of such a community-derived Maori educational entity, shared with me her experiences and opinions during November 1998. Mereana believed that she could only report on education within the Ngati Raukawa area centred upon Otaki. Her overall message was one of hope that the efforts of her people were not going to be in vain. She spoke positively about many of the achievements of the Maori in education and the additional, community-wide benefits that had been derived in adult achievement. She noted that the five kohanga reo each had their own goals and delivery style and affirmed that the calibre of the teachers and the strength of parental commitment and support were the defining factors in the outcomes of these early childhood centres. It seems that the prototype teacher training programme that was set up in the early 1990s was not replicated, so the concept of a national scheme has not been developed further. In Otaki the demand for early childhood education in Maori continues to expand, helped in no small way by the flourishing presence of Te Wananga o Raukawa and its students—some of whom are parents of young children. Finding of teachers is an ongoing problem but many in the community, proud and interested in what is happening, readily provide what support, skills, and knowledge they can to advance the goals of the institutions.

The reputation of kura kaupapa in the area has steadily grown over time. Despite the lack of teaching resources and a similar difficulty in recruiting qualified and able teachers, through the commitment and dedication of the leadership and the depth of community support, this facet of a distinctive Maori educational initiative has thrived around Otaki. Perhaps the clearest evidence of this development can be found in the fact that as the students reached adolescence and parents realised there was little prospect of the local high school being able to offer a continuation of Maori medium education, they decided to keep their children enrolled at whare kura in the hope that not only could the pupils' command of te reo be extended further but that an adequate secondary education could be achieved, too. This experiment continues with support from many volunteers from within the community as well, but, once again, the lack of suitable teaching resources presents a major obstacle in the development of fully autonomous adolescent learners in Maori.

The existence by 1998 of several curriculum statements in Maori, ostensibly for the promotion of a genuinely bicultural Aotearoa-New Zealand within education, has been acknowledged as a welcome development by Raukawa, but it is evident that until the full New Zealand Curriculum Framework Te Anga Marautanga o Aotearoa is agreed and implemented by a supply of trained, competent teachers (for both Maori and non-Maori education sectors) then there is a strong danger that too little will have been done, too late, for the education service to revitalise Maori language and culture. Raukawa does not lack people who are ready to take up the challenge, though, in spite of the widely acknowledged difficulties, for Mereana reports that without any significant publicity there has been no lack of recruits for the teacher training programmes now introduced by Te Wananga o Raukawa. The accreditation of teacher education programmes other than those originally created by the Education Department has given a wider section of the community access to training sites, and Maori educators have grasped this opportunity.

As Raukawa and other communities gave their energy to the consolidation of their successes in building an educational structure in their locality, the national scene was continuing to be wracked by the consequences of the economic and social policies of the government. The media kept supplying a stream of stories which generally reinforced the impression that within New Zealand there was an increasing disparity between the living standards of the most favoured and affluent and those of the less successful and the growing number of considerably disadvantaged citizens. Maori were an easily identified subset of the latter group.

In spite of the improving outcomes for Maori within the education sector in some geographic localities, many other groups were still expressing dissatisfaction by the time a new electoral system returned a coalition government at the end of 1996.

There is no denying that Maori experience poor educational outcomes, higher unemployment, lower income levels, lower rates of house ownership, and poorer health than non-Maori. However, up until now it has been difficult, if not impossible, to assess whether disparities are improving or getting worse. This is because of the variable quality of data collected on Maori outcomes and the ad hoc reporting of it. Overall, the evidence does not provide assurance that the economic and social gaps between Maori and non-Maori are closing. Of greater concern is that the statistics do not provide any signal that there is an impending change in the situation.

Even before he had read these findings, another former colleague, Jim MacGregor, had drawn on his experience as teacher, secondary school principal, one of the founders of Te Wananga o Raukawa, and 30-year advocacy for improvements in the education of Maori children to tell me that he now believes that significant structural change has to be tried. The successive plans for Maori education have been saying the same things for more than two decades. The introduction of nga kohanga reo, and so on, has come about because of Maori initiatives and often with little immediate encouragement (or appropriate funding) from government. Jim believes that as most Maori youngsters are still, and always will be, in the mainstream school system where it appears that they will never be accommodated equitably, then the promotion of self-governing institutions must be worth a try. The saving of the language may be a possibility, but will require remarkable and sustained effort. He makes the point that most present-day teenage Maori display many of the same attitudes as their forebears and that in spite of the taha Maori concept and the writing in of obligations under the Treaty of Waitangi in school charters, it is still only a small proportion of Maori youngsters who benefit from their participation in education. Jim is of the view that the widespread negative attitudes that had grown up about Maori society and culture have continued to prevail among an appreciable proportion of the pakeha population. Jim is sure that most Maori parents would like their children to learn te reo but that the kids often do not wish to do so. Jim thinks that this has a lot to do with the competence, teaching styles, and exam-oriented curriculum of the secondary school language teacher. Maori Studies has low status in students' minds when subject choices are considered. Jim cites with approval the "Tu Tangata" model of Parkway College and other schools that have set out to involve local Maori in the planning and delivery of language and cultural instruction. Thus, the views of Mereana Selby and Jim MacGregor are consistent with the most recent reports, and after talking with them and reading the documents, I have been reminded of what the mid-1980s curriculum review documents stated about the future of education in Aotearoa-New Zealand. For Maori the August 1998 publication must make bleak reading, but the upward trend does provide Mereana and Jim with justification for their optimism and their determination to continue working for the cause that the future of their people seems dependent upon.

References

Annual Report. (1978). Wellington, New Zealand: Department of Education.

Lange, D. (1989). *Tomorrow's schools: The reform of education administration.* Wellington, NZ: Government Printer.

The curriculum review (1988). Report of the committee to revise the curriculum for schools. Wellington, NZ: Department of Education.

New Voices, Second language learning and teaching: A handbook for teachers (1988). Wellington, NZ: Department of Education.

Options for Dialogue

- Discuss again the notes you took while you were reading the article about New Zealand. How did those situations remind you of situations closer to home?
- Which philosophies about learning and life expressed by other writers in this book seem to be reflected in O'Brien's work?

• Bob O'Brien often reminds us that political events in one country have dramatic influences on education in another country. In a discussion about how the education policies in New Zealand have been recently affected by the politics in the United States of America, he said:

The political climate has to be understood if one is to grasp why education systems unfold in the way they do. As I see it, much of the potential for "good" developments in education was lost in the Reaganist takeover of the previous Labour government—particularly after it was reelected in 1987. The major reforms in administration, curriculum, qualifications, and structure which were formalised by 1989 legislation were then distorted and made more controversial when the National Party came to office in 1990 and was in turn dominated by Chicago School monetarist ideology.

What do you think about this opinion? Have you heard other educators or historians make a connection between politics and educational policy? What was said?

Options for Action

• Investigate a minimum of two knowledgeable sources about American Indian Treaty Rights or Immigration Policy for refugees and immigrants in the United States in the past 50 years. Report to your class your findings.
• Obtain permission to visit a history or government class in a middle school or high school. Note ways the teacher assists the students in making personal connections to historical events.
• Investigate the history of education in Australia. How are the situations and events similar to and different from those in New Zealand? Write a comparative essay.

Neil Shepard, Poet and Teacher

Options for Listening

• Briefly write in your journals a few thoughts from the previous essay by Dr. Bob O'Brien which impressed you. What did you learn about the history of New Zealand and the indige-

nous people of that island and the neighboring islands? What did you learn about the relationship of New Zealanders to Britain? What about the educational and other social policies that relate to this history?
- Read the poem about the South Pacific by Neil Shepard.

Following in the Footsteps of Melville
—Neil Shepard

Mostly, he sat on his fat ass
and spun a seafaring yarn
while Fayaway wove white tappa,

Kori-Kori fetched his pipe
and together they taught him
the ancient names of things.

These days, the Marquesans have a name
for men like him: haoie tivava
(white liars). Those who steal
a song, a story from the heart
of things, who leave little in return.
And I'm another. I claim good company:

Melville, Gauguin, Stevenson,
London, Brel, Brookes, and a hundred
more rovers from Suggs to Theroux.

I teach English in the mornings,
write their lives into poems all afternoon,
and learn their songs by evening.

I have a wife, thus no Fayaway.
I own no pipe. I even help
two old ones—two Typee, as Melville

used to say—roll their own smokes,
two dozer men razing old
tohua stones to raise a church—

both drunk on sabbath morning,
as is the custom after custom
has been washed away—not by booze

but by waves of haoies—after
ancient memory has dried up
and mind is a parched landscape.

Then the thirst comes on. Haoies!
Yells one dozer man when he sees
us. Tivava! When he learns

my wife's an anthropologist,
professional apologist
for haoie's sins. You're here to steal

what's left of our memory.
You'll write a book. Make money,
Make money. That's all a haoie

knows. Some of us still know
the ancient tongue—he slurs
through a beer haze. Some still know

the fathers of fathers of fathers
who knew that liar, Melville.
He called us lazy, but where

did our plenty come from?
Only in dreams does everything
grow on trees. He mocked our tongue,

but gibberish is wax
in a conqueror's ears.
Savages, he called us. Who savaged

our lands, our memories?
Who came bearing gifts and syphilis,
doctors and smallpox, missions

and omissions such as
the general provisions of
paradise and hell. Now we

know it well: Make money, make
money. That's all a haoie knows.
Now jungles swallow our tohua stones,

old dance sites and prayer pits.
We're left with absence, silence.
Our lives turned to profit, to live

forever in your books or in
the vacuum-weather of museums.
Make money, Make money.

That's all a haoie knows.

   Note: The Marquesas, a group of six inhabited islands in the South
Pacific form a remote part of French Polynesia. Their language is one of
several Polynesian languages including Hawaiian, Tahitian, and Maori.
Tohua, stone sites elevated above the tropical growth were used by the
ancient Marquesan culture as sites for their social gatherings, dances, and
religious ceremonies.

Options for Dialogue

- In small groups discuss the issues addressed by the poem.
  How do the issues relate to previous information given by
  Dr. Bob O'Brien?
- Discuss your own thoughts about the terms "colonization,"
  "cultural memories," "professional anthropologist."
- Now discuss what you know about colonization and apartheid in South Africa. What brought about the end of apartheid there? Can you name any ways you think the schools in
  that country may be affected by the years of apartheid and
  now by the difficulties that any change of government
  brings?

Options for Action

- Design a project for yourself to use some of your new information and to learn more about an issue you have questions
  about from this chapter.

Carol Masters, Peace Activist and Author

Options for Listening

- Have you ever felt your human rights were violated? Or at the very least, can you remember a time when you were discriminated against and not listened to? Write about one of these situations.
- Brainstorm a list of facts and/or opinions you have heard or learned about over the past few years about the political situations in Central and South American countries. Write down the bits and pieces of information you can remember.
- Carol Masters's story focuses on issues surrounding the United States involvement in Central American conflicts in the late 1980s and early 1990s. In order for you to see that the issues remain of current concern, the following information was gleaned from various newspaper and news media reports in late November 1999.

On November 19–21, 1999 the School of the Americas Watch (SOA Watch) conducted its annual protest at Fort Benning, Georgia, to close the United States Army School of the Americas (USARSA). The United States Army School of the Americas, based in Fort Benning, Georgia, trains Latin American soldiers in combat, counterinsurgency, and counternarcotics. Graduates of the SOA have been responsible for some of the worst human rights abuses in Latin America. Among the SOA's nearly 60,000 graduates are notorious dictators Manuel Noriega and Omar Torrijos of Panama, Leopoldo Galtieri and Roberto Viola of Argentina, Juan Velasco Alvarado of Peru, Guillermo Rodriguez from Ecuador, and Hugo Banzer Suarez of Bolivia.

At Ft. Benning military base on Sunday, November 21, 1999, 4,408 people from around the country risked arrest by crossing the Ft. Benning property line. The Army processed and served "bar and ban" notices to only 65 individuals, most of whom were among the group that led the procession onto the base wearing black mourning shrouds and "death masks" and bearing coffins. Once on the base, they smeared red paint on themselves and lay next to the coffins. The majority of the line crossers were seized and taken in buses to a public park approximately two miles away from the base.

"We will keep coming back in greater numbers until the school is shut down," said SOA Watch founder and co-director Father Roy

Bourgeois. The year 2000 will mark the tenth year that SOA Watch will organize a mass vigil at Ft. Benning (http://www.soaw.org/Articles/99Nov23pr.htm).

• Read the story. Note information that is new to you.

Count Time
—*Carol Masters*

Count time, that time of day twice a day when Seal and the rest of the Hennepin County Women's Section are good girls sitting in their cells waiting to be counted. Why? she wonders, twice a day. It is unlikely anyone will be mislaid.

She consults her wrist. No watch. They've taken her watch. But it is April 16, 1990, and it must be near 7 AM of her first real jail sentence. The internal clock that ticks Seal through the day wakes her even here, a sun under her breastbone rising at five. On the whole, she is proud of herself. The first time she'd been arrested for protesting, the arrest was an accident, she tripped. Klutz of the Western World, her ex-husband Evans called her.

But it was no accident this time. She won't name her accomplices and she will not pay restitution. Why not? She could pay her fine, fly out of jail as she'd flown out of marriage, couldn't she? First there would be a hearing—her unnamed accomplices, her friend Branch and her nephew Jacob, would come. Surely the court wouldn't do anything to little Jacob. Surely, they were supposed to behave in a Christian way, isn't that so? Her chest tightens with fear. So naive, no analysis, Evans would say. Yes, Mom would say, but she is not to endanger the little ones, like Jacob; she is fitting herself for a millstone. What if Seal explained the School of the Americas to her family, as she tried to do to the judge, before he started banging his hammer? Look, she said, the task force reported that men trained right there at Our School in Georgia killed the six Jesuits AND their housekeeper AND her daughter. Seal wanted to be sure the judge knew about the women.

She sits on the floor, cool bile-green tiles in a meditation position. Count time, time to put her historical ducks in a row.

. . .

When she is eight years old, what pulls her from her sweet bed, and she takes her sweet time, is the thought of Sunday comics, their stained glass colors with the Sunday morning light behind them. Sunday School is important, but less so; the colors of Sunday are what call her. Mom takes them in tow, Seal holding the boys' hands crossing 93rd Street, to see the

Sunday school movie *The Life of Jesus* in the church basement. The movie is black and white, but Jesus is lively. She remembers dark eyes, dirt and tears. "When is he going to be crucified?" Seal asks.

Behind St. Luke's movie screen hangs a three-by-five-foot colored print of Jesus, interested if not passionate, knocking at an old wooden door, his pale hand closed in a tentative fist. Her mom puts her arm around Seal so she has to sit still. If she weren't such a big girl, Seal would lean against her, curling into her mom's powdery hot smell. Emeraude. It means green. In the picture, flowers are tucked into a green shade over a fairy-tale cottage door. A Brothers Grimm fairy tale, Seal thinks now, darkness behind that cottage door, some secret festering that could use a good savior to shake and air it out.

Fairy tales, both Evans and Branch called religion fairy tales. Dark ones, priests get killed.

. . .

Not since childhood has Seal been so bored. She supposes, in an average sort of life, one marriage, one divorce, and a not-exactly career, she should be thankful for that. Jail should not be that difficult. She must take stock, know it so her spirit isn't gagging with the effort to reject it. Straight ahead are mustard-colored tile walls, a gritty color, a hint of horseradish color, maybe dirty. She rubs her finger across the tile, leaving a faint shiny trail over a film that, if she peers more closely, is a streaked landscape, whorls and sweeps of scrubbing from its last wash. Sniffing at the wall, she can detect vinegar. That explains some of the smell: the rest of it is cigarette smoke. Ash and vinegar. Her hair reeks of it, from the pillow. She can't leave the smell behind; wherever she goes, down the hall to the common room, across the hall to the lavatory, it rubs against her ears, its tail brushing her nose like an annoying cat.

Soon it will be time for breakfast. Outside, sounds pour into the trees, chuckles and mutterings interspersed with whistles, piercing creaks. Starlings, she decides: morning meeting. Sparrows come afternoons, about the time children are released from the school down the road and orange buses roar past. All these gatherings, communities of sound, Seal can't see. But it's not so bad to be able to listen, to count time from that.

If you'd only listen, Cecelia! Evans said. She has to pay attention to the rules. What if some judge orders never to visit bad-example aunts? Can they do that? Her experience with judges leads her to believe they can do anything they want to. Seal nods emphatically to the blank metal door. She won't mention Jacob. She doesn't want to be taken off the approved list. She'll quit this shit, she won't say that, though it's apropos. No more crossing the line. She'll tell the intake worker, right after breakfast.

. . .

"Mrs. Milner." The blonde seated behind a bare oak desk nods at Seal's outstretched hand but keeps hers attached to a clipboard that she slides toward Seal. "Please sit down, this won't take long. Fill out the top half, you're not obligated to answer the questions 4, 5, and 6 due to privacy regulations but you may do so if you wish. You are encouraged to *briefly* assist us with your answers so that our assessment can be of maximum benefit, sign where I've marked with an X to indicate your agreement that no undue persuasion, influence, or coercion was exercised."

Seal sits, her hands retreating to the company of each other, folded in her lap like good hands. Quickly scanning the top half of the intake form she sees only questions about gender, race, ethnic identity, and age; it doesn't seem like sensitive material.

"I'm forty-five," she says. "No pen." The worker takes the clipboard back, clicks her ball-point into place, checks boxes briskly, then slides the form and pen to Seal for her signature. Seeing more interesting questions at the bottom having to do with psychological profile, Seal poises her pen at the first question. Resident's "affect," state of mind on intake. Do they mean effect? and on what? She doubts her trespasses had any real effect on anyone, but who knows? The street cleaners probably cleaned up the mess, but maybe the Senator caught a whiff.

"That's not for you, please," Blondie says, "I'll fill it in. You just need to sign the release."

Seal blinks, looking for a hint of humor behind the prim wire-rimmed circles.

"Don't you have to ask me some questions, Ms . . . sorry, I don't know your name?"

The counselor sighs, consulting her Daytimer notebook. Seal can just make out tiny notes numbered 1 through 5 under the heading Milner in a neat, squared calligraphy. "It's helpful. This is what we have from the court: Divorced, parents not listed, nephew as next of kin but he's apparently a minor, this won't work. You want to fill me in?"

Seal doesn't remember implicating Jacob. Yes, she reflects, they asked her some few questions downtown, behind the courtroom where the bailiff took her, the judge still pounding his gavel, yes they did that just like the movies, the noise throbbing in her ears still, regular, insistent, interruptive, El Salvador has nothing, nothing to do with the reason she is before this court! No more, this was it, this was jail, and they took away her shoe laces. Seal leans forward, intent on the bridge of the caseworker's nose. A point of intense pain, Evans told her. "Did they tell you about why I'm here? About El Salvador?" She must be made to understand.

Frowning at her notebook as though it were to blame for this omission of information, Ms. Larson says, "I'm sorry. . ."

Seal almost says, 'I'm not,' but can't.

"We *want* to have an idea," Ms. Larson amended, "what's going on with our longer-term residents. We have no interest in keeping you here longer than necessary."

Longer term? She can't help it, Seal's palms itch, beginning to sweat.

When Seal doesn't answer, Ms. Larson puts her notebook down and folds her own hands on the desk. "This concerns me, Cecelia. You know an indeterminate sentence is unusual in this facility."

"How would I know that?" The judge wanted her to do restitution; why? Seal asks, but loses her place in the staredown. Ms. Larson snaps Seal's form into the clipboard, slips her pen tidily into its Daytimer sheath and holds the office door open. Not until she is back in her cell does Seal burst into tears.

. . .

She didn't want to do political work—for a long time, she hadn't realized it was political. She just wanted to help. Evans wrote at times. Why, he asked her, do you want to work at second-class jobs? Do you think what you do makes a difference? She tore up the letter but not the check that came with it. She considered it Evan's contribution to the cause.

But the world's burning, judge. Radiation ticks away at our bones, the ax is laid to the trees, as your Bible says. You've got to do *more* than pay attention, judge. Land mines are sown into a hundred lands like salt, even Central America. Branch showed her a picture once of a nine-year old Salvadoran who'd stepped on a mine, she couldn't tell what color he was, for all the red. No U.S. paper would carry it, Branch said, and there was a reason.

"Did he live?" she asked Branch, feeling foolish.

"She. No."

Is Seal responsible for that? What can she do?

. . .

The guard leads her to the phone in Ms. Larson's office and stands outside; she can see his shoulders and head shadowed against the frosted glass. Her sister is on the phone, long distance, so she is taken from breakfast to the small office.

"Oh, Sissy! I didn't tell them anything! My God, they must have your phone number, O God, I don't know, did they get my address book, how did you find me? Is he all right? Is Jacob all right?"

"Branch told us, of course. Don't be so paranoid, are you getting paranoid?" Sissy sounds more worried about Seal's state of mind than her own boy.

"Is he okay? No, I'm not, I just, you know, didn't want him involved, only he insisted . . . I'm sorry, baby, but you'd be so proud of him."

"You're not making sense, Sealie, slow down."

"I'm sorry, of course." Jacob is okay, Seal thinks, feeling rescued.

. . .

Evans tried to rescue *her*, didn't he, the first time Seal was arrested. He came up from Texas to do it and then get divorced. He appeared, right there in the first jail, December 9, 1983.

How had he known? It was her first arrest, at the Sperry missile plant, and it was by accident. She'd decided to stand there only as long as it took to rebuild a snowfort after Sperry Security bulldozed the women's camp. It was the day that Sperry Pershing missiles were sent to England, and Seal's group had set up a winter tent and a teepee on the war plant's property. The police showed up just as she decided to slip away. She slipped instead into a snowbank.

She hadn't been booked an hour when a female guard unlocked the holding cell. She had been on the point of peeling off her jeans and woolen underwear. Though the cell itself was hot and fusty, she was soaked to the skivvies, shivering. She stood, beginning to follow the guard, who motioned toward Seal's purse and shoes. "Take everything. Your husband made bail."

"My what?" She panicked, looked around for a mirror, ran fluffing fingers through the hair plastered to her skull, awkwardly; she was still handcuffed. "Don't sweat it, honey. He don't care what you look like. Way he talks."

What was the woman saying? She trudged behind the guard, shoelaces untied, shoes squinching and piddling dirty water down the hallway. Then the guard pressed a buzzer, took her elbow, and pushed her through a steel security door into the booking room. With his back to her, a man leaned over the counter on her side, writing. He wore a black leather topcoat that looked as supple as an animal, a large animal, swimming, its pelt slick, catching the light. Evans.

Ten years, of course he'd changed. His face was grim, sour at the moment, but she sensed his anger wasn't at her. He was thinner and more tan than he'd ever been in Texas. He'd lost his youthful plumpness but not the glossy assurance of privilege.

Evans walked to her and took her hands. She was afraid he was going to raise them to his lips, some silly courtly gesture, but he pulled her over to the counter, and laid them on it like an offering. He glared at the officers behind the counter. She'd forgotten there were other people in the room, lots of them, men in blue or white shirts, with ties beside the badges. It was an ordinary office, guys at desks stared morosely at screens, or pecked, or muttered into phones.

A tall gray-haired officer sauntered over, leaned on the counter with both hands straddling Seal's, but he talked to Evans, not to her.

"Okay, Mr. Milner. You want, we can leave them on." He was making a joke, between the guys.

"That won't be necessary."

The cop nodded, took a pair of clippers from a pocket and, with an easy motion born of long practice, snipped the strap that bound Seal's wrists. He held out the white plastic strip and gave another, uncut, to Evans for a souvenir.

. . .

Evans drove her to the apartment, 2B of a fourplex on Portland. What could she do? Her car was back at the peace camp, and his was a rented late-model Volvo that smelled of new leather and vanilla. She felt the heat blowing on her legs, beginning to dry her jeans, then, unaccountably, seeping into her thighs and bottom. It was gradual, so it was a few minutes before she glanced suspiciously at him.

His eyes stayed forward, his long-fingered hands steady on the wheel, nudging the big car into freeway curves as though he'd driven here every night of his life. She saw the upward curve of his lip under the mustache. "It's a heater in the seat bottom," he said. "Nice feature. I drove one of these in Panama, government courtesy, hardly necessary there, but it's a boon in frozen Minnesota, don't you agree?"

Panama? She turned her head back toward the window, flushing, watching the freeway lights swim by, then the darkness of the Mississippi, black but ice-rimmed, beginning to close.

Evans claimed he'd intended to visit before. Now he was in town for a conference at the university. At least they were on the same side again, the side of peace. Or so he claimed. His mother's foundation used the family influence with the chair of the Bipartisan Peace Commission, who it was said had the president's ear. The Milners were key cultural players in the Texas political world, and forged links aesthetic and political with the leaders of the free societies to the south. Wives of junta leaders had visited the Milner room at Big Bayou, had facilitated the fine Bayou collection of indigenous artifacts. An archbishop and two commanders had dined together at the Milners' home. If such personages knew of Seal's existence, Evans didn't mention it.

"What do you think you're doing, Seal? Snowforts, women's peace campouts! Who's the bad guy this time? You're no militant."

Evans didn't have the foggiest idea about her. Mulishly, she seized on the word. "No. Militarism is what's wrong with our society. Language is important, Ev. I should think you'd know that? What are *you* doing in Panama?"

He wouldn't be sidetracked. "Militant. Not military. Nothing's wrong with the word. Forceful. Vigilant. Use the weapons you have."

"Nonviolently, of course." She shifted on the seat, pulling at her jeans' wet patches, trying to dry a few more inches.

His gloved hand smacked the steering wheel, a crack of expensive leather on leather, though he did it without jerking the wheel and the heavy machine hardly shuddered. "Don't be foolish. That's a death philosophy. They want you to be nonviolent, it's easier to maintain control. I was helping Mother," he added, answering her earlier question. "Some loose ends; the school will be moving next year. We needed to move the art."

"I don't get involved in politics," she told him. "I knew about the Euromissiles, and friends of mine were demonstrating." She couldn't stop herself; she wanted approbation. "I went to the Peace Camp to bring them a loaf of bread and tonight just *happened* to be the night Sperry bulldozed it."

"Bad luck, that. Didn't anybody have a bread knife?"

"Jesus, Evans!" Her startled laugh only made her angrier. She was too tired to be a willing target. "Faulty antecedent," she said, and clammed up. So did he, except for whistling between his teeth "Two Good Men," a song that used to make her cry.

. . .

Seal's head aches. There are too many characters populating this jail. She supposes it's nice to have the company, but she wishes they'd get on with it. She wishes she'd told Branch all about Evans before now. He has to understand. On the phone, Branch said she has to hold on until he can drive back, he says she has to leave that place, but she can't, why doesn't he understand? "Branch, the guard's going to be back, I can't talk any more. You hear me?"

"I'm here. What did Evans *do* to you? Beside mess with your head."

"Nothing. It doesn't matter. I learned, that's all."

. . .

It is to Evan's credit that she learned more about Central America, though that probably was not his intention. He taught her that she *needed* to know about it. Evans had visited the army's School of the Americas in Panama and later in 1984, it was moved to Fort Benning, Georgia. Evans helped, in a small way. Evans said the president himself wanted to do everything he could to help the freedom fighters, and that would bring peace. Now she knows that it was all a crock, but she didn't know in 1983.

In 1983, she was shaking with cold and Evans helped her draw a bath. He even lit a candle for her as she eased into the heat, then left her alone. After a long soak, she heard him messing with her kitchen cupboards, rattling paper, clanking a pot onto the gas range! Irked, she pulled the plug and hauled herself out of the now tepid water. The fat candle had shrunk, eating into its wax-pooled interior, but the flame was steadier, shadows peacefully breathing, the world briefly rosier. Seal herself was rosy, steaming from her bath, as she noted, pleased.

Then she swore. No clothes. Terry bathrobe on its hook in the bedroom closet, how inconveniently tidy of her. She was not going to wrap herself in a towel, her towels were less than sumptuous and wouldn't meet. She would be adult about this: she would ask Evans to bring her the robe, please. A timid knock interrupted her plan, and the door inched open.

"Wait," she was going to say, when the robe itself appeared, to her relief, like some wraith needing a body, dangling at the end of Evans' bare arm. But it wasn't her robe, it was something silky. It wouldn't absorb the water, she thought, somewhat disoriented, it would stick to her damp skin. Which it did. They sat on her bed a long while, just to talk, while she dried. Take a chance, he said, be on my side, you never used to worry about picking sides.

Evans' body was so slender; it wasn't fair. He'd grown healthy and thin, she'd aged and sagged. They discussed his body, along with political matters. "Do you work out or something?" She traced his biceps, the line of his muscle as they lay, arranging his arm as she traced down the forearm to the inside of his wrist, arranging it on her hip. She marked the shift of tendons when he closed his hand.

He was busy, he told her, transporting materials, speaking to groups from Texas to Georgia.

"Women?"

He shrugged, seemed irritated. "Not serious ones. Tell me what you're doing. You never answer my letters."

"Come on, Evans. You've written five." She flushed. Five in the last five years, since she'd stopped writing him.

"And you kept them."

"No," she lied.

"Look at this, Seal, I never noticed what your skin does when you tell a fib." His fingers traced the blush spreading between her breasts, and down.

.   .   .

Branch is speaking sharply to her. She can't bear it. She never could bear loud angry voices, scoldings were enough to make her cry. Evans never raised his voice, he mocked her but he didn't shout. She should hang up.

She didn't let him do it. Evans was still her husband, but she didn't let him. She kicked until he had to release her. She didn't care who heard, her landlord, the guys upstairs. The smoke from his breath drove her crazy, her sinuses now swell with it. Everybody smokes in jail, her nose runs constantly. That's what makes the film on the walls, too, though the good little girls scrub with vinegar, leaving a film of whirls and scallops like frost on windowpanes, like hills of snowy landscapes in winter, a country that never was, so clean. She is whispering now, because someone opened the door to see what the noise was, but her voice sounds grainy to her from the stifled cries. She must calm down, she's been hysterical.

"Is that why you never told me?" Branch asks, softly. "You know what the school is for, what it's still for?"

"I know now." Fort Benning, School of the Americas, school for the favored factions, where the training manuals are carefully translated, words precise as cut glass, techniques of pain so meticulously described that there may be no mistake.

Now Branch is gentle again. "His letters, Seal, did he say anything about the school in them?"

"No. I didn't know, I didn't care to know anything about him. He was small potatoes, I think. Just some art things, and the moving, small things." Is Branch crying too? "He stopped, though, Branch! He did it just a little, for the government, to help, but he stopped!"

Evans had nothing to do with the school after 1984. He couldn't have known its graduates would be responsible for killing priests, for massacres in Nicaragua, El Salvador, Columbia. He probably never knew, none of them knew then.

. . .

Evans wasn't the reason for their actions yesterday—hers and Branch's and Jacob's.

Yesterday, the crowds were moved back by the cops in riot gear, as though the scene was set for Hollywood stars to walk, casually, up the middle of Fourth Street, to the front of the Federal Building. No one stopped her. Seal wore an orange highway worker's coverall and a gym whistle. She carried three traffic cones and a shovel.

She blew a shrill blast on her whistle, summoning Branch's truck parked at the end of the block. It was a lovely truck, borrowed from the farm workers' association who asked only that their logo be covered for the day. Branch had taken care of that, creating a new laminated sign in silver, neatly bordered and fastened with duct tape. Its back-up warning beeps chirping officially down the long curb, the truck eased into position. Branch halted, kicked the hydraulic lift on, and Branch and Jacob jumped out. No one moved to question them.

The gate of the dumper swung open as the front end began to rise, an approach quiet and inevitable as the first dawn of the world. Too slow, Seal thought at first, but as soon as that massive pile shifted almost imperceptibly, things happened fast. The first mass of fertilizer whumped to the concrete. Seal and Jacob attacked it, spreading. Jacob's pitchfork worked best, grabbing, adhering to clumps, tossing smelly gobbets toward the doors. Branch heaved and sweated beside Seal until the truck was empty, then he roared off with Jacob according to plan. Only then did the police move in, light dawning that B & S Landscaping were part of the protest.

Seal could have escaped with Branch and Jacob, but as the cops closed in, she took the flat side of the shovel to swirl and smooth a broad swathe of the manure. Then she upended the shovel and, guiding the handle tip through her malodorous medium, she began to write.

. . .

She stopped Evans's hand, but held it where it was. "You want to talk, or not?"

He groaned. "Yep. I have a proposal. I have an ulterior motive for compromising you."

"Sorry, Ev." She sat up. "You can't. I'm already compromised."

"Not yet you aren't. Not thoroughly."

Evans claimed Seal had taught him to act directly, from his heart, without worrying what people would think. Impossible, she never did that. "No Evans, I worry all the time! With you, I just learned who I'm not! Not a wife, a lady. . . ."

He distracted her, she lost her point; he said he learned, too, he was sorry so much was lost in the process. "Your fingers are lost," he said. "Here, let me help you."

His face came down close, almost blocking her vision of his left hand sliding her wrist back toward the bedpost, where the small souvenir handcuff glinted. His smoky breath warmed her lips, his words almost inaudible: "My little *Contra . . .*"

. . .

Branch shouts at her. Branch won't listen, he thinks she's stir-crazy, but she's all right, she was all right then, too. She stopped Evans. He couldn't hold her, not even with a handcuff.

Had she been given the time yesterday, before they arrested her, to write all she wanted in that shit, the dirt would have revealed a lot of her heart's politics: Names. Branch, Mom, Jacob, Evans, her own. Her love would need no translation.

Options for Dialogue

- Please discuss: what were the things about being in jail that most bothered Seal? Would you have been bothered by those same issues and inconveniences?
- Please discuss the choice of conscience and its consequences made by Seal to stand up for her beliefs in this way. Do you admire the character or question her decision? Why?
- What do you do that is conviction-based?
- Look back at the story and together trace the small bits and

pieces of information that you see mentioned as contributing to Seal's convictions. What did Seal learn from these experiences and what evidence do you see of her growth?

- Compare Seal's experience with the jail experience Marv Davidov describes at the beginning of Chapter 9 of this book. What are the similarities and differences?

Options for Action

- Go to a library or research using electronic data bases and find journal articles and newspaper articles about alleged violations of human rights. Read a minimum of two articles about the same country and compare and contrast the information. Report to your class.
- Go to the Website *<http://www.soaw.org>* and read about School of the Americas Watch. Now go to the official Website for the school, *<http://www.benning.army.mil/usarsa/index.html>*. Compare and contrast this information and report to your class.
- View the video documentary, *Voices from Inside* [videorecording], produced & directed by Karina Epperlein (Publication info: Hohokus, NJ : New Day Films, ©1996).

    Abstract: *Voices from Inside* follows German-born theater artist Karina Epperlein into a federal women's prison where she began teaching weekly classes as a volunteer in 1992. Her racially mixed group of women prisoners becomes a circle of trust and healing. Epperlein also talks to the children of the women.
- Go to the Website *<http://www.americas.org>* and investigate all that the Resource Center of the Americas has to offer in terms of informing, educating, and organizing for human rights, democracy and justice. Tell your class what you like most about the site and the information.
- Go to the Website *<http://www.nonviolence.org/wri>* and learn from the War Resisters League where your income tax money really goes. Report to your class.
- Write to Women Against Military Madness (W.A.M.M.) at 310 East 38th Street, Suite 225, Minneapolis, MN 55409; or email at wamm@mtn.org and ask for information about the organization and its activities. Report to your class.

John S. Mayher, Teacher Educator, Author, and Researcher

Options for Listening

- Do you remember how you learned to read? Describe in writing your first memory of reading. Did someone read to you? Do you remember recognizing words, letters? Was it in school? At home?

- In a small group, share your memories and listen to see if anyone mentions philosophies about learning. In your sharing and listening please address the following: Compare and contrast your experiences. What did the experiences of your group members have in common? How were they different? From considering the experiences of your group members could you say there is only one way to learn to read? Why or why not?

- Read the essays by John Mayher. What philosophy/philosophies of learning underlie his beliefs about literacy instruction?

Political Action Now: Do We Dare?

—*John S. Mayher*

These are unsettling times—for research and researchers. Some of us who sit in our concrete towers (literacy researchers never merited ivory) survey the classrooms of the land and find, mostly, that things are as they have always been: teacher-centered (Cuban, 1993), monologic (Nystrand et al., 1997), test obsessed, and filled with skills and drills. Others take a somewhat more optimistic view and see the impact of whole language, writing process, literature circles, and other progressive methodologies actually happening in various places in ways that their originators might recognize and endorse (Pearson, 1997).

But the politicians of the land see the world very differently. (In my original draft, I typed ploticians, perhaps a more accurate label.) From one side comes the cry of national (and higher) standards, from another: beware of the federal monolith controlling your children. And, most strangely of all, come the efforts to legislate a single approach to the teaching of beginning reading. And, most ironic of all, the same people who are sponsoring the bill are opposing the federal role in standards! This act, called, with no hint of irony, the Reading Excellence Act, is designed to control reading instruction and reading research. (The latter is particularly insidious, since it is designed to restrict the kinds of research which are "scientific" and therefore can be used as self-fulfilling evidence to support the instructional program. As Allington and Woodside-Jiron (1998) have pointed out, the "30 Years of Research" paper by Bonnie Grossen (1997) which lurks at the bottom of much of this is virtually identical to the rationale for a proposed commercial reading text series (Grossen, n.d.).

The need for the single systematic, out-of-context phonics approach is supposedly justified by the findings of review of the research on reading which purports to show that "about 40% of the population have reading problems severe enough to hinder their enjoyment of reading" (Grossen, 1997, p. 4). What is scary here is that because this review is apparently sponsored by the National Institute of Child Health Development, it has taken on a prestige that has enabled it to pass into the popular press as fact. Thus Brent Staples is able to write in the *New York Times* (1998).

> Conventional wisdom has it that human beings are neurologically wired to read and learn to do it automatically. But an ongoing, comprehensive study by the National Institutes of Health is telling a far different story. Begun in the 1960s; the National Institute of Health study shows that 4 in 10 children have trouble learning to read. About half of these children have such grave difficulty that they fall behind early in school and stay behind. (Grossen, 1997)

Staples is reporting the claims accurately; however, Allington and Woodside-Jiron (1998) have critiqued in detail what the NICHD "review" actually does and found that the claims themselves are nowhere supported by the data cited in the studies "reviewed." At best, the 4 out of 10 figure derives from a population who have already been identified as being at risk for reading failure, so what is surprising is not that so many from this "troubled" population have trouble but that so many do not. And, notice also the NICHD review has become an "NIH study" and Staples, like the review, then goes on to bash whole language instruction for "jettison[ing] the drill and practice component that 40 percent of American children need to learn reading" (p. 65).

Leaving aside the merits or demerits of the review on which these claims are based and the distortions of whole language contained in the review and subsequently in Staples's article, one fascinating thing is that the approach "needed" by 4 of 10 children is now going to be foisted on 10 of 10 by law. Now I'm an uncommon sense/whole language guy myself, but no one I know ever proposed either that an uncommon sense approach should be legislated as the ONLY way or even that it couldn't and didn't include as much instruction in sound-letter correspondences (phonics) as children seemed to need. Our view was child centered and learning centered.

That may indeed be the trouble, but even more likely it stems from what James Moffett observed 30 years ago and wrote about in *Storm in the Mountains* (1988), when he wondered why a method of beginning reading teaching had gotten tied up with politics. His conclusion: the culprit is meaning and its radical indeterminacy. The phonics advocates had correctly ascertained that by focusing on meaning and, especially, on the transaction between reader and text as a meaning making process (Rosenblatt, 1978), meaning-based approaches to reading had loosened the text from its determinate moorings, and no longer could anyone go unchallenged when they said: THIS is what it means. And even deeper still, Moffett recognized that parents were worried about losing control and authority over their children.

Could this still be the issue? Under the smokescreen of handwringing about reading failure and declining test scores, could people really be trying to bring back meaning control? Given the other stances of many of those who are advocating these laws, it seems like the storm in the mountains is spreading across the land but deriving from many of the same sources: the fundamentalist churches, their right-wing political allies, and their fellow travelers in the education marketplace. They dearly want monopoly control here, or they would be willing to let their ideas be tested in the educational marketplace.

It is, of course, a losing battle; the genie of meaning soon escapes even from the bottle of phonics, but while it is being tried, what will be the continued cost for America's children who in fact have been drilling and skilling far too much even in these days when whole language supposedly swept the land? The whole language approach certainly doesn't predominate most places I go in NYC or its suburbs.

But more important in this context is what are researchers and organizations of researchers to do? Do we stand idly by and say this too will pass; do we study it as a fascinating phenomenon?

I'd say: that won't cut it. We have to try to act.

We may not have much impact: educational professionals in these debates have come to be regarded by policy makers as "the blob." We are not cited in the NICHD review, and we have not been consulted by the Congress as it moves to pass the Excellence in Reading Act.

And our own internal disputes and disagreements, which we have viewed as a sign of health, cause even our potential allies to throw up their hands in despair about our effectiveness in communicating with people who really live in a soundbite world. We are loath to write papers with subtitles like "What we now know about how children learn to read."

The single answer, the single solution is very tempting in soundbiteland.

Can we compete? Can we get through? We are students of language and literacy. Can we use our knowledge to simplify as well as acknowledge complexity? To make the case for multiplicity of approaches? For meaning? For real excellence?

Hard to say, but the recent standards debacle suggests not. We certainly have not yet been effective. If we really lived in an ivory tower, I'd say okay, let the politicians act, we'll just observe and critique. As Kress (1995) has argued, however, that academic role will no longer suffice.

We can't abandon the children, nor can we abandon our colleagues who are teaching them in their fight to preserve their professional judgments. I'm pleased to say that during the time I was writing this paper, the NCRLL board voted to join the IRA, the NCTE, and NCRC in formal opposition to this legislation.

This is a start, but it is not the answer.

References

Allington, R., and Woodside-Jiron, H. (1998). Thirty years of research in reading. . . . When is a research summary not a research summary? In Goodman, K. (Ed.) *In defense of good teaching: What teachers need to know about the reading wars* (pp. 143–157). York, ME: Stenhouse.

Cuban, L. (1993).*How teachers taught 1890–1990* (2nd Ed.). New York: Teachers College Press.

Grossen, B. (1997). *30 years of reading research: What we now know about how children learn to read—a synthesis of research on reading from the National Institute of Child Health and Development.* Santa Cruz, CA: Center for the Future of Teaching and Learning. Available at <*www.cftl.org*>.

Grossen, B. (n.d.). *The research base for reading mastery-RA*. Eugene, OR: University of Oregon Press.

Kress, G. (1995). *Writing the future*. Urbana: NCTE.

Nystrand, M., et al. (1988). Opening dialogue in Moffett's *Storm in the mountains* (pp. 6–12). Carbondale, IL: Southern Illinois University Press.

Pearson, P. D. (1997, September). The politics of reading research and practice. NCTE *Council Chronicle.*

Rosenblatt, L. (1978). *The reader, the text, the poem*. Carbondale, IL: Southern Illinois University Press.

Staples, B. (1997). Special ed is no scandal. *New York Times Magazine*, September 21.

Research, Politics, and Mutual Respect

—*John S. Mayher*

When I wrote my fall "President's Message" (to the National Conference on Research in Language and Literacy) we were all in the throes of the debate on the "Reading Excellence Act" which was then under consideration by the House. In the ways of Washington, the bill was substantially modified before it was passed, and as of this writing (early March 1998), it has not yet been acted upon by the Senate. Lots of different agendas were and are in play in the bill, including those who do and don't want national testing, those who do and don't believe in the exclusive power of phonics as the way to teach reading, and those concerned with a thought police atmosphere which seems to be spreading eastward from California in the area of permitted approaches to teaching and teacher education in reading.

For those of you who haven't committed it to memory, I'll remind you that I expressed my concerns about these directions and urged researchers and teachers to take an active role in shaping the debate, in trying to get through to our elected officials, and in generally being willing to help stem the "phonics is the ONLY way" tide. And, indeed, I was happy to see that the NCTE Convention in Detroit saw a more active stance being taken than I've ever seen before from Sheridan Blau's Presidential Address (published in the February 1998 issue of Language Arts) to a variety of sessions discussing how to be active and referring frequently to the Allington and Woodside-Jiron (1997) critique of the NICHE research review (Grossen, 1997) that I had referred to in my "Message."

As has been usual in my experience of doing professional writing, I've gotten generally positive feedback both from my friends and from others who stopped me in the convention corridors or had reason to talk with me since the convention. But this feedback has not been unanimous, since I got a long and critical letter from Patrick Groff, the essence of which is included in this issue. While I was and am offended by his patronizing tone and implications that I must be a know-nothing, the issues he raises are sufficiently important to be worth a second look. I was not surprised by the substance of his pro-phonics position—I've seen that before over the years—but I continue to be surprised that the qualitative/quantitative debate was resurrected one more time in such pejorative tones.

I certainly know that there are lots of people around whose assumptions about knowledge and knowing and about the way we search for truth are rigidly fixed in a positivist paradigm. Indeed I think most of the nonacademic world is still so inclined, and this makes them comfortable with reports of research that stem from that paradigm. It was more surprising to me to find such a position being taken within our community, however, where I thought the last two decades of case study, qualitative, naturalistic and small number research had at least opened up the range of possibilities for acceptable research.

Further it still strikes me as irresponsible for what purports to be a review of research (Grossen, 1997) to ignore thousands of studies—books, dissertations, and monographs—simply because they didn't fit the experimental paradigm. Never has there been a clearer indication of what Thomas Kuhn was talking about when he said that researchers from different paradigms simply talk past each other and can find no common ground on which to meet.

To accuse me—or Groff—of being ideologues misses the point. Of course we have ideological positions, and indeed one of the major insights of research and theory of the last half of the twentieth century has been to explain why people read the world differently depending on their experience, social class, gender, and so on. But the point of research is to try to struggle with those biases and find ways to keep them within bounds so that we can understand better how the world works. It is not sufficient simply to assume, as Groff and Grossen seem to do, that experimental research has no such biases—and hence is scientific—while qualitative approaches do and therefore can't be scientific.

Sadly, this kind of name-calling and mutual incomprehension is not limited to language education researchers. While I was writing this, the winter issue of the *Review of Educational Research* featured a group of special educators insulting each other in very similar tones over exactly the same issue. But we can take no comfort in being similar in this area.

It seems to me high time we found a way to get beyond this. To learn mutual respect, to understand the standards of quality that various approaches have developed, and above all to stop calling each other names. The children of America deserve all of our insights into the reading and learning and teaching processes, and we shouldn't be satisfied with any single lens, however useful, as the sole way of looking. And if we ever expect to affect the political debates that are still raging around the country, we need to first find a way to put our own house in order.

Perhaps it's time for the professional organizations involved to confront this issue in sponsoring effective forums not for debate, but for conversation, not for confrontation, but for mutual exploration of the assumptions and standards we each hold dear. Not all research is useful in any paradigm, but it is not the paradigm itself that should be held responsible for poor research. So we need to do the hard work of philosophical analysis of each of our approaches to develop better paths to mutual comprehension. We won't deserve to be listened to by the public, by parents and by politicians if we can't even learn to listen to each other.

References

Allington, R., and Woodside-Jiron, H. (1997). *Thirty years of research in reading: When is a research summary not a research summary*. Albany: National Research Center on English Learning and Achievement.

Grossen, B. (1997). *30 years of reading research*. Santa Cruz, CA:

Center for the Future of Teaching and Learning. Available at <*www. cftl.org.*>

Options for Dialogue

- Please discuss in small groups: Why do you think the teaching of reading has become a political issue? What does John Mayher say is the deep reason for the controversy?
- David Pearson, preeminent reading researcher, states that "much of the current literacy crisis is manufactured. The question that must always be asked is: who benefits from the crisis?" Discuss your opinions about this.
- Who do you think benefits from the controversy around reading instruction? What conflicts are involved when researchers like Grossen, as described by Mahyer, are authors of and consultants for a very specific series of reading texts?
- Think of a metaphor that would describe a skills-based, phonics worksheet approach to teaching reading (skill and drill approach). Think of a metaphor that would describe an approach to reading pedagogy in which the goal is the creation of meaning by individual readers of the text. Discuss what philosophy of education would be most related to one perspective or the other.

Options for Action

- Interview a professor of literacy education at your college or interview an elementary teacher about her/his views on the most effective way to teach reading. What are the philosophical foundations of that view?
- Find another issue in which philosophical foundations and beliefs have been drawn into political debate. Ask the same questions: who benefits from one perspective or another? Who loses?
- Apply this process to the political climate of your college and university. What foundational beliefs support sides of an issue? What are your beliefs?
- Do further research on the controversy around the teaching of reading. Some sources are listed here. Share your findings with the class.

Paley, Vivian, G. (1995). *Kwanza and me.* Cambridge, MA, and London: Harvard University Press.

Martin, G. (1995). *Star teachers of children in poverty.* West Lafayette, IN: Kappa Delta Pi.

Paterson, F.R.A. (1998). Mandating methodology: Promoting the use of phonics through state statute. In Goodman, K. (Ed.) *In defense of good teaching: What teachers need to know about the reading wars (*pp. 107–125). York, ME: Stenhouse.

Routman, R. (1996). *Literacy at the crossroads.* Portsmouth, NH: Heinemann.

CHAPTER ELEVEN

Bringing Communities and Classrooms Together

To synthesize what the readers' experiences may have been and to connect the material to the ongoing political, historical evolution of events, we again ask you to participate in problem-posing activities related to the final contribution from a Turkish scholar and a culminating essay by the authors. Because of the importance of the information, some of the problem-posing activities are interspersed with sections of the essay for the purpose of reflection, discussion and feedback. By now you, the readers know that we, the authors, feel that all teaching and learning takes place in a community of learners. The communities include all students' families, schools, local communities and world communities. We teachers create the context for learners to pose questions and encourage the consideration of the strengths of students and their families and the consideration of the barriers they face daily.

Options for Listening

- Read the introduction to the following essay by Dr. Engin Demir and list any terms you question or are unfamiliar with.

Cennet Engin Demir, University Professor

Secularism and Education in Turkey

—*Cennet Engin Demir*

Turkey is the only country in the Middle East where secularism has become the official ideology of the state. The term "secularism" was used in the West to refer to a specific policy of separating church from state starting from the mid-nineteenth century. The word "secular" has been used with the meaning of "the temporary world" in all protestant countries. The policy of secularism in Catholic countries is more often expressed by the term "laicism" implying the distinction of the laity from the clergy. However, both terms are used to refer to opposition or separation of the church and state. The church represented the highest authority over the spiritual sphere and the state represented the highest authority over temporal matters. Berkes (1998) defines the secularization or laicization as the "transformation of persons, offices, properties, institutions or matters of ecclesiastical or spiritual character to lay and worldly position" (p. 5). He argues that the basic conflict of secularism is often between the forces of tradition, which tend to promote the domination of religion and sacred law, and the forces of change. Therefore, secularization constitutes a fundamental aspect of the whole modernization process that is change in the values and traditions of the society (Kazamias, 1966).

In Islam there have been no discrete concepts of church and state; that is, religious and political institutions. This is because religion and the state were believed to be fused together; the state was conceived as the representation of religion, and religion as the essence of the state (Berkes, 1998). The core of the tradition, which would be challenged in Islamic countries by the forces of modern civilizations, was Islam. Therefore, it should be pointed out that Turkish secularism does not have same meaning as Western secularism, which includes the separation of church and the state. Rather it is a reform called *"laiklik"* (laicism) in which religious practice and religious institutions are regulated and administered by the state (Berkes, 1998; Olson, 1985). Thus, "the aim of laicizm in Turkey was the 'modernization' of all aspects of culture, state and society that had their roots in traditional Islamic concepts and traditions" (Olson, 1985, p. 163). In the case of Turkey, the term "modernization" refers to "the process of transforming Ottoman Islamic Institutions, concepts and a way of life into those of secular, constitutional republic" (Kazamias, 1966, p. 17). As argued by Inkeles and Smith (1974), modernization is essentially a social psychological process through which a country becomes modern only after its population has adopted modern attitudes, values and beliefs. Therefore, in the process of modernization, the Turkish Republic has attempted to create changes in the values and traditions of the Turkish society which were based on Islamic way of life.

Sociologists have emphasized the modernizing influence of education on values, beliefs, and behaviors. It is education, particularly schooling, that has, perhaps, been the most important agent for transforming a traditional society into a modern one. Accordingly, the entire modernization movement of Turkey has been an experiment in education; how to create new values, new ideologies, new human beings, or new Turks (Kazamias, 1966). In a more restricted sense, formal education or schools have been considered to be crucial agents for Western ideas and actualizing the modernizing goals of both the Ottoman and Turks. As a result, to understand the modernization process in Turkey, it is essential to examine the modernization, in particular, the secularization of education. The pathway from an Islamic (i.e., essentially private system of schools and an essentially Islamic content and mode of thinking) to a state, secular system (i.e., one with an emphasis upon a modern curriculum and modern pedagogy) is described and discussed in this paper.

Options for Dialogue

- Discuss your list and assumptions and suppositions with a partner.
- Please discuss how the concept of secularism in Turkey is different from the concept in the United States and other Western societies?

Options for Action

- Collaborate to look up definitions of terms on the lists.
- Now collaborate with classmates and devise a list of important historical and political events and changes in the United States during the twentieth century. Discuss the effects of these events and changes on education.

Options for Listening

- As you read the historical background of Turkish governments' attempt to create a secular society, create a graphic time line or drawing that documents important events in historical development from the eighteenth century to the present.

Historical Background

Secularism and Education in the Ottoman Empire

To understand the development of the secularization process in Turkey, one must go back to the Ottoman empire period. In the Ottoman period, the Islamic religion was a unifying element in society and the very basis upon which the Ottoman state rested. Thus, the Muslim state was by definition religious. For all sects of the community the *Seriat* (divine law) was the righteous way of living leading to God. It included law, moral principles, and the creed to which every Muslim should subscribe. Accordingly, religious schools and religious instruction in schools were unquestioned premises in the Ottoman theocratic ideology (Kazamias, 1966).

However, beginning with Selim III (1789–1807), a series of reformist sultans and statesman attempted to make major changes in the Ottoman society in an effort to cope with changing internal and external conditions. Because education was considered as the prime agent for accomplishing the aims of modernization and Westernization, significant reforms were made in it. This was the first attempt to eliminate the control and supervision of *Sheyh-ul-Islam* (the highest religious authority) on education. In 1838 Mahmud made a public statement concerning secular education. Briefly, he declared that, "religious knowledge served salvation after death, but science served perfection of man in this world"(cited in Ergil, 1988, p. 15). The new school which was called *rushdiye* (senior primary school) was founded for adolescents. Its purpose was to provide a link between the "religious education" of the *mekteps* (elementary schools) and the "worldly" education of the schools of higher learning. A special school called the *Mekteb-i Maarif* (school of secular learning) was established in 1839 to educate a limited number of boys to be employed as government functionaries (Berkes, 1998). However, students entering these new schools lacked even basic knowledge and proper reading of recently published Turkish books. This was a consequence of the defectiveness of the primary education system, because primary education was still under the religious realm covered by the *Seriat*.

While there was a persistent traditionalism and religious education in primary education, the reform movements in higher education were radical and effective. In this period, the earlier School of Engineering (the

Muhendishane) as well as other new schools were permanently
established. No traditional institutions possessed enough power to close
down the new schools. On the contrary, the engineering school, the
medical school, and the military academy attracted the potential students
of *medreses*. As a result, *medreses* were finally brought to a position
where they had to close their own doors. This was a noticeable aspect of
the secularization trend in Turkey (Berkes, 1998).

The years between 1840 and 1870 are significant in the modernization
process of Turkey. The road which was charted by Selim III and Mahmud
II was followed by their successors. Four months after his accession to the
sultanate in 1839, *Abdül-Medjid* and Ottoman ministers declared the
famous *Hatt-ı Serif* (Nobel Rescript). This was the first constitutional
document of the Islamic world, although it was not meant to be a
constitution (Ergil, 1988).

The declaration of this rescript initiated a new era of reforms known as
Tanzimat (reformation). The *Tanzimat* period was characterized by
attempts to set up a modern administrative framework and a graded
system of schools different in many respects from the traditional
institutional arrangements (Kazamias, 1966), because education was seen
as an integral part of the overall reform movement and as a component of
the creation of a modern state. The educational system of European
countries, especially that of France, was used as a model for changing the
educational system of that time. As Bernard Lewis (1961) pointed out, the
effect of changes from *Tanzimat* on education was: "to set up new
schools, with teachers and curricula outside the scope of the *ulema*
(doctors of Islamic theology) and the religious sciences which they
cultivated, and thus prepare the way for a system of secular education.
The creation of a separate Ministry of Education confirmed the removal of
this important matter from the sole jurisdiction of the *ulema*" (p. 114).
The *Tanzimat* period was successful in creating *Rushdiye* (senior primary
school), *Idadiye* (preparatory secondary school), and in training teachers in
a more Western tradition. As a consequence of reform attempts in
education, a new type of bureaucrat at the high levels of administration
and the various government offices emerged. During the emergence of this
bureaucratic elite, Western styles of education became increasingly
important. However, the elites of the more traditional religious
institutions namely the *ulema* still maintained a strong position in
educational, cultural, and political spheres. In addition to conflicts
between Westernizers and traditionalists a new intellectual force known
as the Young Ottomans appeared in the middle decades of the nineteenth
century.

Another period which is worth noting in terms of the modernization of
education is the period of *Meshrutia* (constitutional period) which was
declared by the Young Turks in 1908. The active discussion of political life

by the Young Turks lead to discussions about educational philosophy and strategies. Therefore, between the years of 1908 and 1918, several steps were taken to modernize the education system: (a) primary schools were made compulsory and free; (b) additional taxes were taken to finance primary education; (c) some steps were taken toward the unification of education (i.e., eliminating the difference between *medrese* education and modern schools); and (d) the education of women became widespread. Along with these, some steps were taken to improve *medrese* education. In addition to Arabic, Turkish and Persian languages were introduced into the curriculum. Although there were many reforms made for the modernization of education, the *medreses* were never touched. All modern schools were founded without touching the *medreses* (Weiker, 1981).

Secularism and Education Under the Republic

Following the collapse of the Ottoman Empire in 1918, there was a struggle against victorious Allied Powers following World War I, and an internal revolution which substituted a republican form of government of the existing Ottoman Islamic theocracy for a new-nation state, Turkey (Ergil, 1988). A few years after the modern Turkish Republic was established, a reform program based on secularism or *laicism* was implemented. "The aim was to disestablish Islam in Turkey, to limit the powers to matters of belief and worship" (Lewis, 1961, p. 412). The Turkish revolution was not only a political event, but also a social, cultural, and economic revolution (Saeed, 1994; Weiker, 1981). Its aim was not merely to overthrow a political system, but to transform the entire fabric of the society along modern, Western characteristics (Kazamias, 1966).

As mentioned before, the Ottoman State rested upon Islamic religion and religious schools. Moreover, religious instruction in schools was an unquestioned premise of Ottoman theocratic ideology. However, Mustafa Kemal Ataturk (the founder of the Turkish Republic) and his fellow revolutionaries thought of such an education as an obstacle in the modernization of the Turkish society. As a result, the new government took over several crucial steps to disestablish Islam from law and education, to remove Islam as the official religion of the state, and to reduce its influence among the Turkish people in favor of a "scientific mentality" (Guvenc, 1998; Weiker, 1981).

In 1923, the Ministry of Education took over the administration and control of all religious schools and all their means of support (endowments and funds). In the same year, the teaching of religion was prohibited in all state schools. The abolition of *Caliphate* in 1924 was followed by the acceptance of *Tevhid-i Tedrisad Kanunu* (The Unification of Education Law). Accordingly, all *medreses* and other separate religious schools were closed and a centralized curricula was implemented throughout the country. The principle of co-education (boys and girls attend the same school) was introduced to elementary school. Then, the office of *Seyh-ul-Islam* was eliminated and replaced by the *Diyanet Isleri Baskanligi* (Presidency of Religious Affairs) under the control of the prime minister so that the state would control the appointment, training, and salary rate of religious personnel (Davison, 1998; Mardin, 1977). The Unification of Education Law helped to solve the problem of training religious personnel. Measures to improve the quality of religious personnel included establishment of some training schools for *imams* (prayer leaders) and *hatips* (preachers) which were called Imam Hatip schools. At the same time, the foundation of the Faculty of Divinity at Istanbul University intended to serve as the center of a new modernized and scientific form of religious instruction that was more consistent with a secular, Westernized republic. However, as a result of university reform, the Faculty of Divinity was closed in 1934. Between the years 1930–31 all *Imam Hatip* schools had to be closed because of the lack of financial support from the state (Weiker, 1981).

In 1927, religious courses were removed from the primary and secondary school curriculum. Although religious courses continued to be taught in village schools, their content included modern ethical principles rather than the doctrine of Islam (Tekeli, 1985). Students were taught values such as being hardworking, being auspicious, participating in public life effectively, and being honest and virtuous to meet their spiritual needs in public life. In this positivist view of religion, science vs. dogma, rationality vs. mysticism, good/beneficial vs. sin/pious deed was emphasized. Therefore, positivism became a primary philosophy of education (Saeed, 1994).

The Unification of Education Law created a legal basis to control the missionary schools and schools of minorities. The strict implementation of secular education in Turkish schools was also applied in these schools. Any type of religious education was forbidden by the state. The Koranic seminaries and *evkaf* (religious endowments) as well as non-Muslim religious institutions such as Patriarchate of the Greek Orthodox Church came under state control, and their curricula and personnel appointments came under stated inspection (Shaw & Shaw, 1977). However, the prohibitions made by the state regarding religious education were reduced after World War II.

One of the most revolutionary and important steps towards the religious re-orientation and re-education of Turkish people was through language reform. That is the Arabic alphabet was replaced by the Latin alphabet. The goal was to purify the language from its Arabic, Persian, and Islamic influences. Turkish written with the Latin alphabet was believed to be more modern, practical, precise, and less difficult to learn. In fact Ataturk believed that few people understood the Arabic language because it was used more by the elite, while the middle and lower classes used the less-developed Turkish (Saeed, 1994). As a result of this situation, only 10% of men and less than 1% of women were literate at the time that the Republic of Turkey was founded. The Romanization of the Latin alphabet had pedagogical, cultural, nationalistic, and religious implications as well. Because it severed the ties of the Turks to the language and script of the Koran and to the Arabic and Muslim World, it contributed to the consolidation of secularism (Gole, 1997). The state attempted to transform popular and folk culture through education. To these ends *Halk Evleri* (People's Houses) were established and literacy campaigns were engaged. Since the population was largely illiterate, education in the new alphabet had the effect of drawing a distinct line between the old and new identity (Tekeli, 1985). Moreover, in 1929, Arabic and Persian were prohibited in the curriculum of secondary schools and history books were rewritten with major emphasis placed upon the ethnic background of the Turks (Kazamias, 1966).

   In addition to these radical reforms in education, some reforms, which could have implications on education, were made in the civil and legal code in an effort to create a modern secular Turkish nation state. In 1928, Article 2 of the first Constitution of the Republic of Turkey, which had made Islam the state religion, was amended, and in 1937 the principle of secularism was incorporated in the Constitution (Ergil, 1988). Other official arrangements were made to Turkify Islam, such as using Turkish rather than Arabic at devotions and introducing Turkish to the *ezan* (daily calls to prayer). According to Mustafa Kemal Ataturk, all the people should learn of their religion in their own language, without having a need to read the explanations through self-styled interpreters in an incomprehensible book (Berkes, 1998).

   A secular civil law was adapted from Switzerland to complete the break with the Ottoman and Muslim past. Additionally, the Western calendar was adapted and the *fez* (Turkish hat) was outlawed in 1925 (Gole, 1998). In fact, all men were forced by law to wear European-type hats, the traditional garb of local religious leaders was outlawed, and wearing a veil was discouraged for women (Olson, 1985). That same year, Statute 2413 regulated the dress codes of civil servants, which required them to dress like their partners in civilized nations of the world (Arat, 2000).

   The Muslim institutions that were considered to be particularly backward and/or a political or economic threat to the success of the new Turkish Republic [such as *tekke* (dervish brotherhoods, and the religious *turbe* (shrines)] were closed and their property was appropriated by the national government to be turned into museums or were utilized for other state purposes.

At the same time, several reforms were made to enhance women rights. Indeed, promoting women's rights and promoting women to public citizens can be considered as a vital component of Turkish modernism. The removal of the veil, the establishment of compulsory co-education for girls and boys, and increased civil rights for women (such as electoral eligibility, voting, and the abolition of the *Seriat* [divine law] guaranteed the public presence of women (Göle, 1998).

1940s and 1950s: Corrosion of Secularism

The issue of religion or the role of Islam in the new state was quite inactive until the 1940s. With Turkey's transition from a one-party to the multi-party system (from 1940 to 1950), the government became more sensitive to the demands of people, and religion again emerged as a political and cultural issue. In fact, religion became a political slogan for vote-getting and the official attitude toward Islam had softened. As a matter of fact, religion was still an important part of the lives of people, especially those in the villages (Kazamias, 1966; Lewis, 1961; Tapper, 1994; Tekeli, 1985). As a result, one of the most openly discussed questions was that of religious education. After a debate in the Grand National Assembly in 1949, courses in Islam were permitted in the fourth and fifth grades of elementary schools. At first the courses in religion were to be optional and only for those children whose parents had requested such instruction. Since most parents had asked for such courses, they soon became compulsory for all Muslim children in the fourth and fifth classes, except in cases where parents would ask in writing that their children be excused from attending them. In 1950, the religious education was made compulsory in secondary schools unless parents made a specific request to have their children excused.

Two other developments in religious education during this period were significant. In 1949 a Divinity Faculty was opened at the University of Ankara under the control of the Ministry of Education. Government scholarships for attending the school after graduation from high school were provided for a large number of students. At the same time *Imam Hatip* schools for the training of religious leaders were re-established with a six-year course following five-year elementary schools (Akşit, 1994; Guvenc, 1998) and more mosques were built. In the 1950s, "the Democratic Party came to power with the support of an Islamic (*Sunni* Orthodox) reaction to secularism and the agrarian majority" (Güvenc, 1998, p. 61). The Democratic Party allowed the *ezan* (daily call to prayer) to be read in Arabic instead of Turkish and excerpts from the Koran to be read on the radio. The tombs of sultans that were closed in 1925 were reopened. There was even some loosening of restrictions regarding wearing religious garb (i.e., the fez, the veil and traditional garb of local religious leaders). Since 1950 there has been a dramatic increase in special courses of approximately a year's duration in the reading of Koran. In 1953, compulsory religion courses were added to the ninth and tenth grades of primary schools. In 1956–57 religion (Islam) and ethics courses were reintroduced to middle schools (6th, 7th and 8th grades).

In 1960, Institutes of Islam were established in different provinces. The Democratic Party also increased the budget allocated for the Presidency of Religious Affairs. As a result, the influence of Islam in public life increased dramatically in the 1950s and continued to rise in the 1960s. Almost all of the political parties supported or turned a blind eye to the rise of Islam (Schankland, 1999).

After a military intervention in 1960, a new constitution was prepared; it was ratified in 1961. Compared to Turkey's two previous constitutions, this was the most liberal. In this constitution, the religious course, again, became optional unless parents requested their children to attend it. In 1962, the Higher Islamic Institute was opened and the Department of Religious Education was established within the Ministry of Education (Akşit, 1994).

The number of *Imam Hatip* schools increased rapidly to more than 250 during the 1970s when the pro-Islam National Salvation Party participated in coalition governments. During the 1970s, political parties continued to compensate the principle of secularism for their own interest and use Islam to influence masses (Narli, 1999).

1980s and 1990s: The Emergence of Turk Islam Synthesis

After the military intervention in the 1980s, generals aimed to restore a strongly centralized and secular Turkish state on the one hand, and recognized the societal role of Islam and attempted to use religion to support a secular agenda on the other. The 1982 Constitution especially laid down secularism as an unchangeable and permanent aspect of the Turkish state. Because the military, although secular in orientation, regarded religion as an effective means to counter socialist ideas, it authorized the establishment of 90 more *Imam Hatip* schools and required that education in "religious culture and ethics" became a mandatory course of study (Narli, 1999).

It can be argued that the implementation of religious education aimed to restore religious authority to the state in the face of increasing numbers of Turkish people attending private religious education offered by *tarikats* (religious brotherhoods). Religion that was provided through the state was conceptualized as a unifying factor in society. For example, Minister of Education Avni Akyol (1990) wrote that it was the obligation of the state to provide education in all regards, including religion. Secularism, he defined, "is not the separation of spiritual and temporal" (p. 10) rather "one of the important purposes of secularism is also to prevent the misuse of religion for special goals and interests" (p. 11).

As a result, a plan termed "Turk Islam Synthesis," which had the goal of creating a common culture, was prepared. The creators of this ideological orientation claimed that "as a result of having a pragmatist and positivist education based on a materialistic world view, Turkish youngsters have turned out to be rootless and undecisive individuals participating in anarchists activities" (Olcen, 1993). It can be argued that, in reality, the "synthesis" was a deceptive cover-up for the restoration of Islam because it was based on two hypothetical premises: "(a) there is an unchanging core of culture; and (b) that core is religion (or Islam)" (Guvenc, 1998, p. 80). In accordance with this plan, educational programs have been revised and rendered compatible with the teaching of Islam. One of the indicators of how the Turk Islam synthesis has been an ideology of the state and its power has been the publication of textbooks and their content. Between 1984 and 1986, Islamic publication companies published textbooks, which included knowledge emphasizing Turkish nationalism, Islamic cooperation againts non-Muslim societies and depreciation of democratic values (Ozil & Tapan, 1991; Saktanber, 1994a). Although the Turkish Republic was looking to the West for inclusion as a member of the European Union, it was simultaneously moving towards an increasingly political Islam between 1986 and 1996 (Guvenc, 1998). Therefore, the principle of secularism began to be discussed by everybody everywhere in Turkey.

In the general election of 1995, the Islamist *Refah Partisi* (Welfare Party) emerged as the leading party with 20% of the popular vote. Forming a coalition government was inevitable. The Welfare Party formed a coalition with one of the center right parties. This government attempted to amend the constitution to remove legal obstacles blocking the way to an Islamic Republic of Turkey. As a result, generals from the army and the National Security Council expressed their detailed suggestions on February 28, 1997 which is known as *"28 February Decisions."* They declared that Islamic fundamentalism was the biggest threat to the security of the country and they initiated a process to limit the growth and power of fundamentalist Islam. They accused the Welfare Party of using education as a way to ensure the survival of its ideology and of infiltrating the civil service (Schankland, 1999). They suggested that any Islamic activity should be strictly under the control of the state. They also proposed that courses regarding the study of the Koran should come under the direction of the Ministry of Education rather than through the Directorate of Religious Affairs (as they used to be). Moreover, the *Imam Hatip* schools should be made ineffective by introducing a change in Turkish Education in which compulsory education was extended from five to eight years. This meant that all pupils between the ages of seven and fifteen years had to go to similar nonvocational schools for eight years and the middle level (6th, 7th and 8th grades) of *Imam Hatip* schools were inevitably abolished. In July 1997, after a hot debate on the issues between secularism and Islam, primary education was extended to eight years and termed the "uninterrupted eight year schooling." In the same year, the Welfare Party was confirmed as being guilty of acting against the constitution of the Republic and closed in 1998 (Schankland, 1999).

Options for Dialogue

- Using your time lines, discuss with your class what you learned about the events as they relate to modernization in general. Come up with answers as to why you believe the author stated, "the principle of secularism discussed by everybody everywhere in Turkey?"

Options for Action

- Research other countries which have undergone tremendous changes during the twentieth century and report on the effect these changes have had upon education in those countries.

Options for Listening

- List all educational debates you are aware of in your own educational context (state, nation, etc.)
- As you read the last section of the essay, note which of the educational debates in Turkey relate to those in your experience. Note the ones in Turkey that are not on your list . . . why not?

Contemporary Debates on Secularism in Education

Secularism, its interpretation and its implementation has been among the most debated issues of contemporary Turkey. The most hotly debated issues which indicate the difficulties and barriers experienced in the efforts toward becoming a secular state include the: (a) *Imam Hatip* schools (b) headscarves (*başörtü*), and (c) the policy of the Ministry of Education on religious education.

Imam Hatip Schools

The problem of the education of religious leaders has ranked among the most commonly discussed issues in republican Turkey. Although it was temporarily solved through the acceptance of *Tevhid-i Tedrisat Kanunu* (the Unification of Education Law), the problem re-emerged with the transition to a multiparty political system in the 1940s and the 1950s (Akşit, 1994). To understand the present debates about secularism and the role of politics on religious education in Turkey, one must take a look at some statistical data on the development of *Imam Hatip* schools.

As mentioned before, *Imam Hatip* schools were found to train unenlightened and enlightened *imams* (prayer leaders) and *hatips* (preachers) (Guvenc, 1998; Akşit, 1994) compatible with the ideology of the new Republic. For this purpose, twenty-four *Imam Hatip* schools and one Faculty of Divinity were opened after the acceptance of the Unification of Education Law which abolished all of the *mekteps* (traditional elementary schools) and *medreses* (traditional colleges). However, the *Imam Hatip* schools were closed in 1932 because of the lack of financial support from the government and the Faculty of Divinity was closed as a result of university reform in 1934. Between 1946 and 1949, twenty-five years after the abolition of *medreses* during the period of transformation from single-party to multi-party politics, the Republican People's Party started a discussion of the education of *imams* (prayer leaders) and *hatips* (preachers). In 1946, ten short-term Koran courses were opened in various provinces. In 1951, a year after the Democrat Party came to power, seven middle-level (6th, 7th and 8th grades) and *lycée* (high school: 9th, 10th and 11th grades) level *Imam Hatip* schools were opened under the jurisdiction of the Ministry of Education (Akşit, 1994).

In 1960, after the first military coup, it was recommended in the Seventh Educational Convention that fifteen of *Imam Hatip* schools, which were not serving the purposes defined by the law, be banned. Instead in 1962, twelve new schools were opened (Güvenc, 1998). In 1965–1969, when the Justice Party representing the central right was in power, forty more middle-level *Imam Hatip* schools were established. In 1971, after the second military intervention *Imam Hatip* schools were converted to three-year vocational *lycées* to follow attendance in the three-year middle schools. In 1972–1974, only graduates of middle schools were admitted. In 1974–1975, when the Islamist National Salvation Party was in the coalition government with the secular Republican People's Party, the first cycle of three years was reinstated and the number of middle-level *Imam Hatip* schools went up to 101 and *lycée*-level to 73 with 49,000 students. In 1977–1978, when the Justice Party, National Salvation Party, and National Action Party were in a coalition government, the number of middle-level *Imam Hatip* schools rose to 334 and *lycée* level to 103, with total of 134,517 students. In 1987, there were

376 middle-level and 341 *lycée*-level *Imam Hatip* schools with approximately 240,000 students (Akşit, 1994).

The establishment of *Imam Hatip* schools did not stop, although it has been criticized throughout 1990s. In the 1995–1996 academic year there were 561 *Imam Hatip* schools with 492,000 students. In the 1999–2000 academic year there were 604 *lycée*-level *Imam Hatip* schools with a total of 134,224 students (66,776 female and 67,448 male) (*Ministry of Education Statistics*, 2000). There are several reasons for the decrease in the number of students in the *Imam Hatip* schools in the year 2000 compared to 1988. First, the duration of compulsory primary school was expanded from five to eight years in 1997. As a result of this reform, all of the middle-level *Imam Hatip* schools were naturally closed. Second, although *Imam Hatip* schools were established as vocational high schools to produce religious functionaries such as *imams* and *hatips* and candidates for recruitment into Higher Islamic Institutes and Faculties of Divinity, they have been transformed into an alternative *lycée* whose graduates have entered various departments of national universities and become civil servants as well as *imams* and *hatips* by the Directorate of Religious Affairs. As a result, secularists (laicists) opposed the *Imam Hatip* schools because of the curriculum implemented in these schools. In addition to the standard secular *lycée* curriculum, *Imam Hatip* schools offer 11 to 18 hours of professional (Islamic) studies such as Arabic, Hadis [sayings attributable to the Prophet Muhammed], Islamic history per week. They argue that there may not be so much the weight of Islamic studies, but the fact that standard *lycée* courses were offered with a built-in Islamic worldview made all the difference (Guvenc, 1998). For example, students are taught modern biology, but they will not accept the theory of evolution because of their Islamic worldview. The laicists fear that the detailed Islamic training which the *Imam Hatip* schools offer is far deeper than might appear on the surface (Schankland, 1999). According to research, completed by Piar Gallup with 1085 *Imam Hatip* students in 9 provinces, 80% of the students suggested that Islamic principles should be included in the legal system. Sixty percent of the students accepted the idea that men and women should attend different schools (Copeaux, 1998). Therefore, these schools have been perceived to be functioning as breeding-grounds for radical Islam by the laicist (Akşit, 1994). Considering this the laicist think that the graduates of *Imam Hatip* schools should be kept away from having jobs in government offices other than in the Directorate of Religious Affairs. As a matter of fact, the number of pupils trained at these schools far exceeds any possible need the state's administration of the Directorate of Religious Affairs might require.

On the other hand, Islamic groups such as *tarikats* (religious order or brotherhoods) and Islamist political parties tend to use *Imam Hatip* schools as channels for the recruitment of new members and as a means of creating new Islamic *ulema* (Akşit, 1994). As a result, laicists argue that the purpose of establishing *Imam Hatip* schools is just political and it has nothing to do with training *imams* and preachers. One of the indicators stated by the laicist is that these schools are not founded only for the training of religious personnel since girls are allowed to attend as well. However, in Islam, women cannot be *imams* or preachers. Officially, these schools are defined as a category of "vocational" schools and are administered similarly to technical high schools for both girls and boys. This provides the legal basis for enrolling girls. Another indicator is that the students of *Imam Hatip* schools are mostly oriented to departments of public administration and faculties of teacher education by their supporters so that they can have an opportunity to disseminate their worldview to large groups of people which may be regarded as a threat to the secular republic. It is claimed by the secularist that by establishing *Imam Hatip* schools a pseudo-legitimate way was found to restore the old *medrese* which means to go 80 years backwards in efforts of establishing a secular and democratic Turkish nation-state (Akşit 1994; Güvenc, 1998).

Consequently, it was decided by the Council of Higher Education (*YOK*) that since *Imam Hatip* schools are vocational high schools, and the graduates are going to be *imams* and *hatips* they therefore can only attend the Faculties of Divinity. However, this decision was counter to the equality of educational opportunity principle of the Turkish education system. Therefore, the students who attend *Imam Hatip* schools are awarded an extra point to the score of the standard University Entrance Examination results, only if they choose to compete for the Faculties of Theology. At the same time, graduates of the *Imam Hatip* schools are not allowed to apply to any military officer training schools, which are totally secular. As a consequence, students of *Imam Hatip* schools frequently transfer to normal high schools so that they will be eligible to apply to other faculties and departments at universities. However, supporters have systematically been attempting to gain special concessions for *Imam Hatip* graduates to be able to attend military officer training schools.

Başörtü (Headscarf) Dispute in Higher Education

In order to maintain secularism, Islamic groups have been kept under tight control. Until after the 1960s, this has, at times, compromised the dictates of a pluralistic democratic order. With the provisions of civil liberties by the 1961 Constitution, Islamic groups began to operate legally (though their activities were still technically banned). Especially in the 1960s, they emerged in the political and social scene in Turkey, as a result of gradual liberalization and economic development (Arat, 1995). Several reasons are identified by social scientists in explaining the rise of Islam: (a) migration from rural to urban areas increased dramatically so that choosing the Islamic way of life was a response to the life in metropolis (Toprak, 1981); (b) Islam filled the psychological vacuum left by the secular Kemalist ideology after its attempts to remove Islam from people's lives (Mardin, 1971); and (c) it was a postmodern reaction to Turkish modernization which allowed Islamic groups to assert themselves (Arat, 1995).

As the Islamists continued to increase their power through the 1980s, they started to challenge the principles of Turkish Republic, including secularism. Owing to an increased number of Islamic groups and their visibility in the public realm with their alternative life styles and institutions (Saktanber, 1994b), there has been an increase in the public expressions of Muslim devotional exercise. Parallel with this, female university students began to cover their heads and necks with large scarves and wear long, shape-concealing overcoats to demonstrate their commitment to Islam. Consequently, as identified by Arat (2000), "the most tangible, emotional, and prolonged confrontation between the state and the Islamic groups took place around the *başörtü* (headscarf) issue" (p. 1). The participants of the debate constitute two opposing orientations: "(a) Turkish nationalism versus Muslim identity; and (b) Secularism *(laicism)* versus Islamic society" (Olson, 1985, p. 165).

As mentioned before, a dress code of civil servants was established in 1925 which required employees to dress like their partners in the civilized (Western) nations of the world. The formal adoption of European dress legally allowed women to unveil (Toprak, 1981). After the 1980 coup, the new government which was installed by the army introduced "Dress and Appearance Regulations." The new regulation prohibited men from wearing beards and long hair, women from wearing mini-skirts, low-necked dresses, and headscarves while on duty in public agencies, offices, and institutions (Olson, 1985; Ozdalga, 1998). This was also applied to educational organizations (i.e., including students), since all universities and most schools at the lower levels were public institutions. Thus, parallel to the regulations made by the government, the Council of Higher Education issued a regulation in 1987 forbidding female university students and professors to cover their heads. Thousands of female students, supported by men, organized protests and engaged in political activity which was designed to defend their right to cover their heads in the manner consistent with Islamic dictates. At the same time there have been widespread, secular and popular demonstrations against the Islamification of politics. These frequently conclude with mass rallies at Ataturk's tomb. The issue continues to be an argument between the two groups.

In the following years, Islamic women have insisted on attending universities with their heads covered. Citing the freedom of religious expressions guaranteed with Article 24 of the 1982 Constitution and

Article 10 which prohibits discrimination before law due to religious belief of differences in language, ethnicity, gender, etc., the women claim that wearing headscarves is or should be their right. They also assert that the prohibition of headscarves obstructs their right to education, which is protected by Article 42 of the Constitution. Another argument which is raised by the proponents is that women are particularly liable to discrimination because men, who share the same beliefs with women and think that women's head covering is a dictate of religion, are unquestioningly admitted to universities since their heads are uncovered (Arat, 2000). Therefore, those who are Islamic use arguments which are used by the present constitutional secular system in order to achieve the benefits recognized by the existing polity (Ozdalga, 1998).

On the contrary the *laicists*—the Turkish social democrats who claim that the heritage of Republican reforms include that of secularism—are against head covering. They claim that wearing a headscarf in an official space is a political rather than a personal statement (Schankland, 1999). Similarly, in their decisions, the Council of State and Constitutional Courts have argued that wearing headscarves is not an innocent custom; rather it has become the symbol of a worldview opposed to the fundamental principles of the Turkish Republic and opposed to women's liberation. Therefore the head covering is judged to be against secularism and women's rights (Arat, 2000). They have argued that it is evident that in some cases, fundamentalist and other Islamic groups have been using protests against the ban of headscarves for their ideological benefit. They have also been providing support for female university students who are unable to finance their education if they cover their heads at university (*Ministry of Education Statistics*, 2000, p. 15).

Regarding the headscarf issue, one question that comes to mind is: How can young women, born and raised in a secular society and educated in a secular school system, become followers of Islamic movements (Acar, 1994)? One explanation lies in the socioeconomic characteristics of these students. Many of the Islamic girls and women are from small towns and provincial cities of these lower middle-class. These groups are still among the most conservative in Turkey. The education system, established after the foundation of the Republic and the social and economic changes that took place between 1950 and 1980, provided opportunities for those children from small towns and from the lower- and middle-class families to benefit from educational opportunities. Especially in small towns, many girls were sent to *Imam Hatip* schools by their parents because of the moral values represented by those schools. As a result, some of these girls who identified themselves with the conservative and patriarchal values of their family and community entered universities. Such values are often in harmony with Islamic thought (Acar, 1994). Educated women from middle and upper-middle socioeconomic status groups who were not supporters of Islamic activities also benefited from republican reforms.

The motives of female students who have decided to defy the headscarf ban are complex. Some are tired of being harassed in public spaces by men and, as a consequence, they value the protection that covering may offer. Others may be motivated by the convictions and influence of their spouses or family. Still others are awarded grants or a place in lodgings by Islamic charities in return for wearing headscarves in public (Acar, 1994; Schankland, 1999; Ozdalga, 1998). In general, it can be argued that headscarfs for them symbolize taking part in the Islamic movement and asserting an Islamic identity. It is not only a political symbol, but it is also a symbol of piety and *namus* (virtue) to many women, as it was in the traditional past (Narli, 1999).

The headscarf ban itself neither promotes liberal values nor political participation in Turkey. The debate on the headcarf has contributed to the democratic process to the extent that it has challenged the current concept of secularism and the parameters of political participation. Moreover, it has allowed people to recognize the nature of Turkey's democracy (Arat, 2000).

Ministry of Educations Policies on Religious Education

A third debate about secularism and education is the providence of religious education by the state and the Islamification of the content of primary and secondary school curricula, especially in textbooks. Education under the Republic has always had a political flavor. In Turkey there has been an indirect politicization of education through the determination of what general values should be stressed. One of the aspects of the controversy was whether religion should be taught in schools. As mentioned before, following a military coup, the 1982 Constitution made religious education compulsory starting from fourth grade of elementary school through the completion of secondary school. Critics argue that a secular state should not teach religion in public schools.

About 99% of Turkey's population are Muslim, primarily *Sunni* (Orthodox). In addition to the Sunni majority, there is a significant *Shia* minority, of which an estimated 12 or 15 million are *Alewis* (a heterodox Muslim Shia sect which are recognized as a distinct legal school within the Imam Shia tradition). Their rituals include men and women praying together through speeches, poetry, and dance. The Alewis lifestyle is more secular compared to other Islamic sects in Turkey. However, in public schools, the Sunni (or Orthodox) version of Islam alone is taught rather than a general education, or objective information about religion (Güvenc, 1998). This becomes a Constitutional paradox. While Article 24 of the

Constitution guarantees unalienable freedom of religious expression, the third paragraph said that religious culture and ethics are compulsory in primary and secondary schools.

Non-Muslim minorities "recognized" by the government to be covered by the 1923 Lausanne Treaty (Greek Orthodox, Armenian Orthodox, and Jews) are exempted by law from Muslim religious instruction if they provide written verifications of their non-Muslim background. These students may attend courses with parental consent. However, other non-Muslim minorities such as Catholics, Protestants, and Syriac Christians are not exempted.

The influence of the Turk-Islam synthesis can be seen in the curricula of primary and secondary schools which is developed by the Board of Education. Specifically, the content of history books promotes a rightist, conservative, and nationalist ideology, which it implicitly terms the Turk-Islam Synthesis. This trend redefines the Turkish identity with religious as opposed to Kemalism which values the republican nationalism (Copeaux, 1998). For example, in the *History of Revolution and Ataturk's Principles* textbook, written by Su and Mumcu (1990) and approved by the Board of Education, while explaining the principle of *laicizm* it was stated that Islam is open to secular thought by nature. Similarly, the authors have provided examples from the Koran to explain the benefits of *laicizm* for Turkish society (Aslan, 1994). In the middle school *Citizenship Education* textbook, which was written by Dal, Cakiroglu and Yazgan (1987), the message conveyed to students is that only religious people are decent people while describing a good citizen. In the same book, the rules of Islam are considered among the rules which organize the social life (cited in Nas, 1994). Turk-Islam Synthesis, as an ideology of the state and politicians, has penetrated to other textbooks as well. It can be argued that the discourse of textbooks in primary and secondary schools is no longer secular. However, after the "28 February Decisions," the Ministry of Education initiated an attempt to clean the Islamic components of the textbooks.

Conclusion

Secularization has been the major aim of the Turkish modernization process and, although the achievements have been many, secularization remains a major problem. To what extent reformers have succeeded in secularizing the new nation or education system and the minds of people remains unclear. Several major aims of secularization obviously have been accomplished: (a) the formal power of religious functionaries is forever ended; (b) the usefulness of secular education has been realized; and (c) scientific mentality and secular thinking characterizes a large proportion of Turkish population. For example, according to research results, 67.2% of Turkish people disagreed with the statement that political decisions must be made in accordance with Islamic principles. In addition, the statement that secularism must be continued has been accepted by 77.3% of the population (Carkoglu & Toprak, 2000). Moreover, the majority of Turkish people want to be a part of contemporary Western civilization which is mainly democratic and secular. Another indicator of the penetration of secularism in daily life is women's physical and social visibility in the public realm. Secularism, under the Republic, pushed for the emancipation of women from religious practices such as veiling and the segregation of sexes. Ironically, women have played a central role in the rise of Islam as well. The dramatic increase in the number of women wearing the headscarf in the 1980s and 1990s has indicated the re-Islamization of personal relations, public spaces, and daily practices (Gole, 1997).

On the other hand, Turkey could not have achieved the purpose of the separating religion from the state, which is accepted as essential for being completely secular. Although *Laiklik,* by definition, is to separate religion and state, Islam has never been separated from the state in Turkey (Rustow, cited in Davison, 1998). As a matter of fact, separation of religion and state was never attempted in its Western sense. Rather, Islam was put under the control and made subservient to the state authority. This happened rigidly during the early years of the Republic especially between 1923 and 1946, but gradually softened from the 1950s through the 1980s (Toprak, 1981). According to Ernest Gellner (1981) it became "a didactic secularism," moralistic and pedagogical, teaching and imposing a modern way of life (p. 68). In general, it can be argued that certain aspects of Kemalist secularism have implied political legal and educational restrictions upon religion, while some others such as the existence of the Department of Religious Affairs within the government, the expenditure of public funds on religious affairs, and the providence of state controlled religious education have seemed to be inconsistent with a secular state (Berkes, 1998).

Research on political and general socialization leaves no doubt that schools are extremely important agencies for the inculcation of values and attitudes as well as specific knowledge and skills (Weiker, 1981; Tekeli, 1985). The Turkish Education System has clearly achieved a great deal in its contribution to Turkey's modernization, secularization, and development. Therefore, if there is a potential threat to the understanding of secularism coming from Islamists, among whom are some women who cover their heads, the state can try to expand and improve the quality of its primary and secondary education. The education should emphasize rational and scientific thinking and encourage creativity rather than rote learning and memorization. In addition to this, the article of the Constitution which amended the mandatory religious course in schools can be abolished. An optional religion course can be offered, which provides general information about religion rather imposing the values and practices of a single sect. Moreover, the Ministry of Education can leave the training of *imams* and *hatips* to the Directorate of Religious Affairs.

In short, to achieve complete secularism, the state must completely strip itself of religion, must stop controlling and financing it with the expectations of establishing a moderate Islam in Turkey, and must keep in mind that Islam is impossible under a secular state.

References

Acar, F. (1994). Women in the ideology of Islamic revivalism in Turkey: Three Islamic women's journals. In R. L. Tapper (Ed.) *Islam in Modern Turkey: Religion Politics and Literature in a Secular State*, pp. 280–303. London: I. B. Tauris & Co Ltd.

Akşit, B. (1994). Islamic education in Turkey: Medrese reform in late Ottoman times and Imam Hatip schools in the republic. In R. L. Tapper (Ed.) *Islam in Modern Turkey:* Religion Politics and Literature in a Secular State, pp. 145–170. London: I. B. Tauris & Co Ltd.

Akyol, A. (1990). *Laiklik ve Din Öğretimi (Secularism and Religious Education)*, Ankara: T. C. Milli Eğitim Bakanlığı.

Arat, Y. (1995). Feminism and Islam: Considerations on the journal *Kadin ve Aile*. In S. Tekeli (Ed.) *Women in Modern Turkish Society: A Reader*, pp. 66–78. London: Zed Books.

Arat, Y. (2000) *Islamist women, their headscarves and democracy in Turkey*. A seminar given at Bogazici University, September 2000, Istanbul.

Aslan, E. (1994). Ortaogretimdeki "Turkiye Cumhuriyeti Inkilap Tarihi ve Ataturkculuk" ders kitaplari ("The History of Revolution and Ataturk's Principles" textbooks in secondary schools). In Ozil & Tapan (Ed.). *Turkiye'nin Ders Kitapları (Textbooks of Turkey)*, pp. 175–204. Istanbul: Cem Yayınevi.

Berkes, N. (1998). *The Development of Secularism in Turkey*. Boston: Routledge.

Carkoglu, A., & Toprak, B. (2000). *Turkiye'de Din Toplum ve Siyaset (Religion, Society and Politics in Turkey)*. Istanbul: TESEV.

Copeaux, E. (1998). *Turk Tarih Kitaplarinda (1931–1993), Turk Tarih Tezinden Turk Islam Sentezine (in Turkish History Books 1931–1993), From the Thesis of Turk to Turk Islam Synthesis)*. Istanbul: Tarih Vakfi Yurt Yayinlari. *Cumhuriyet*, December 30, 1996.

Dal, K., Cakıroglu, O. & Yazgan, A. I. (1987). *Ortaokullar icin Vatandaslık Bilgileri III (Citizenship Education Textbook for Middle Schools III)*. Istanbul: Milli Egitim Basimevi.

Davison, A. (1998). *Secularism and Revivalism in Turkey: A Hermeneutic Reconsideration*. New Haven: Yale University Press.

Ergil, D. (1988). *Secularism in Turkey: Past and Present*. Ankara: Foreign Policy Institute.

Gellner, E. (1981). Muslim Society. Cambridge University Press.

Gole, N. (1997). Secularism and Islamism in Turkey: The making of elites and counter-elites. *Middle East Journal,* 51 (1), 46–58.

Gole, N. (1998). The freedom of seduction of Muslim women. *New Perspectives Quarterly,* 15(3), 43–51.

Guvenc, B. (1998). *History of Turkish Education*. Ankara: Turkish Education Association.

Inkeles, A., & Smith, D. H. (1974). *Becoming Modern. London:* Heinemann Education Books.

Kazamias, A. M. (1966). *Education and the Quest for Modernity in Turkey*. Chicago: The University of Chicago Press.

Lewis, B. (1961). *The Emergence of Modern Turkey*. Oxford University Press.

Mardin, S. (1971). Ideology and religion in Turkish revolution. *International Journal of Middle East Studies,* 2: 25–42.

Mardin, S. (1977). Religion in Modern Turkey. *International Social Science Journal,* 29:279–297.

Ministry of Education Statistics, 2000. Ankara: Milli Egitim Bakanlığı Yayinlari. *Milliyet,* May 9, 2000.

Narli, N. (1999). The rise of Islamist movement in Turkey. *MERIA Journal,* 3(3), 95–113.

Nas, R. (1994). Ortaokullar için vatandaşlık bilgileri (Citizenship education for middle schools). In Ozil & Tapan (Ed.) *Turkiye'nin Ders Kitapları (Textbooks of Turkey)*, pp. 215–227. Istanbul: Cem Yayınevi.

Olcen, A. N. (1993). Islamda Karanligin Baslangici ve Turk Islam Sentezi (The Start of Darkness in Islam and the Turkish Islam Synthesis). Ankara: Ekin Yayınları.

Olson, E. A. (1985). Muslim identity and secularism in contemporary Turkey: "The headscarve dispute." *Antropological Quarterly,* 58 (3), 161–168.

Ozdalga, E. (1998). *The Veiling Issue, Official Secularism and Popular Islam in Modern Turkey.* England: Curzon Press.

Ozil, S., & Tapan, N. (1991). *Turkiye'nin Ders Kitaplari (Textbooks of Turkey)*. Istanbul: Cem Yayinevi.

Saeed, J. (1994). *Islam and Modernization: A Comparative Analysis of Pakistan, Egypt and Turkey*. Connecticut: Praeger.

Saktanber, A. (1994a). Muslim identity in children's picture books. In R. L. Tapper (Ed.) *Islam in Modern Turkey: Religion Politics and Literature in a Secular State*, pp. 171–188. London: I. B. Tauris & Co Ltd.

Saktanber, A. (1994b). Becoming the "other" as a Muslim in Turkey: Turkish women vs. Islamist women. *New Perspectives on Turkey*, 11, 99–134.

Schankland, D. (1999). *Islam and Society in Turkey*. Cambridge-shire: The Eothen Press.

Shaw, S., & Shaw, E. K. (1977). *History of the Ottoman Empire and Modern Turkey*, Vol. II. Cambridge University Press.

Su, M. K., & Mumcu, A. (1990). *Lise ve Dengi Okullar icin Turkiye Cumhuriyeti Inkilap Tarihi ve Ataturkculuk (History of Revolution and Ataturk's Principles: A Textbook)*. 10. baskı. Istanbul: Milli Egitim Basimevi.

Tapper, R. L. (1994). *Islam in Modern Turkey: Religion Politics and Literature in a Secular State*. London: I. B. Tauris & Co Ltd.

Tekeli, I. (1985). Osmanlı Impatorlugu' ndan gunumuze egitim kurumlarinin gelisimi. (The development of educational institutions from Ottoman Empire to present). *Cumhuriyet Donemi Turkiye Ansiklopedisi (The Encyclopedia of Turkey: Republican Period)*, no. 3. Istanbul: Iletisim Yayinlari.

Toprak, B., (1981). *Islam and Political Development in Turkey*. Leiden: Brill.

Weiker, W. F. (1981). *The Modernization of Turkey: From Ataturk to the Present Day*. New York: Holmes & Meier Publishers, Inc.

Response

The poem, "Belief," which introduces Chapter 2 of this book, brought to our attention the endurance of human faith and creativity in the context of an ever-changing world. In Beibei, China, faith and the moon outlive tourists and the karoake bars, at the same time as they are changed by them. Matt Russell, a young man teaching in China wrote to us:

Being in China isn't just about discarding your old ideas about it before you went there, but also discarding what you thought about it the day before. Just as my speaking English to the kindergarten class proved to them that the world is a more complex place than they had imagined, I realized in China that any given person, place, or thing is always much more complex than it first appears, and "understanding" something is nothing more than a step in the direction of realizing this fact more completely. It made me realize that in trying to truly understand anything, we're all basically like kindergartners, rubbing out clumsily formed letters with a pink eraser that never completely erases, writing slightly less clumsy letters on top. (Russell, 2000, np)

In writing this book we, the authors, are learning as we write, and we ask you, the readers, to continue the investigations that you have begun here. Schooling in these times is an experience in dissonance between two forces: on the one hand, a trend towards a global homogenization which brings people and countries closer than ever, and, on the other hand, the affirmation of what is specific and particular. This tension obviously has implications for decisions about teaching: are we concerned with the education of the citizen for a globally patterned culture or for a particular cultural identity? Why are we not concerned with both?

Mary Oliver (1984) asks in one of her poems, "Tell me, what is it you plan to do/with your one wild and precious life?" (p. 22). It is a challenge to us as learners, educators and the creators of our lives. None of us lives or works in isolation and we draw our inspiration from a global community.

James Baldwin wrote in 1962, "The purpose of art is to lay bare the questions which have been hidden by the answers" (p. 17). Painter and teacher Ali Raza, a native of Pakistan who currently resides in the United States, illuminates Baldwin's statement by telling how he paints with many active questions in mind, including:

What is the relationship between the practice of art across global and regional boundaries? What happens to an image's significance when it crosses cultural boundaries? What has been filtered and lost in art forms during the post-colonial era in South Asia? What form of values in art can be studied to revive and modernize? While living in a multicultural, post-capitalist society, to whom am I addressing my work? (Raza, 2002, n.p.)

Raza believes that teaching is closely related to his work as an artist because it provides access to the critical thinking that gives rise to these questions. His process is like that of many teachers who create curriculum and teach with active questions in mind—questions that relate to the content of this book. We end with the hope expressed by Freire.

> I like being a human person because even though I know that the material, social, political, cultural, and ideological conditions in which we find ourselves almost always generate divisions that make difficult the construction of our ideals of change and transformation, I know also that the obstacles are not eternal. (Freire, 1998, p. 55)

References

Baldwin, J. (1962). *Creative Process.* New York: Ridge Press.

Freire, P. (1998). *Pedagogy of freedom : Ethics, democracy, and civic courage.* New York: Rowman & Littlefield.

Oliver, M. (1984). *American primitive.* New York: Little Brown.

Raza, A. (2002). Idea into image: An exhibition of five Pakistani painters at the Indo Center of Art and Culture, New York.

Russell, M. (April, 2000). Personal communication. Duluth, MN: University of Minnesota, Duluth.

Studies in the Postmodern Theory of Education

General Editors
Joe L. Kincheloe & Shirley R. Steinberg

Counterpoints publishes the most compelling and imaginative books being written in education today. Grounded on the theoretical advances in criticalism, feminism, and postmodernism in the last two decades of the twentieth century, Counterpoints engages the meaning of these innovations in various forms of educational expression. Committed to the proposition that theoretical literature should be accessible to a variety of audiences, the series insists that its authors avoid esoteric and jargonistic languages that transform educational scholarship into an elite discourse for the initiated. Scholarly work matters only to the degree it affects consciousness and practice at multiple sites. Counterpoints' editorial policy is based on these principles and the ability of scholars to break new ground, to open new conversations, to go where educators have never gone before.

For additional information about this series or for the submission of manuscripts, please contact:

Joe L. Kincheloe & Shirley R. Steinberg
c/o Peter Lang Publishing, Inc.
275 Seventh Avenue, 28th floor
New York, New York 10001

To order other books in this series, please contact our Customer Service Department:

(800) 770-LANG (within the U.S.)
(212) 647-7706 (outside the U.S.)
(212) 647-7707 FAX

Or browse online by series:
www.peterlangusa.com

THOMSON DELMAR LEARNING'S
NURSING REVIEW SERIES

Psychiatric Nursing